How to Spot

LIES

Like the FBI

How to Spot
LIES
Like the FBI

Protect your money, heart, and sanity using proven tips.

Mark Bouton

Cosmic Wind Press
CWP

Mark Bouton

How to Spot Lies Like the FBI

Copyright © 2010 by Mark M. Bouton

First Edition, *Cosmic Wind Press (CWP)*

Although this book was reviewed and approved for publication by representatives of the Federal Bureau of Investigation, Washington, D.C., the ideas and opinions expressed herein are strictly those of the author.

Photographs by Patsie Sweeden, Topeka, Kansas.

Technical assistance by Mary Kate Denny, Los Angeles, CA, Denny Photo; Chad Bouton, Senior Research Engineer, Battelle Global Health and Life Sciences, Columbus, OH; and Carol Yoho, website designer, Topeka, KS.

ISBN 978-0-615-37186-3

LCCN 2010906725

Dedication

This book is dedicated with gratitude and love to my uncle, Robert "Bob" Bouton, who is always supportive of the family and has been a great advocate of my writing.

Mark Bouton

Author's note: Many of the tips and techniques for detecting lies are intentionally repeated throughout the book. This is done to assist the reader in remembering the various signals of which he should be aware. It is also written in this manner to remind the reader to be alert for "tells" from the person with whom they're conversing in all areas of concern, including body language, facial expressions, and verbal indicators.

Masquerade

Having no bona fide costume to wear,
No fangs, or hats, or pantaloons,
He yanked Halloween
By its black-orange sleeves
And pulled it inside out.

He set aside his pasted smile
Purged pseudo laughter from his throat
And spent the day unmasked,
Disguised as himself.
No one guessed who it was

And he won first prize
For scariest costume.

Naomi Patterson
from *Living Out Loud*, a book of poems

Acknowledgments

Many thanks to the members of the WriteStuff group who posed for photographs depicting various mannerisms that occur when someone lies. The helpful models included Dennis Smirl, Phil L. Morris, Carol Feierabend, Larry S. Wilson, Pat Bonine, Steve Laird, Kristine Polansky, and Elizabeth de Ford.

Thanks also to the members of the Kansas Author's Club and Kansas Writer's, Inc., who encouraged me to pursue and complete this book.

I appreciate the patience and co-operation of my family in allowing me the time to research and write this book. Thanks to Ellen Byers Bouton, Ben Byers Bouton, and Daniel Bouton.

This book would not have been possible without my experiences serving as a Special Agent for the Federal Bureau of Investigation. I was privileged to work with many dedicated and intelligent members of the law enforcement community, including the FBI, DEA, U.S. Customs, U.S. Secret Service, U.S. Marshal's Service, U.S. Border Patrol, sheriff's and police organizations, Texas Rangers, Kansas Bureau of Investigation, local constables, Royal Canadian Mounted Police, Interpol, Scotland Yard, Inmigracion Federales de Mexico, Policias Nacionales de Mexico, CID, OSI, NCIS, and the BATF. Much of the information in this book came from their expertise.

Mark Bouton

Contents

Chapter Lineup:

Chapter 1 – Why Try to Spot Lies?   8

Chapter 2 – The Eyes as Windows to the Truth   26

Chapter 3 – The Psychology of Lying   48

Chapter 4 – Detecting the Spoken Lie   77

Chapter 5 – Lying in Our Society   129

Chapter 6 – Let the Buyer Beware   155

Chapter 7 – Body Language of Liars   176

Chapter 8 – How Lying Affects Daily Life   225

Chapter 9 – Summary: Ten Secrets to Spotting Lies   243

1

Why Try to Spot Lies?

Someone will lie to you today, and even though you may doubt his veracity, you might not have the skills to catch the fib. Your auto dealership may say you need a major repair job. Your boy friend may swear he had drinks with his cute secretary "as thanks for her help on a project." The teenager who borrowed your car may lament, "Some jerk smashed the fender while I was parked at the mall." Wouldn't you like to detect such lies, and not just suspect them? Then take heart—I can show you how to perceive those falsehoods and others.

As an FBI agent, I worked criminal cases and national security matters across America for decades. I contacted more than 100,000 people, analyzing each discussion for truth or falsity. Detecting lies helped me escape tight spots and even saved my life. I'll describe some of those situations as examples of the deadly deception that's out there. And I'll explain many techniques that you can use to spot harmful lies. I believe your life will improve when you learn to identify lying, and with practice, you should become a pro at it.

In my job, I encountered many situations where spotting lies was crucial. But no matter what your vocation or avocation, you'll run across more deceit than you now realize. It's a sad situation, but even if you choose to ignore some of the falsehoods told you, obviously it's to your advantage to know when someone is trying to hoodwink you.

While in the FBI, I identified the Oklahoma City bombers due to their deceit; tracked the travels of a kidnapper posing as a CIA agent; interviewed the head of the Heaven's Gate cult (leader of the largest mass suicide in U.S. history); survived an attacker wielding pistols and pipe bombs in revenge against the government; and caught a phantom burglar who stole money from a locked bank vault. I'll explain how I analyzed those cases and others as examples of how to detect dishonesty. You may not be solving crimes, but you'll be happier, more secure, and more self-assured when you can determine truth from lies.

You need the information given here if you've:

    lost family or friends due to politicians' lies.

    suspected your significant other cheated on you.

    lost much of your money to a slick stock broker.

    been overcharged for repairs or services.

    lost your retirement funds due to a corrupt CEO.

    had a house foreclosed owing to lies by a banker.

    been taken by a con man.

If these or similar events have happened in your life, then this book will help you. It's not just to point a finger at someone and denounce them as a liar. The purpose is to make you more aware of what's going on in the world so you can better protect yourself, your loved ones, and your belongings.

From news reports, we've become aware how many powerful people are liars, and how devastating it's been to everyone's livelihood, financial security, and personal safety. This book will show the prevalence of lying, the psychology of deception, and many specific methods for detecting dishonesty. I'll describe the benefits you'll receive from being able to recognize falsehoods. And I'll provide a mnemonic based on the phrase *To Spot a Lie,* to help you recall the techniques we'll discuss. By the book's end, you'll be a human lie detector.

➢ **Deception is everywhere.**

Psychologists tell us people are always lying. In my work, I learned that hustlers constantly pull swindles and con games to separate people from their savings. Criminals use many ruses and excuses to deny their guilt. In one psychological test, 91 percent of participants admitted to lying daily. I believe those were the ones answering honestly. The true figure is likely higher. And oddly enough, it's quite often our friends and relatives and loved ones who are doing the deceiving.

Lying in one form or another is a time-honored means of self-preservation used by every insect, plant, and animal on the planet, including Man. They all practice devious techniques to safeguard themselves and their offspring. Camouflage, impersonation, misdirection, protective coloration, and mimicking are the veritable minefield of non-truths laid down daily.

Rampant deception is the norm in our world. Headlines exclaim the fraud and trickery of our leaders and advisors that have devastated our economy, wrecked the housing market, destroyed retirement savings, killed job security, and demolished our financial well-being. On a personal level, you must be wary of financial advisors who promise high returns on your money, repairmen of every type, and salesmen and advertisers whenever they open their mouths.

Do you recall those notorious lies where the speaker was later exposed? "I'm not a crook!" "I did not have sexual relations with that woman!" "Iraq has weapons of mass destruction!" They're so high profile they need not be attributed. (Okay, a hint: they were all U.S. Presidents.) And pro sports stars, night show hosts, and reality show celebs regularly have furtive scandalous affairs.

Then there are the lies we've been fed over the years, spoken by more than one CEO or corporate spokesperson, such as, "No scientific medical proof shows that cigarettes can cause cancer or other diseases." They got away with that one for a long time. "This diet plan will melt the pounds away for good." That canard continues, and America's weight gains do also. "Gasoline prices are a function of supply and demand." Or maybe as Jay Leno, the late night talk show host, said about those ever-rising gas prices, "I'm no economist, but here's a thought: maybe the oil companies are just trying to screw us."

History shows that deception starts wars, breaks hearts, costs jobs, destroys fortunes, and brings civilizations to the brink of ruin. Throughout time, man's deceitful tendencies have permeated our culture and drastically affected human interactions. The philosopher Diogenes of Sinope, even using a lantern, could not find an honest man in ancient Athens. And the destructive lies of Hitler caused fifty million civilian and combat casualties. It can and will happen—your boss, child, or dearest friend will try to fool you. Studies show that some of the most destructive deceptions are performed by those people closest to you.

Will you catch the betrayal? Some fibs can be trivial, even polite, such as, "Oh, I love your new short hairstyle." Or maybe, "Yes, that dress is really slimming on you." But other dishonest comments can damage your health, emotions, or finances.

Say your stock broker acquires some of your investment money by "churning" your portfolio (buying and selling stocks with little or no planning in order to collect the commissions). Or an auto mechanic or carpet salesman or plumber gyps you out of substantial funds. Don't you want to know when they're trying to hand you a phony bill of goods? Then study this book, and I'll give you some expert tips for perceiving fraud.

> **When lying starts.**

We learn to lie in our childhood. Dr. Harriet Goldhor Lerner, in her book, *The Dance of Deception,* Harper, New York, 1994, states, "Children conceal information from their parents and engage in deception for many reasons." She says that a child may keep secrets as a means of avoiding punishment for his misdeeds. It's also a way for him to assert his separateness and individual personality.

Research shows that around age five a child will first tell a successful fib. It's then that he realizes he is an independent being and that his parents are not all-knowing. By the time a youngster reaches adolescence, he's striving hard to be a detached individual. He will often scorn his parents' values and regulations, wanting to make his own decisions about life. And

11

he'll use deceit as a way of avoiding parental control. As the father of four sons, I've heard many times, "I'm sure I handed in that assignment." Or, "Everyone got a low score on that quiz." Or, "I really studied for that test, but I just got nervous."

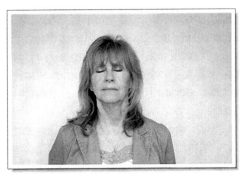

Hiding something? Hmm. We'll see.

➤ **Those little white lies.**

We all seem to develop as individuals who are a bit less than honest. And, indeed, much lying that goes on in everyday life is not intended to harm anyone. Everyone has told small fibs meant to make another person feel better about himself.

Many lies are harmless and are used only to make interactions with others go smoothly. Charles V. Ford, M.D., says that white lies are "basically social lies that serve to lubricate interpersonal relationships."

We've all practiced this form of pretending. We've complimented someone on their clothing or creative project when we weren't really that impressed. We'll say, "You really nailed that karaoke song," when the audience had cringed in pain. We tell these fibs in order to get through the day without hurting anyone's feelings or causing a fistfight. Social fibs can be harmless or destructive, but they're certainly accepted practice in our culture.

➤ **Oh, the lies I've seen.**

In my law enforcement career, as I spoke with tens of thousands of people, my objective was to collect information about federal crimes. I dealt with bank robbers, killers, kidnappers, con men, and embezzlers. Other contacts involved burglars, salesmen, prostitutes, strippers, and businessmen. And then there were cops, scientists, clergy, engineers, and psychiatrists. What did they all have in common? They'd all bend, twist, or just plain fracture the truth. It's like the old joke: How can you tell when someone's lying? Easy, it's when his lips move.

But why do most of us develop into effective liars? For as many reasons, I would venture, as there are raindrops in a thunderstorm. There are numerous types of liars among us, and people have different reasons for telling falsehoods in diverse situations.

People will fib to protect themselves from harm or punishment. This comes from the basic instinct of self-preservation we all possess. In addition, some people lie to defraud others and to gain something of value. A third type is the pathological liar who will use deception without needing a specific reason. Such a person will lie occasionally, frequently, or habitually, and in varying degrees.

Besides the fundamental causes for deception, I think there are multiple choices we make concerning how we relate to others, including how truthful we may be. Don't you have your own standards for the way you interact with your child, mate, best friend, relatives, and bosses? Then you likely have different levels of truthfulness with co-workers, neighbors, golf buddies, poker friends, and party pals. Circumstances affect the stories you relate and in what manner you do so.

There are not only these societal links that affect how we tell a story, and how much private information we may broadcast, there are also our own upbringings and our life experiences that shape how forthcoming we are in our dealings with others. I know that by mingling with those from the underbelly of American society, I became more suspicious of people and more alert to spot deception. We're all affected by our history, as well as our ongoing daily encounters.

Drug users and alcoholics are practiced liars. Often times, their entire family shares in a communal lie to cover up the addiction from outsiders. And the addicts deceive themselves by insisting that they don't have a problem, they're not hooked, and they can quit smoking or drinking or using drugs anytime they want. We see a lot of this denial among Hollywood celebrities on the television show "*E*" ("*Entertainment Nightly*"), or from other such media watchers of the beautiful people.

An expert in lie detection, Stan B. Walters, says the factors that exist in any situation involving deception are choice, opportunity, and ability. The person must first make a conscious choice about trying to deceive you. Opportunity refers to whether you give him an opening by not paying close attention to what he's saying, or by not knowing how to spot lies and deception. The ability to deceive is determined by the liar's intelligence and communication skills. Thus, we must be alert to analyze each discussion for the likelihood of deceit.

❖ **Nothing but the truth.**

In one case involving two bank robberies by the same man, the defendant showed up at trial with a belated alibi. A friend of his claimed that he and the suspect had been at the Laundromat™ for about six hours (lots of dirty undies and such, I guess), including the time that one of the robberies occurred. It was a pathetic performance, with the witness reciting his sworn testimony as though he'd memorized it. And during pauses before and during the testimony, the witness and the subject gazed at each other and grinned like a couple of demented hyenas, both giggling to themselves at times, with the shared knowledge, I suppose, that they were really putting one over on the jury, and that the robber would get off Scot free.

I didn't think much about how it would affect the case until the judge ordered a recess after the man's testimony. While I stood in the hallway, I was approached by the president of the bank that had been robbed. He was pale-faced and jittery. I said hello and waited to hear what was on his mind.

The bank president had been in the courtroom and heard the

testimony, and he was panicking. "That man couldn't have robbed our bank," he said, "the witness said he was at the Laundromat™ during that time." I realized the banker was absolutely serious.

"Don't worry about it, sir," I said. "The witness was lying. Our subject was the man who robbed your bank." Then I reminded him that three of his tellers had identified the man from a photo lineup, that he'd been identified by a passerby who saw him exit the bank, and that he was arrested with a shirt in his car trunk that matched the photo of the robber at the bank (and it sure hadn't been laundered). A sawed-off shotgun was found in his car that matched the weapon shown in the bank surveillance photos. Also the photographs taken by the bank camera looked like the man, and they had been identified as being him by people who knew him, including testimony by his own mother.

Now the president settled down. But he was shocked to learn that someone would get on the stand in federal court, swear to tell the truth, and then just plain lie. I'd been to quite a few trials, and I wasn't surprised. But it does go to show that some people are very trusting when someone tells them a story.

I dealt with falsehoods my entire career. And I've studied the techniques that have been developed over the years to detect when someone is lying. Many of the criminals I interviewed had faced situations where their parents were either onerously strict, or absent in fact or because of drug use, alcoholism, or just plain ignorance and ineptitude.

Such children grow up having to defend themselves both at home and on what mystery writer Raymond Chandler termed "the mean streets," by hook or by crook. Lying as a means of avoiding punishment and even for survival's sake becomes a way of life for them. Even those who don't turn to crime may use deceit to deal with various situations in their lives.

Defensive? Unresponsive?

> ➤ **Coping with lies.**

There are many ways to deal with the false statements, ex-aggerations, and fantasies with which you're bombarded daily. You could become cynical and mistrusting of everyone you meet. But I see that as a self-destructive behavior that harms you much more than it hurts others. I believe that you're best served by doing what all the creatures of this world have done for millions of years. You must observe, learn, and adapt your behavior in response to what's happening in your surroundings.

Dr. Jo-Ellan Dimitrius says a reward of being able to detect deception is that you become a more caring and compassionate person. I've noticed that having the ability to decipher why people perform the acts they do makes me feel less angry with them. When you understand why individuals stretch the truth, you become more empathetic.

This could be important in your life. Maybe you can help someone you're fond of overcome their tendency to be untruth-ful and defensive. By being able to listen to them and evaluate what they're saying, you'll know better how to deal with them.

> **Our batting average.**

With so many falsities surrounding us daily, how good are we at detecting them? A compilation of psychological tests by Dr. Alfred Vrij showed the accuracy rate of people being able to detect lies was 44 percent. And these were situations where the observers were watching closely to ferret out untruths. Added to that poor average, I think a number of lies will slip by us due to our inattention or because of our basic trust of others.

We all have an "inner sense" that helps us deal with the chiselers and con men we run across. Still, in these times of super hype and grossly fraudulent business practices, I believe everyone should learn as much as possible about how to spot deceit. In a later chapter, I'll explain various schemes and scams and stratagems that con artists use, but for now, don't be concerned. You can use the techniques for catching lies that you'll learn in this book quite effectively in the tricky commercial arena, as well as in your ordinary personal interactions.

❖ **Always watch your back.**

Though most of you won't be arresting anyone, I'm telling this anecdote to remind you to always be alert to what's going on around you. Anyone can run into trouble in restaurants, schools, or their work places. Out-of-control people are a menace to us all. Also, con men, pickpockets, and armed robbers can approach you unannounced at any time. It pays you to be watchful of the people in your surroundings.

Early one morning in San Antonio I joined an FBI raid team that crept up to a trailer to arrest a dangerous felon. An agent forced open the door, and SWAT team members swarmed inside. Together with a couple of other agents, I entered hard on their heels. But the SWAT team quickly handcuffed the man, with no incidence of violence, so there was a general feeling of relief and a job well done.

After the arrest, we began to search the place. An agent was assigned to watch the fugitive while the rest of us inspected the filthy, smelly, trash-laden trailer. Crusted plates were piled high in the sink and on countertops. Magazines, beer bottles, and heaping ashtrays cluttered a coffee table. The floor was littered with fast food wrappers and crumpled cigarette packs. Martha Stewart would have fainted dead away.

During the search, I saw the agent who was guarding the subject start to walk him across the trailer. "What are you doing?" I asked him. He said the guy had to use the bathroom. In truth, this is a common occurrence following an arrest.

But as I studied the man, he looked nervous, but he wasn't giving any signals such as a pained face, jittery legs, or tight lips. Also, he wasn't staring at the bathroom in a yearning way, but he kept glancing around, seeming to watch who was where, and what they were doing. He didn't show the discomfort of a man who really needed to go, and he was blinking more rapidly than normal, which is a sign of deception. I suspected he was putting on an act, and I wondered why.

"Wait a minute," I told the agent, and I stepped inside the small bathroom. The toilet smelled of stale urine, and the washbasin was streaked with dark stains. But I wasn't interested in the décor or cleanliness. I was checking for a reason the felon might want to get in there besides performing the usual bodily functions.

The window was too small to wriggle out of. There was nothing in the tub but mildew and soap scum, and I found no objects hidden in the toilet tank. That left only the cabinet under the washbasin where something might be stashed.

On my knees, I opened the cabinet doors, and peered inside. There was the usual—toilet tissue, bottles of cleaner, shampoo, soap, and some crumpled cloths—and there, as I moved the rags aside, lay the reason for my unease about the man's fakery: a loaded 9mm semi-automatic pistol, dark and menacing. I snagged the weapon and exited the bathroom door. Displaying the gun, I said, "Think you can pee without this?"

When the fellow saw it in my hand, he got a hangdog look. I'm sure he had intentions of wreaking havoc with that pistol. But because I followed my intuition about his strange behavior, and then noticed some clues of deception, it wasn't to be.

➢ **Know the clues.**

To protect yourself from duplicity, I suggest you should be educated beyond using hunches to decipher it. Anyone can find himself in a decision-making quandary in critical situations. Every person should know the latest methods of lie detection to better enable him to make sound decisions.

Dr. David J. Lieberman says a truthful person will expect to be believed, but a liar may worry about "the integrity of his façade." Thus, he may ask you, in so many words, if you believe him. I've come across many such storytellers, and they seem quite eager to present themselves as forthcoming and co-operative. A truthful person, on the other hand, will be more interested in making sure you understand what he's trying to say, not whether you perceive him as a pillar of honesty.

When I interviewed one of these prevaricators, it would often be a battle of wits to get him to "come clean" and tell the truth. Many times I couldn't do it. When I would win the skirmish, it was often because I managed to box in the person by disproving his lies with evidence to the contrary. Appealing to the man's conscience seldom worked, as this type of suspect usually had an anti-social personality, and he would feel no emotional effects from conning or hurting or even killing another person.

This kind of liar would often, when cornered, skirt the issue with a new explanation of why things appeared as they did, but were simply misunderstood. I found it was only after years of interviewing such people that I became somewhat accomplished in being able to cut through the "tangled web" they'd weave.

You've probably run across some of these people, and you were likely left with a feeling of "What just happened?" or "What did he say?" They can easily confuse you because their individual statements seem to make sense, but the whole story just doesn't hang together. When you begin to feel like Alice in Wonderland, you should start to doubt, question, and try to perceive what's really happening.

I'll describe the methods I learned over years of dealing

with deceptive people. Of course, it can be difficult to know who and what to believe. As we've seen, there are many types of liars. Fortunately, they all exhibit characteristics and mannerisms you can identify that indicate they're trying to trick you.

> **Detecting lies.**

Modern life is complex. You never know when your identity, money, and safety might be at risk. As a result of having been exposed to many types of deceptive practices, we've all developed radar antennae for being able to ascertain certain kinds of lies, and we've learned how to deal with them. A few individuals are astute at it, just as a small number of folks are unaware of practically anything that's going on around them. Some of us are too trusting. Others are too cynical. Only a scant percentage of people know most of the techniques that we'll discuss in this book.

In my job as an FBI agent, a major part of my work was to search for, identify, and be able to prove the truth of a matter. In short, any lie that was presented to me, by a person or document or crime scene, was an obstacle in the performance of my duty. Learning to uncover the truth of what happened became the sought-after Holy Grail of each case I investigated in order to bring it to a logical conclusion.

We can learn to observe and interpret another's body language, even while we're also listening to what he says and watching his facial expressions. Messages are sent by a person's posture, gestures, and movements. We must become attuned to the "microexpressions" that flash across a person's face for a fraction of a second and signal his true emotions. Such an expression often precedes another expression that the person wants you to see. The first expression, which is an automatic one, is the true one.

A microexpression of anger.

Humans are much better at reading the significant signals given by other people by using their unconscious brain, says Dr. Smith, than they are by working with the conscious intellect. He believes that natural selection, perhaps as a reaction to handling complex social interactions, would favor those who could distinguish the wheat from the chaff of social intercourse. I think that's likely, and it's in our favor to have the underlying judgment of our unconscious to alert us to suspected untruths. However, we also need the conscious understanding of signals that indicate stress or lying in order to pinpoint the questionable statements in a person's story.

I think we can improve our abilities to "read" other people and determine their mind-set, uncover their motivations, and predict their actions. We simply must study the behavioral indicators found in this book. There are various verbal and non-verbal patterns that even practiced liars can't keep themselves from doing. We'll learn these signals so as to be forewarned about any dishonest remarks being delivered our way.

It's always a good policy, when questioning someone you suspect of being untruthful, to keep your "virtual poker hand" close to the vest. Don't confront a suspected liar with the information you know that indicates he may be twisting the truth. He'll often just tell you another lie to explain why your evidence doesn't mean what you think. Then you're stuck without any ammunition. You've fired your single shot pistol, and now you're empty. Instead, you should question the person about the situation in such a way that he can't later use certain alibis, because you've already made those excuses unavailable.

I cringe when the specialists on the television show *CSI* go to a suspect and say something like, "We found hairs from the murder victim on your tennis racket. How do you explain that?" Then the suspect will say, "Oh, Melissa and I played tennis a few days ago. She broke a string on her racket, and I loaned her one of mine. She had dandruff, you know, and I saw her scratching her head with the racket several times."

You must be clever and trap the liar so that he can't dodge your questions. Ask if he saw Melissa within the past week and what they did together. Eliminate any possibility that they'd played tennis, and thus any excuse that she'd had some contact with his racket before he bashed her on the head with it.

This technique is essential to use in any situation where you're trying to evaluate the veracity of someone's comments. You should never let your emotional involvement override your rationality in framing your questions and in sorting through the value of the responses you receive. Always be aware to use your common sense and keep your wits about you when seeking the truth of a certain matter. Prepare yourself by analyzing what questions you need the answers to, and plan your strategy for eliminating any false replies, so you'll nail down the essence of what actually happened.

When I entered the Bureau, I went through the 14-week training period at the FBI Academy in Quantico, Virginia. There, I learned interview procedures for eliciting the truth. And I discovered many more once I started working in the field. I picked up techniques from partner FBI agents, other federal agents, and local police officers when they interviewed suspects. Talking with criminals taught me other ideas. I've also studied methods for recognizing deceit, and reasons why people lie, just because I've always been fascinated with the subject. I'll pass on all these techniques to you in this book.

You'll review the body language people display when they

practice deception, and the verbal slips, facial expressions, and other "tells" people exhibit when they try to mislead. Also, you'll learn to listen for tell-tale phrases of deception. If you learn the clues, you'll know what's going on in any discussion. You'll know who to trust and who to be leery of.

Even though your reasons for discerning the truth probably won't involve mayhem (although, in today's bizarre world, they might), I feel it's important for you to learn how. You should study ways to question others more effectively. Your awareness of what's going on around you will definitely increase as you explore the psychology of lying.

Dr. Smith theorizes that not only does _lying to yourself soothe the stresses of life,_ but it also helps you to be _better_ able to _lie to others._ He believes that _self-deception_ is probably necessary for _psychological equilibrium._ I don't believe you'd go crazy if you never told another lie, but it's possible everyone around you might. And though many have lauded the virtue of truth-telling, I prefer the more patently "honest" comment by Jerome K. Jerome, "It is always the best policy to speak the truth—unless, of course, you are an exceptionally good liar."

You'll learn to be aware of your surroundings, including the types of people in the area. Your concentration will focus on what people actually say, and you'll watch them for signs of deceit when they say it. Being alert to how someone looks and sounds and acts when he talks to you will help you determine his veracity. Also, you should be careful to avoid seeing and hearing only what you want, as that's a form of self-deception.

One shortcoming many of us have, says Dr. Dimitrius, is that we often evaluate people based on their race, national origin, sex, age, appearance, and economic status, including trappings such as their clothing, jewelry, and vehicles. You should never allow any preconceived notions about a person affect your judgment about their truthfulness. Honest folks come in all shapes, sizes, and colors. As do liars. So, you should just analyze the reliable indicators that tell you when people are being less than candid.

It's necessary to accumulate and assess a certain amount of information about a person before you can make a judgment about his usual patterns of behavior, and therefore be able to note any changes from those patterns that might reflect a false response. If a person is presumably telling the truth, such as when he's being questioned about his background information, he will act in a particular way. However, if the questioning concerns wrongdoing by that person or by someone else about whom he has knowledge, he'll often change his actions considerably.

I always took this idea into account when interviewing someone in a criminal case. I'd first ask about personal items such as his age, address, job, and so forth, to establish rapport with him, and also to see how he acted while answering questions when he was fairly relaxed. Then when I asked questions about the crime, I could tell when he got stressed. By establishing a baseline of the man's behavior, I was able to tell whether his voice, gestures, posture and other factors changed while he was under pressure. At that point, I could be reasonably sure whether he was guilty and/or he had some knowledge of the crime.

In our daily exposure to lying, I've found that we must look out for ourselves and be aware that few people we deal with have our best interests at heart. Perhaps you don't want to be skeptical about people, but you do need to realize there are many psyches you'll deal with, and that people have myriad reasons to falsify, excuse, and sidestep in their dealings with you. To detect those falsehoods, it should help you to know the techniques I've learned from my study and experiences.

I'll furnish examples to show how these skills work, including photographs showing lying "tells." And I'll depict how various methods have helped me during my years of confronting known and suspected liars. Through anecdotes, I'll show that what I'm discussing has a basis in fact in the real world.

The information in this book will help you deal with whatever lies you hear. Just study the techniques discussed and be willing to evaluate the deceptive comments people make. You'll feel more aware and confident about controlling any situation you're in. And, like an FBI agent, you'll develop the expertise necessary to spot those lies that could hurt you.

2

The Eyes as Windows to the Truth

> **Look 'em in the eye.**

We all know the adage about how you can spot a person who's telling a lie by looking him in the eye. Supposedly, if he flinches, or won't look directly at you, or looks away quickly, he's probably lying. That does have a kernel of truth to it. I've interrogated criminal suspects who would avert their eyes from me every time they told a lie.

But when it comes to staring a person in the eye and discerning whether he "speaks with forked tongue" or is telling it straight, there's a problem. It's not a strong indicator because there are many reasons someone might not hold his gaze when he speaks to you. Studies have shown that it's natural for people not to maintain constant eye contact when talking. Around 60 percent direct involvement during a conversation is the norm.

Cultural or ethnic backgrounds can create a difference in how much connection a person keeps through his gaze. A person's personality type, whether introverted or extroverted, can affect the duration of contact with which they feel comfortable. Also, con men and habitual liars, knowing they'll seem more honest, will force themselves to look their victims directly in the eye as they lead them down the primrose path.

We tend to get a first impression of people by watching their eyes. When people avert their gaze, or stare at us too hard, or lock eyes with us, giving us a "come hither" gaze, we get decidedly different reactions. Let's consider some situations.

❖ **What's in a glance?**

The Shah of Iran, Mohammed Pahlavi, was deposed in 1973, and made an emergency trip to the United States for his personal safety. Word came that the Shah would be landing at Kelly Air Force Base, San Antonio, Texas, and FBI agents should be on stand-by to provide security. I got called at 3:00 a.m. with instructions to head for the base.

My assignment was to meet the Shah and Empress Farah at the elevator and to take them to the floor where they'd be staying. I waited beside a locked elevator until they arrived. The Shah and the Empress were attended by six bodyguards and six large Dobermans on leashes. That assemblage was far past the capacity of the elevator. We decided that the Shah and the Empress and two bodyguards would ride up with me. The other bodyguards and the doggies had to wait for the next run.

The bodyguards regarded me with dull, lifeless looks in their eyes. The Shah gave me a brief glance when I pressed the elevator button. It must have been one of those looks that royalty gives regular people—blank and expressionless and not registering human contact. His posture was rigid, and he wore a custom-fitted light gray suit, tie knotted neatly, coat buttoned. This was about 4:30 a.m. I was wearing a suit and tie, too, but I was on duty. Maybe he thought he was, too.

Then I glanced toward the Empress. She was attractive, wearing a colorful dress, and was more animated than the Shah. She looked me directly in the eye and gave me a smile. I sensed immediately that she was a warm and open person. Of course, the Shah had more reason to be guarded in his contacts, and I know he had a lot on his mind, but if I were to consider the candor of one or the other of them, my first impression would be to feel more trusting of the Empress. A direct and <u>genuine gaze</u> can go a long way toward <u>establishing good faith.</u>

➢ **You could have fooled me.**

In a test conducted by psychologists Allan and Barbara

Pease, volunteers were instructed to tell lies to other people in interviews. Of the volunteer liars, 30 percent looked away from the people as they lied to them. But 70 percent kept strong eye contact with their victims as they sought to deceive them. The victims believed 75 percent of those who looked into their eyes, and they didn't believe 80 percent of those who looked away. Clearly, the amount of eye contact was misleading.

So, the old saw that says "looking them in the eye" is a good lie detecting method doesn't wash. Just because someone is gazing into your baby blues doesn't mean they're giving you the straight skinny. It may be a means of deceiving you.

Aversion of the eyes each time a person answers a question that might incriminate him may indicate evasion, but I prefer to watch this sort of person for other signs of nervousness to validate the possible signal. He may also clear his throat or swallow often, and he'll find it hard to sit still in his chair, often moving his legs to point toward an exit.

When I talked with this kind of individual, I always felt that he'd eventually realize he couldn't continue fabricating lies to wriggle out of the jam he was in. So I fully expected that he'd either 'fess up or shut up or lawyer up. Such a liar reminds me of Thomas Fuller's quote in *Gnomologia*: "Trust him no further than you can throw him."

Another indicator of evasion is when a person's eyes dart from side-to-side. This means the man's mind is subconsciously searching for an escape route to get away from you and your questions. It signals that you've hit upon a question that he doesn't want to answer truthfully.

However, be sure not to confuse this darting of the eyes with a simple looking off when someone is formulating a response to your question. Glancing away can not be construed as being deceptive. Many people gaze afar when talking with close friends. I know I can concentrate on devising a complex response far better by looking away from a person than by continuing to stare into his eyes. The distancing provides for better concentration and a more coherent response.

Another factor to be aware of, according to the Pease's, is when men view something they find exciting, such as a hot-looking woman, a certain part of their body can increase to three times its normal size. Women also show this extreme pupil dilation, but it's most pronounced not when they observe a man's studly bod, but when they view a mother with a child. So, when you see pupil dilation, try to narrow down the cause.

When a person's eyes dilate, it can mean she's spotted something she considers to be favorable. Have you ever noticed that many professional poker players wear sunglasses? That's not only because they're cool to the max, it also hides the dilation of their pupils when they get a killer hand. The enlarging of the pupils can indicate the person is captivated by the way you look, but it can also reflect anxiety, and this phenomenon appears often when a person is lying. So, it's a good indicator to watch, along with other signs of deception that may be given simultaneously

> **Those loving eyes.**

And we're not even safe when gazing into the adoring peepers of our significant other. Dr. Lerner says that women are known to fake orgasms in order to please a man, to keep the relationship strong, or just to "get it over with." That's a sad revelation, but I suppose that some women just can't be satisfied with five minutes of bliss. Those misty eyes are saying, "Yes, yes," but it seems the lady's heart may be saying, "No, no." So, there's yet another mystery in the art of prevarication.

> **Eye shifts tell a tale.**

Indicators that show what a person is thinking include shifting of his eyes. I've learned techniques of what to watch for from several sources over the years, and I think they're worth your knowing. Psychologists Richard Bandler and John Grinder conducted scientific tests that they claim verify the psychological basis for the phenomena.

When you ask a person a question that requires him to check his visual memory about an event, he'll often pause and his eyes will shift upward. If he's trying to recall what happened, and he's recreating the scene in his mind, his eyes will shift upward and to his left (your right, as you look at him).

Eye shifts up and to his left signal truthfulness.

If the person is trying to make up a story which won't get him in trouble, his eyes will shift upward and to his right. This indicates he's creating it on the fly. He's imagining all or a significant part of the incident.

Eye shifts up and to his right show he's lying.

Also, if you ask a person to remember a particular sound she heard during a conversation or altercation, her eye shifts will tell you whether she's recalling an actual sound, or whether she's manufacturing it. If she's conjuring up a phony sound (the town clock striking three as she arrived at the bank), and she's integrating the sound as part of her story, you have reason to think her tale may have lots of other holes in it, too.

Perhaps you ask someone to recall what another person said, or how many gunshots she heard, or what a man's voice sounded like on the phone. If she is searching her memory for an auditory sensation, her eyes will shift to her left, toward her ear. This is because she's accessing the temporal lobe for an auditory memory. If she's making up a sound she didn't hear, her eyes will drift toward her right ear.

Eyes look toward right ear; making up lies.

Another sign that a person is trying to access a true memory and not just creating an answer she hopes sounds plausible is when that person stares straight ahead, "into space," with an unfocused look. Whatever answer she comes up with after that would likely be truthful. You'll see this type of eye fixation performed by actors in movies when the story switches to a flashback scene.

Just be aware that there are a small percentage of people whose eyes shift in the opposite mode. So, to be certain the interviewee is not one of them, ask him a couple of questions that you know the answers to, and see which way his eyes shift when he's answering truthfully. Then you'll have a baseline of his behavior in order to be able to distinguish whether he's telling the truth or lying.

This principle of eye shifts also applies to sensations of

emotion, taste, and smell. Ask a person something like, "What did the liquid that the man threw on your fur coat smell like?" If her eyes shift downward and to her left, she's truly trying to access what the aroma was, and her story is fortified. If her eyes lower and shift to her right, she's trying to come up with a believable reply.

I've run across tearful responses when interviewing people. Sometimes I take their crying at face value as a sign that they're overwhelmed and emotionally freaked out. I also think tears can show frustration and fear. So, there can be many emotions signaled by a person turning on the waterworks. You'd do well to watch for other "tells" that verify whether a person is being genuine in revealing their feelings, or whether they're trying to trick you into being sympathetic to them.

❖ **The dead don't lie—or do they?**

Concerning the lies or truths shown in people's eyes, I recall the time I looked into the eyes of a dead man and the totally surreal happened. It was a hot day in South Texas, and I was searching for a fugitive. The man had killed someone in Kansas and fled south. A person who knew the subject tipped us off that he was staying with a relative at a certain address.

I was the only agent in town, as my partner had just left on vacation. So, I drove to the police station and asked a couple of detectives to help me find the murderer. We left for the house around noon, with the temperature nearing 100 degrees, the sun blazing, and the air suffocating.

The fugitive was said to have traveled by bus, so there was no car outside the residence. One of the detectives knew the owner of the home, and he called her at work, getting permission to search it. We slipped into the house, seeking the killer.

As we walked into the empty living room, the detectives turned left and headed for the kitchen. I turned right and moved along a hallway. There were two bedrooms and a bath off the hall. I searched the first bedroom, then the bath. No one was there. I listened for sounds from the detectives' endeavors, but heard nothing. There was no air conditioning, windows were closed, and no fans whirred to move the air.

I was sweating and felt nervous about searching by myself. But I forged ahead, checking the next bedroom. There was no one in the room, or under the bed, or in the closet. But I noticed a large shelf in the top of the closet that held a stack of sheets and quilts and blankets, all folded neatly, probably four feet deep. I'd never seen so many bedclothes. But it struck me that it was possible, just possible, that the man could be hiding up there.

It seemed unlikely, as I saw no ladder or footstool or any way he could have climbed up there, much less be among the bedclothes, all folded perfectly over him. But a voice in my head reminded me that in training school the instructors told us about fugitives who had hidden in dresser drawers, refrigerators, and crawl spaces underneath the house. In short, we'd been advised to always search any space into which a human body could possibly fit.

I sighed, wiped sweat from my forehead, holstered my revolver, and reached up to the humongous pile of bedding. I pushed my arms into the stack, going all the way to the back of the closet. First I tried about five inches from the bottom, then ten inches, and so on. When I reached about two-and-a-half feet, I felt a hard object. I pulled some bedding aside and thrust my hand in so I could better feel what it was. Then I touched something wet.

What the hell? I thought. And I moved some more sheets and blankets aside. When I'd cleared about a four-inch gap, I could see what it was. Black, slick, wet human hair and a man's forehead, ashen gray, motionless. *Oh, my God,* I thought. *He's killed someone else and stuffed the body into the top of this closet.*

So, I tugged more bedclothes out and dropped them to the floor. Now I could see the man's head, which resembled a wax figure. His face was taut, eyes closed, purplish lips motionless. *I suppose I should get the body down,* I thought. And then, as I stared at the man's rigid face, his eyes flicked open. They looked glassy, like marbles. In a heartbeat, my hand went from near his chin to my holster and back, with my gun barrel pointing two inches from his face. "Get down from there," I said. "I'm FBI. We have a warrant for your arrest."

In that instant, I'd realized that the "dead guy" was the fugitive we sought. He'd hidden under all those covers, in the top of a closet, on a stifling, muggy day, in a house with no cooling. And he'd nearly died from his efforts.

I sensed a feeling of relief on his part when he climbed down from the top of the closet and some color returned to his face. And I have to note that paying attention to the eyes brought me success in doing my job. It might even have saved my life, or his.

➤ **A blink in time.**

Rapid blinking of the eyes usually indicates nervousness and deception. The normal blinking rate is once every five or six seconds, with the eyes closed for a brief one tenth of a second. But when people are feeling anxiety, such as when they're lying, they'll blink at a faster rate. The blinking rate performed by nervous, and possibly deceptive people, can increase from the normal ten blinks per minute to four or five times as high. Sometimes, when I asked suspects the tough questions about their guilt or innocence, I've seen them flap their lids so fast I thought they might singe their lashes.

Also, when someone closes his or her eyes for an extended period of time, it's a good indication they're being deceitful. Once a suspect I was questioning about a bank robbery was clamping his eyelids shut for such long intervals that I thought he might fall asleep. And sometimes a person's eyelids will flutter during such interludes, showing nervousness.

Eyes closing too long show she's lying.

A suspect's eyes may lift at the end of a spoken sentence. This could indicate a false statement, especially when the voice and head also go up in conjunction with the eyes. This person's conviction about what he's just told you is not strong, especially not as solid as he may be trying to convince you it is, likely because he's fibbing.

A similar sign of deceit is when the person being questioned rubs his eye. Men often do this heartily, making it seem casual and nonchalant. Actually, it's a psychological "tell," as the man's brain is sending him a signal to hide from his own deception or to block out your distasteful image as a tough questioner.

It's also a part of a trio of indicators that come from the monkey triad that sees no evil, hears no evil, and tells no evil. As we'll see, all these signals will be given by a person who's trying to hide the truth from you or avoid answering your questions. Think of the triad as a way to remember those moves that signal he's showing deception.

Rubbing his eye is hiding from you.

> ➤ **Other signals to note.**

When someone doubts what you've said, she'll narrow her eyes, furrow her forehead, and lift one eyebrow. If you've seen the wrestler and actor known as "The Rock" display this look, you'll never forget it. It's a classic sign that tells it like it is.

Another look that can be interpreted through watching someone's eyes is that of surprise. When a person is taken off guard, you can read it in her eyes. If someone is startled, astonished, or shocked by something that's said or done during a conversation, she'll open her eyes very wide.

This reaction will show the sclera (the whites of the eyes) above the iris. And the lower jaw will sometimes drop, which makes her lips come apart. This is a look most of us can immediately analyze.

If someone is surprised by information she would know if she were guilty of an act, then you have reason to believe she's innocent. On the other hand, if you tell someone certain facts about a situation that would be shocking to most people, and she shows minimal or no real reaction, then you'd have cause to be suspicious of her. She could be involved in the irregular activity in question, and you'd want to keep checking it out.

It can be useful to note surprise.

Anger can also be spotted through the aspect of a person's eyes. A person who's mad will stare at you with a tense look. Her eyelids will narrow, giving a "snake eye" gaze. I've had subjects get angry with me during an interview, and it's a simple matter to detect. But I was just doing my job, so I would try to defuse the situation and move forward. If it seems incongruous for someone to get <u>angry</u> with you when you're asking <u>straightforward questions,</u> it may be because they feel pressured to either admit wrongdoing or to lie to you.

If a person is embarrassed by a situation, they may give you a sideways glance. People who have an eye twitch or spasm are usually tense and feel under stress. A person who feels ashamed will often look downward to avoid eye contact. Any of these may be indicators that they've been lying to you.

If a person is telling the truth, but he's been accused falsely of lying, he'll tend to offer strong and undeviating eye contact. The muscles around his eyes will be relaxed, showing no signs of stress, and he'll fix you with a direct gaze. In this case, I think he's trying to beam the thought into your brain that he's being honest and, damn it, you should believe him.

Admittedly, it's often difficult to observe eye movements. And let me repeat that you need to be watching and listening for other non-verbal and verbal clues to deception, as well. In fact, it's best not to base your assumption about lying on just one indicator. I suggest you raise your antenna when you spot one sign, then be aware to notice whether other signals of deceit are given to support it. You're looking for clusters of indications as to a person's veracity or mendacity at that particular moment.

> **Good vibrations.**

Besides watching a person's eyes, you should keep your other deception detecting senses fully alert. Use your intuition, your hunches, the vibes you get when dealing with a person. Psychoanalyst Robert J. Langs states that an individual's "deep unconscious system" was designed by nature to quickly and accurately size up other people. I believe we should pay attention to clues of deceit that we see, and any subjective feelings about a person's truthfulness we get while talking with him.

Any vibes about his truthfulness?

> **The power of the unconscious.**

Studies show that most of our mental work is done by the unconscious mind. Say someone throws a ball at your face— you'll likely react with reaching up your hand to stop it. Your conscious mind hasn't had time to work out that Jack has just cocked his arm and flung a baseball in your direction and that, if you don't flinch or cover up, the ball will probably hit you in the face. Do you think President Bush had time to consciously analyze the shoe throwing incident? No, but his dodging reactions were good.

Your unconscious mind has been structured through millions of years of development from our ancestors seeing some object or insect or animal's paw headed toward their faces. The brain has learned the best way to handle the situation to survive the onslaught, and it knows you need to duck or throw up a hand, or you'll get smacked. And so we do, without conscious thought.

While the unconscious mind is at work, receiving all the stimuli out there and translating which actions may affect our well-being, it will select the proper emotion to protect us in the situation. What if you're suddenly threatened by a man waving a gun in your face? The unconscious may decide you should experience fear and either freeze or try to run away. Or it may select anger and aggression, so you'll try to grab the gun and punch the man in the face. You respond emotionally to a situation before your conscious mind can make any kind of rational decision. Anger or fear will come over you before you have had time to assess the situation logically.

And emotions are usually displayed through facial expressions or body language. Thus, the person with the gun stuck in his face may jerk his head or body, his jaw may drop, and his eyes may open wide from fear or from being startled. If he's angered, his jaw muscles may tighten, face redden, eyes narrow, lips compress, muscles tense, and fists clench. Some facial aspects are easily recognizable to each of us. In situations where you're trying to assess whether a person is lying or being truthful, watching for expressions and body language can assist you greatly.

Once again, if the look only shows for a fraction of a second, then changes, you can be sure that the first expression indicated the true emotion the person felt. He was signaling through his brief aspect exactly how he was responding to your question or to whatever situation was presented to him. And those fleeting looks will likely seem incongruous with what the man is saying.

Such quick changes in a person's mien that last only a split second are shown simply because every basic emotion has its own characteristic pattern of expression. These reactions occur involuntarily before the individual can control them. Often these will seep through a liar's deceptive façade and momentarily slip across his face. Then these signals can be picked up and analyzed by an observer's unconscious neural circuitry that is expressly dedicated to this purpose.

Most often, the person will be totally unaware of having given away his inner feelings through the look on his face, as it was an unconscious reaction. But the expression does reflect that he or she is undergoing stress, conflict, and inner turmoil. And these are exactly the emotions that a liar would be feeling

It's a useful approach to suggest to the interviewee that he knows about the matter at hand. Preface your questions with phrases such as, "What happened when . . . ?" or "Tell me about . . ." It's better to be positive and confident in an interview and not seem as if you're fishing for information. I found that if I knew something about how a crime was committed, I could get more information from the interviewee. I'd ask about specifics I knew the answer to already. If the man lied, I'd call him on it. If he told the truth, I'd ask something I didn't know, with more confidence that he might give me the right answer.

> **Cool is the rule.**

Also, when trying to get at the truth of a matter, I've found that it pays to stay composed and think about all aspects of the situation. Remember what it is that you want to know. Don't be distracted by off-topic statements the interviewee makes. Don't get upset by insinuations that you are to blame for something having gone wrong, when you know that's not the case. Keep focused on the subject at hand. Listen to the content of how the person answers the questions, while watching and listening for other signs of untruth, and think about the consequences of the answers.

It never hurts to be pleasant and courteous at the beginning of an interview or conversation. This may keep the interviewee from withdrawing from conversation or becoming confrontational to the point where no information of value will be obtained. You can always get tough later if you think it will help you get the answers you seek.

Don't ever drop a line of questioning until you've taken it to a logical conclusion. The only exception would be if you're trying to throw the person off stride by thinking you've gone on to a new topic, and then suddenly come back to the original line of questioning. This can sometimes be effective for assessing truthfulness. If the interviewee seems tense and nervous when you're dwelling on certain questions, then seems to relax when you switch subjects, you have a good indication he's been deceptive before. Then you can return to the topic later and pin him down.

Also, be thorough. I've seen many interviewers ask some perceptive questions, getting helpful answers, and then fail to follow through, to ask the last couple of questions that would nail down an admission. They simply don't skewer the liar as a matador would kill a bull. Maybe it's because both parties are uncomfortable. Maybe it's because it's embarrassing to box someone in to where he'll have to admit he's been lying. But that's the nature of the beast. Often the truth is discovered through a painful process.

Another problem with incomplete questioning is that it fails to get to the kernel of truth. The result of this hesitancy is that the previous statements of admission will probably be denied or explained away with another barrage of false accounts at a later time. After all, if you don't strike when the iron is hot, the person has had time to think. He can develop some "better" answers, much like when you think of clever retorts in a dispute that's been over for an hour.

Of course, police interrogators are often trying to determine if people are guilty, or to judge whether they're reliable witnesses. One way of doing this is that propounded by Sir Arthur

Conan Doyle, the author of the Sherlock Holmes mystery series. He wrote, "How often have I said to you that when you have eliminated the impossible, whatever remains, however improbable, must be the truth?" I must agree that sometimes that's more effective than pursuing any number of hunches.

➢ **Watch the mouth.**

When a person tightens or compresses his lips, he may be irritated or put off by what you're saying. He may also be, in effect, "biting his tongue," just waiting to refute what you're telling him. However, pursed lips can otherwise mean he's merely contemplating what you're saying. Nodding of the head while he's listening will signal that he agrees with you.

Some people try to mask their emotional reactions by controlling their aspects. They project a stony visage, or what's sometimes called a "poker face." When you observe this look, you can be sure the person is trying to conceal something, and you should be alert to watch his non-verbal movements and listen to the content of his speech. I've seen some real deadpan expressions when I interviewed men or women in jail or prison. I suppose the philosophy of not showing any weakness while you're behind the wall carries over into interviews by a lawman.

➢ **What the face can tell us.**

Some facial movements or expressions that you can spot when a person is lying are muscular jerking in the face; blushing or blanching, which signals nervousness; and twitching of the small muscles around the eye, which can show that a person is stressed or uncomfortable. Other related signals are excessive sweating and respiration changes, such as hyperventilation.

Similar actions include "adapters" such as fiddling with one's hair, which indicates nervousness and possible prevarication. Eye rolling is a sign that a person finds what you're telling him to be incredible or ridiculous. A clenched, tight jaw means the person is unhappy with you or what you're saying to him, and he's angry about the situation. An aloof, deadpan expression means the person is not interested in what you're saying, and probably not that taken with you, either.

But can we read expressions with confidence as to their meaning, even with people from other countries and cultures? The answer appears to be "yes." Dr. Linda Camras studied the facial expressions of Japanese and American infants. Both groups gave the same looks to show the same reactions.

We can all make countless expressions which have significance to others, and each of us can correctly interpret the meanings of those looks. We instinctively know how to communicate using nonverbal signals. When we analyze it, we realize that some very complex emotions can be shown through expressions. And, of course, we've been reading them since we were in diapers, so we usually receive the messages loud and clear.

Since people understand the meaning of expressions and how to make them, then those who are trying to deceive others, such as con men and fraudulent salesmen, are good at faking them. One example is the charming serial killer Ted Bundy. His good looks, false congenial manner, and phony smile aided him greatly in persuading women to let down their guard, which was a deadly mistake.

Psychologists say that cultural differences don't seem to affect the basic human expressions and their interpretation by those who observe them. This is good news in your quest for detecting deception. You can be confident that expressions are universal to all men, regardless of where they're born and raised, and in what type of cultural environment they live. The smile remains a signal of happiness and good will wherever you travel. And a frown is a universal downer.

Even the most primitive cultures were found to use and to identify the same expressions, whether used by inhabitants of New Guinea, New Zealand, or New York. Dr. Paul Ekman believes that our evolutionary heritage must be instrumental in producing nearly identical facial expressions for basic human emotions around the globe. He denotes this phenomenon as being "species-constant learning."

Psychological tests have shown that some people are especially good at reading faces. And it's been estimated that people can make over 10,000 expressions. In general, women are better at interpreting these looks than men. In fact, one study has shown that men make less than one third of the expressions that women use when communicating. Also, men are not as aware of the looks shown by others with whom they converse.

When someone grins at you, but her mouth and lips look tight and unnatural, you're getting a phony expression. We've all seen this on occasion, and I know that it makes me feel uncomfortable. This fake grin is shown when a person doesn't like you or really doesn't want to talk to you. The person will also have a dull look in his eyes, as if he's not really all there. But, in some circumstances, it could be that he fears talking with you because he'll have to manufacture a lie to stay out of trouble.

People who give tight-lipped smiles are not presenting their real feelings. Although they may say, "No, I wasn't there," or "I don't know anything about that," they're not thinking those things. But they feel obliged to say something and to fake a smile. They're trying to avoid discussing the real topic.

A genuine smile will affect both the mouth and the eyes, with a crinkling of the skin beside the eyes. A fake smile will involve only the lower face and mouth. This is because a true smile is generated by the unconscious mind and affects different muscles of the face than an intentionally constructed one.

When someone's angry with you or the situation, but trying to suppress it, he will instinctively tighten his lips. In addition, with this type of anger, you'll often observe a reddening of the cheeks, neck, and ears. The muscles of the face will also tense with the effort. If you're asking a person something at the time, he may be upset or irritated because he'll have to either lie to you or admit to an act he doesn't want to acknowledge.

➢ **A smile can go a mile.**

Dr. Smith notes that people are hardwired to be able to deliver a phony smile, where there are no wrinkles and crinkles beside and beneath the eyes. He states that even babies give strangers a fake smile but reward their mothers with the genuine item. And if someone is giving you a false smile, then you'd be best advised to be wary of whatever he says. He might be giving you some other hogwash to boot.

Person giving a phony smile—beware.

The smile looks pleasant, but it involves only the mouth. The muscles that control the eyes (the *ocularis oculi*) are not being used. The muscles around the eyes are controlled by the subconscious mind. When those muscles are not in play, the person is not giving you a genuine expression. Compare this photo to the next one to see the difference in the expressions.

Now here's a smile you can trust.

Another type of smile is the twisted smile. This is where an eyebrow and one side of the mouth are raised, but the other eyebrow remains still and the other side of the mouth turns down. It looks as if one half of the face is smiling and the other half is frowning. This is only given in the Western world, and it signals sarcasm.

A drop-jaw smile is just what it sounds like. The jaw lowers and the teeth are revealed, and the person tries to look jovial. However, his eyes are not twinkling or crinkling. This is another fake smile. To me, it seems as if the person looks ill. It's what might be termed a sickly grin, but with the teeth showing.

> **Other meaningful expressions.**

When a person is being stone-faced during questioning, he's trying to hide his facial expressions from being read. This disguising of his aspect helps to hide his thoughts. It's a good time to carefully observe his body language, because the hands, arms, and legs will now become more expressive than normal. So, you should be able to read what the man's thoughts and feelings are in the situation.

An additional facial expression to be aware of is one where people who feel disgust will involuntarily wrinkle their noses. I've seen this one shown on the television show *Lie to Me*. And as a perceived antagonist for the criminals I've confronted, I've experienced the look in person many times. Someone may display one of these aspects because they don't care for you or because they feel distressed by the question you've asked.

Research has shown a person's pupils will constrict when they look at something or someone they find unpleasant. Their eyes will widen when they're surprised or placed in a confrontational situation. A person will squint at something he perceives negatively. Sometimes an individual will lower his eyebrows when spotting a threat or some unlikable person or situation. Be aware of what look you are getting when you approach someone with your ideas, comments, or questions.

Any blocking of a person's eyes when he's listening to you should be seen as a signal that he doesn't like what you're saying. This can include a quick touching of the eye, rubbing or holding the eyelids closed, or a delayed opening of the eyelids after blinking. I've seen this blocking done many times in interviews with subjects who had committed a crime. They weren't too keen on my discussing the matter and trying to implicate them.

Eyelid flutter indicates an individual is having an internal struggle with receiving or delivering information. This reaction, of course, could be caused by guilt and worry that he will be caught lying. I've noticed this movement during interviews with suspects who were later proven to be guilty of the crimes in question.

So, try to remain aware of the varied eye movements and their meanings. This can be helpful to you whether you're trying to determine a teenager's veracity, or trying to break down the seemingly sincere protestations of a vicious criminal. Knowledge of these shifts can even come in handy if, on occasion, you're trying to get a straight story from your significant other.

Using common sense, listening to what's said and what's not being said, and watching the eyes, facial expressions, and body language a person projects can give you a solid basis for judging the accuracy and truthfulness of any comments he makes. In short, pay attention to expressions, as well as what's being said and done. It's all grist for your lie-detecting mill.

3

The Psychology of Lying

➤ Why do we all lie?

There are many self-serving homilies about this, including that we fib to protect the feelings of others. Or maybe we're just trying to be polite in a civilized society. After all, it wouldn't do to tell Fred, a colleague at work, that his breath smells like a goat's, and he drinks too much, and we despise his entrails. So, we sort of "go along to get along" in this cultured civilization of ours.

The concept of lying came about in the human species, says Dr. Smith, when they gathered together in larger numbers than the single family unit. Of course, they probably originally did that for protection, division of labor, and social contact. But when you collect more than a few individuals together in a social situation (living together, working together, "getting down" together), the number of possible interconnected social relationships spirals exponentially. Smith says once you get 20 people together in a group, the number of possible social interactions exceeds one million. That's a lot of interactions to be considered when you're trying to figure out the best plan of action to follow.

These complicated social systems create a need for people to be smarter in order to keep up with all of it. Smith believes the Darwinian theory of evolution would suggest that nature would select for any changes in the brain that would make the cerebral cortex larger, thereby providing for higher intelligence. Since I have trouble keeping track of the complicated interactive situations in my personal life and in the social order in which I operate, I have to concur with his ideas.

The theory of brain development is treated by Dr. Ford, who notes that as societies developed there was an increasing interplay between deceivers and those trying to avoid deception. He thinks this may have contributed to the large increase in brain size during human evolution, especially in the later stages. The prefrontal lobes of the brain are known to contain the interconnections and feedback loops among the major sensory and motor systems. The prefrontal cortex that takes information from both the conscious and the unconscious parts of the human brain is the most recently evolved portion of the brain, and within those lobes are integrated all the activities of the brain that affect our behavior.

A fact that seems to bolster this belief is that any damage to the prefrontal lobes often results in impaired social judgment in the injured person. This is seen quite often in criminal behavior studies. Such injuries are thought to cause hostility, impulsiveness, lack of self-control, and aggression.

It's well-documented that sociopaths don't feel the emotions of empathy, guilt, and remorse. Thus, such a person does what he wants to do, then can rationalize his actions afterwards. These types are committed to their own interests, they crave power, and they don't hesitate to lie to gain their goals. Jef Nance states that 8 percent of the general population fits this description, with them making up 40 percent of the prison inmates, and committing 90 percent of violent crimes. These are the types of people you want to identify quickly and stay away from, if at all possible.

> **Social interactions.**

In the earlier stages of the development of human societies, Smith notes that women were gathered together doing tasks around the campground during the day, and the development of language would have enabled them to better organize their work. It would also have aided them in "facilitating social networking." He believes that women would have done multitasking better if they could talk about things while still using their hands to do work.

Studies show that women are better in today's world at performing multiple tasks at one time than are men. Haven't you seen a woman driving, applying makeup, and talking on her cell phone? The neurons will fire up in many different sections of women's brains in order to do these tasks. And when we look at men's brains? No, not so much. Fewer parts of their brains light up as they perform fewer tasks at a time.

Did you ever see a man installing an auto part into his beloved vehicle? His whole existence, both mental and physical, is wrapped up in the job at hand. And probably women will never understand that a football game is like an intense chess match that must be studied in depth from the incipient kickoff until the last seconds tick off, without interruptions requesting he take out the trash, put in a light bulb, or drive to the store for milk.

The phenomenon of gossip aids people in learning about the social group, finding out who they can trust, and helping them to form alliances. Dr. Smith suggests that probably the evolution of language made it possible for humans to live together in increasingly larger groups. And in relation to gossip, language can be used to deceive and manipulate others, as well as merely pass on information. Once the social pastime of gossip became entrenched, it was not long until malicious gossip came along. Of course, Cicero understood this phenomenon and stated, "One does not have to believe everything one hears." Perhaps he also anticipated television commercials.

Caesar saw another side of this situation, and he included some perceptive psychological understanding by saying, "Men quite gladly believe what they want to believe." I have to agree that this has likely always been so. We all have our own interpretations of how the world operates. We have our personal unshakable ideas about what's really going on in life. William

Cowper noted that, "Each man's belief is right in his own eyes."

Francis Bacon added a dimension to that thought by saying, "Man prefers to believe what he prefers to be true." Of course, someone always has to be cynical on any subject, and Montaigne fills this role for us with his comment, "Nothing is so firmly believed as that which we least know." I do know a few folks who would fit into that category, but their names will be omitted to protect the guilty.

> **Various purposes for lies.**

Dr. Ford notes that lying can be a form of aggression. One may lie to another person with a belief that the other does not deserve the truth and with a feeling of contempt that the other is not smart enough to detect the lie. In a psychological study of a teen gang subculture, smartness was defined as the ability to dupe or con others successfully. Clever deceit is considered cool by this subgroup, and it is decidedly lame to be caught in a lie. But even though skill in lying is valued, it is not considered good for group survival to lie to each other. There's a code of honor among thieves and gangbangers.

Lies are used frequently to maintain power, such as when governments develop secrecy about weapons, economics, and industrial research. They vigorously protect against thievery of this top secret knowledge, and they spread misinformation to decrease the power of other people who want to be "in the know." When a person is able to tell many successful lies, he or she achieves a sense of superiority and a feeling of dominance.

> **Types of liars.**

Some people lie for the "fun and games" aspect of fooling someone else. They feel a sense of power by being able to pull off a deceitful scam. I believe that practical jokes are a form of this type of lying. This form of "kidding" often has a basis of underlying hostility and aggression. The joker receives a thrill by deceiving someone else, thus achieving a sense of cleverness and superiority. Several shows on television demonstrate the juvenile glee experienced when the perpetrator is able to "punk" someone else.

There are many types of liars we must watch for, according to Dr. Dimitrius. She notes that most people will lie occasionally to avoid punishment or other unpleasantness that might ensue if they were to admit to doing something wrong. I've found that these people, when you talk with them face-to-face, will usually feel uncomfortable about lying to you, and they'll manifest various types of body language that signal they're not giving you the whole truth and nothing but.

A person who lies more often and doesn't feel the guilt felt by a normal person is called a "frequent liar." And then some other people really get in the groove by lying constantly. Termed "habitual liars," these folks don't much care what they say, and they don't show many signs of distress when they lie. But Dimitrius says their stories are often confused and inconsistent. It's always wise to pay close attention to what someone tells you and to analyze whether it makes common sense and is logically sound.

Another type is the "professional liar," such as a shifty auto mechanic or a seasoned con man. These people will lie to you as a means to an end—to get your money. And they've told their packaged stories so often that they come across as very smooth and relaxed and honest in their presentations.

Dr. Dimitrius looks at three meaningful items as a way of understanding a prospective juror: compassion, socioeconomic background, and satisfaction with life. She says this helps her avoid making snap judgments based on stereotypes and bias, which should also be a goal of anyone seeking to determine someone's veracity. Personally, I'd tend to be more trusting of the word of someone who is compassionate concerning others instead of a person who is uncaring and self-centered. I know of no scientific tests that have tried to compare this character trait with a tendency to tell the truth, but my gut instinct and experiences in dealing with people leads me to that conclusion.

Regarding a person's socio-economic background, I've seen firsthand that desperate people tend to commit criminal acts. And then they lie about whether they've done so. Not to say that I haven't investigated cases where well-to-do suspects have broken the law. We've all seen the headlines and heard the stories of heads of huge corporations and Wall Street firms who have cheated and lied and defrauded others. Greed, materialism, and self-importance will lead men to do wrong. But many of my cases involved those who were perched on the lower rungs of the economic ladder.

❖ Brother, can you spare a dime?

There was a bank robbery in Kansas where, according to witnesses, after the man robbed the bank, he left with a bag of loot in hand and made his escape on a bicycle. It signaled to me that the robber might be a bit desperate. Also, he was described as being disheveled-looking and poorly dressed.

It happened that a sheriff's deputy entered a convenience store shortly after the robbery, after having heard about the incident over the police radio. He'd noticed a bicycle leaned against the building outside, and he observed a man buying some cigarettes who fit the description of the robber. He detained the man, called for backup, and the responding officers decided to take the fellow in for questioning.

I'd interviewed people at the bank, getting a description of the robber, how he acted, and how much money he'd taken from the bank, down to the exact dollar. A detective informed me over the phone how much money the suspect had on his person when arrested, and it was very close to what had been stolen. So, I asked what else the man had with him. I was informed about his purchase of cigarettes, and was also told that he had two bottles of unopened vodka in his possession.

I visited the convenience store and a nearby liquor store. The clerks in both places told me that a man matching the robber's description had just made purchases in their respective stores. I got copies of the register tapes to see how much money he'd spent at the two stores. When the subtractions were made, it resulted that the suspect had cash and purchases in his possession of exactly ten cents more than had been stolen from the bank. The poor guy was down to his last dime.

In my interview of the suspect, he began by lying about his involvement, but I noted signals of deception, such as the darting of his eyes, dropping of the volume of his voice at the end of his sentences, and his fiddling with an empty cigarette package during the interview. I reminded him matter-of-factly that he matched the description of the bank robber, he'd been identified by two tellers when police took him by the bank for identification, and that he'd undoubtedly show up on the bank surveillance tape.

Also I pointed out the circumstantial evidence that he'd been located by an officer in a store close to the bank, with a bicycle, and in possession of money and purchases matching the bank's loss. He finally sighed, gave a "look at the heavens mercy stare," and admitted to me that he'd robbed the bank because he'd been desperate for money. Some criminals even I have to feel compassion for. It's a tough world out there.

People who have had to claw and struggle for everything they have, says Dr. Dimitrius, tend to be hardened, stingy, defensive and insecure. They also don't care to reveal much about themselves. In regard to lying, I would expect these types of people would be less trustworthy in what they say to you.

On the other hand, people who have always had their needs met as they grew up are more confident, generous, forgiving and open. So, I'd say you can usually take this sort of man's word to the bank. However, Dimitrius makes the point that those who are given everything without exception may not have the personal drive to accomplish tasks on their own, and they may be self-centered and materialistic.

You might be able to think of some well-publicized examples of this type of person. So beware of people who are so rich they don't think the rules of society apply to them. They may well be prone to exaggeration, excuses, and exculpatory remarks that are totally spurious.

Concerning people's satisfaction with life, Dr. Dimitrius believes that someone who's been able to accomplish the goals he set out to do is more satisfied with his life than those who have failed in their efforts. A successful person is more optimistic, forgiving, and upbeat about life, including supporting others and being more forgiving of others' faults and shortcomings. People who have not attained their goals, however, are more pessimistic about life in general. They're apt to feel like victims who place blame on others or fate and who tend to be bitter and angry people. They can be negative and vengeful. I'd be far more inclined to be trusting of what the more upbeat person says.

➤ **Do you remember?**

People recall events in different ways. Hartley speaks of some people being sequencers. These folks relate situations as they correspond to their memory of the actual order of events. If you interrupt them to ask for specifics about one event, it may confound or confuse or irritate them. Even though you're more interested in some events than others, you should let people relate a situation in the way that they recall it the best, even if you have to be patient and wait for the information you want to know.

Other people may recall situations according to the time of the events that occurred. A time-driven person might relate his day by telling when he got up, when he went to work, and what time the SUV slammed into the rear of his Cadillac. He may even have a good idea of how long certain events took to transpire.

An event-sensitive person will recall the main situations that happened during his day, not necessarily in exact order. He will often not tell his story sequentially. And he may dwell longer on the more important happenings, not even mentioning items of lesser importance to him. You may have to go over certain parts of his story several times to assure you get the information you need about all the events that happened.

➤ **Creative lying.**

Walters mentions a method of lying he calls "creatively disguising reality," or "bargaining." This occurs when a person makes a statement that has some elements of truth in it, but he glosses over and dresses up and substitutes enough fiction in the statement to make the result palatable to the person he's trying to fool. It's an attempt to disguise reality, as well as a means of evasion, which are just ways of not telling the truth.

Of course, it's only human nature to avoid acknowledging events in life that embarrass a person or that he finds distressing. Leon Festinger calls this particular occurrence "cognitive dissonance." The person is basically constructing a personal fantasy, or suffering from delusional thinking.

I can imagine someone who is sitting in jail, having been arrested for a serious crime, engaging in this type of cogitation. And I have to believe that any statement a person would make in this situation would be self-serving, subjective, and likely inaccurate. Dr. Dimitrius says that people tend to brainwash themselves into believing what they've said, or at least in justifying to themselves why they said it.

Be alert for a situation where a suspect describes the actions in question by using soft expressions which lessen the severity of what he did. Your teenage son may say he wasn't speeding, he was just "keeping up with the traffic." Your significant other may claim that he wasn't yelling, he was just "raising his voice" to make a point. Your daughter may be late for her curfew because some events happened that made her "run a little late." Your friend may have had "only a few drinks," just to be social. And, of course, we know from a great deal of experience that politicians never tell lies, they are just "quoted out of context," or perhaps, at worst, they "misspoke." Sometimes even bizarre non-occurrences such as phantom "sniper fire" may crop up during political ramblings.

Many such comments can be disproved by simply addressing them using common sense. When you discuss the statement with the deceptive person, you should point out contradictions in what he said (either within the statement itself or with the known elements of the situation). Also, ask him about missing information. Ask for expansion and clarification of any parts of the statement that seem vague. Using these tactics should allow you to deconstruct the story the person is trying to foist on you.

Wish-fulfillment lies are common in children ages four to seven years old. But for some people, this type of lie is continued into adulthood. These fantasy lies appear to give gratification to the teller, and this kind of illusory lying is often used by persons who can't or won't make the effort required to complete the necessary steps to accomplish the goal they dream about.

I believe this type of person sometimes appears on television programs such as *American Idol* or *America's Got Talent,* where some contestants with little or no musical or dancing or acrobatic ability seem convinced when they describe their talent to the judges that they're going to win the contest over thousands of others. They have no grounded reason for so believing, but only find rationale within their own fantasy world.

Then the moment of truth arrives, and they must face the judges and the TV audience displaying their strange form of ineptitude that really stinks on ice. When the judges cringe and the audience boos and crosses their arms in disdain, the contestants are visibly shaken, sometimes crushed. They simply don't understand why their rare "talent" isn't recognized.

People lie to implement the pursuit of their own needs and wishes. And sometimes they do so to further the needs of others. Most people don't wish to hurt other people's feelings. And using a harmless form of deception can help them protect the sensibilities and the sensitivities of others. After all, what does it cost someone emotionally to complement another person on a hideous new necktie or suit or dress?

Passive-aggressive behavior is a type often spoken of in the literature about psychological behaviors. A person thus afflicted will have feelings of aggression toward another individual or toward society. But instead of directly attacking the source of his aggravation, he'll use destructive techniques against himself. It's often a way to combat the assertive personality of another person who he feels is trying to control him. By the passive-aggressive person's behavior and insincere words, often including exaggeration of the problems he's facing, he's trying to make the other person feel guilty for mistreating him.

I believe the person with this type of personality is quite aware that he's using overemphasis as a means of avoiding direct confrontation with another. But then, Cicero noted, "A man is least known to himself." So, perhaps we all stride forward in life in a state of oblivion, armed with the shield and sword we were given at birth.

Psychiatrists talk of a *grandiose self*, by which is meant the fantasy self that's been developed by people of low self-esteem. Their actual accomplishments, even though they may be of high standards, will never measure up to the expectations of their fantasy achievements. Thus, they will exaggerate and deceive others and themselves when discussing their activities past and present.

A pathological type of liar may act as an imposter, playing out various career or pastime roles in which he has little or no expertise, as a means of achieving a sense of identity. This type of deceiver will feel gratification when he is believed by others about the false role. He's also trying to convince himself that the deception is true.

❖ **Say what, now?**

I ran across a person like that when I was working in Texas. I don't know what his exact background was that made him so unusual, and I'm not even sure that he realized what he was spouting wasn't exactly the "truth" as most of us would evaluate it. But I did have the occasion to interview Marshall Applewhite, leader of the Heaven's Gate movement, in the early 1970's. He and Bonnie Lu Truesdale Nettles had rented a car in Houston, Texas, and had failed to return it as scheduled. They were still driving it several days after the due date when they were stopped by police in Harlingen, Texas. It wasn't long before the police decided they weren't sure what to do with him, and that maybe the feds would be willing to take him off their hands.

I drove to the police station and talked with the problematic couple. The FBI didn't handle one-car thefts, unless there were exacerbating circumstances, such as that the vehicle had been used in a bank robbery or the like, so I didn't really have a way to charge them with anything. But I could soon see what troubled the police about Applewhite.

The man exhibited a peculiar serenity that was rather unsettling. But I'm rather calm and collected myself, so I wasn't bothered that much by his demeanor. I tried talking with him about the stolen car, but he wasn't really concerned with making any statements about that, other than that he still had the car because he was on a mission and hadn't yet completed it. Then he began to tell me how he was trying to recruit people to join him in his quest to prepare for the recycling of the Earth. He explained how he had come to Earth on a spaceship, and how a spaceship would return to retrieve him and his followers. They'd be taken away from Earth while it was being cleansed and rejuvenated.

I asked him if he had any followers and where they met. He said he was attempting to recruit people, and that they had no set meeting place at that time. His voice was steady, he looked me in the eye as he spoke, and he was articulate. He was obviously under no stress—a very cool person. And I noted one of the strangest phenomena I can recall in my years of observing people's physical appearances. His eyes had a pronounced gleam to them which I've never seen with any other person before or since. It was as if someone were shining a tiny flashlight into his eyes, with the light being reflected outward. It was a pure, white light that seemed to glitter.

I took a break from questioning him to ask the involved police officers if they'd found any narcotics in his possession, and what they thought about his possible drug use. They said they'd found nothing, and they didn't sense that he was high on anything, but they did think he acted in an unusual manner. I told them I agreed with their assessment, and I returned to the interview room to see what would happen next.

Then the discussion became repetitive, with Applewhite

sticking to his guns about the spaceship that was coming for
him. This was before the movie *E. T.* had arrived on the cultural
scene, so that couldn't have influenced him. And I knew of no
federal law against believing that a spaceship was coming to
pick you up, so I finished the interview, advised the police there
was no viable federal charge that could be brought against him,
and left the station.

And that would have been the end of one of many strange
encounters that I had during my years in the FBI, except that
Applewhite came back into the news and back to my attention
many years later. It seemed that he'd been able to convince a
number of people to join him in a rather monastic existence in
Oregon, and later, California, as they waited for the spaceship to
arrive for them. At one time, he had a following of about 200
people. His group had dwindled, Bonnie had passed on, and
Applewhite and his devotees were still waiting. Most impor-
tantly, everyone still believed his big lie.

Then an event happened that convinced Applewhite that the
time for the spaceship embarkation was at hand. The Hale-Bopp
comet lit up the sky in 1997. I remember watching it blaze
across the darkness in the evening and marveling at its size and
brightness and its long, vivid tail. Applewhite and his followers
were also excited, as they became certain that behind the comet
was the spaceship they'd awaited for so long. And all they had
to do at that point was to abandon their earthly bodies so they
could be picked up.

So, Applewhite and his following of thirty-eight people
gathered in a rented mansion in Rancho Santa Fe, a suburb of
San Diego. They were all dressed in black shirts and sweat-
pants, wore black-and-white Nike tennis shoes, and had arm-
bands that stated they were members of the "Heaven's Gate
Away Team." They drank a liquid consisting of Phenobarbital
and vodka, then lay down in beds all over the house and peace-
fully died. This was the largest mass suicide ever recorded in
U.S. history.

When the news came out, I remembered Applewhite's

name, and naturally, the story about the spaceship had stuck in my brain. And then I saw an article about him in *Time* magazine. He didn't look that much different. He was bald in the recent photo, but then he had worn very close-cropped hair when I'd seen him in Texas. And I'm sure that most people thought the glitter in his eyes was reflected from a flash used by the photographer who took his photo, or a light in the room. But I knew the truth of that matter.

> **More strange deceptions.**

Another type of person I ran across during my career in the FBI was the one given to schizoid fantasy. This person uses avoidance of real world situations with which he feels unable to cope. In order to deal with life, he builds a fantasy world in which he's the star player. Often this will become an obsession that he's a kind of secret agent, somehow affiliated with the FBI, or Central Intelligence Agency (CIA), or the National Security Agency (NSA). He'll feel compelled to make contact with the FBI in person. But when he tries to explain his connection with these "secret" agencies, which ideas seem real and logical to him, his story will fall apart with the slightest bit of fact-checking.

Of course, there are many variations on this theme, and the person might fantasize about his hidden wealth, or his many exotic adventures, or his (imagined) success with numerous gorgeous women. Once these people try to operate in the real world, they're fairly easy to detect. Still, it was said in the *Rubaiyat of Omar Khayyam* that, "A hair perhaps divides the false and true." Thus, one man's fantasy can definitely be another's truth. And also we should consider a comment by Goethe, "They say that dissimulation is a crime, yet we live by dissimulation." So before we cast stones at others, perhaps we should examine our own faults and weaknesses.

> **Psychological problems and lying.**

Psychologists think that pathological lying is likely affected by both biological and developmental problems. Perhaps brain dysfunction or psychological disorders leading to incomplete personality formation will add to the tendency to lie. Bad parenting, sexual or physical abuse, and other such stressors may inhibit personality development. And poor impulse control often seems to be a characteristic possessed by pathological liars. This type of person also seems to lack empathy for others. He will have difficulty in establishing close relationships with others, and he will tend to lie to them in order to project an image of himself that is untrue.

Or, he may lie to himself about what his personality and true self is really like, thus developing a type of narcissistic behavior and attitude toward life. He will be battling feelings of inadequacy or of not being accepted by others, and he will create a fantasy in order to attempt to project a self that is more intelligent and gifted than he really is or feels he is. Thus, all statements he makes will be influenced by his psychological need to maintain his self-image, which definitely affects the truthfulness of each remark.

A type of person that Dr. Glass classifies as a "seducer" will present many false signals. She will use charm and animation to win you over and to get what she wants. She's full of overblown compliments. She'll stretch the truth to make you feel good about yourself. She manipulates people who are drawn to her. If she's caught in a lie, she'll likely be able to wriggle out of it with her clever patter. She'll say and do whatever it takes to control the situation and you and to obtain her goals. A seducer will have a relaxed posture and will often tilt her head toward the person talking and nod at what they're saying. She'll probably toy with her jewelry or twirl her hair around a finger, and she tends to lean in close and to touch the person with whom she's talking.

Another anomaly to watch for is what Dr. Dimitrius terms a "rogue action." She points out that people are creatures of habit, and that when they perform an action that seems out of character for them, any comments they make or avoid making related to their different behavior could be worth taking a close look at. If a normally talkative colleague seems suddenly silent on a particular subject or on a certain occasion, it could be that a guilty conscience is bothering him.

Pay attention to analyzing his statements. Also, always remember that people of good character can act in socially or morally unacceptable ways. And be aware that bad folks can occasionally act like saints.

➤ **Personality type affects lying potential.**

Dr. Ford identifies five types of personalities where people use deception as a characteristic behavior pattern. These are the borderline, antisocial, histrionic, obsessive-compulsive, and the narcissistic personality disorders. Let's examine them.

People with borderline personality disorder are disenchanted troublemakers. Their lives are ruled by impulsiveness, and they don't adjust well to normal activities or relationships. They have low levels of serotonin, and they often are plagued with problems with drugs, alcohol, or other types of aberrant behavior patterns. They have strong mood swings, and they'll sometimes have fantasies that they'll recount to others as being the truth. And like the sociopath, they have little regard for the well-being or feelings of other people, so they will manipulate others through their casual lies.

The person with an <u>antisocial</u> personality disorder will exhibit deceit, as well as disregard for others. He will have problems both at his workplace and in his interpersonal relationships. He's prone to have <u>run-ins</u> with the police, in fact, he'll often have trouble with any type of <u>authority</u>. He'll have difficulty adjusting in the military service. He <u>doesn't get along</u> in organizations where he has <u>bosses.</u> He seems to find it <u>difficult</u> to deal with <u>frustration in attaining his desires.</u> Some sociopaths become con men, criminals, or even serial killers.

The person with this personality disorder also manifests sexual promiscuity and has problems with relationships. He uses complicated and extensive patterns of lying as a way to attain his goals. People with antisocial personality disorder constitute about 2 percent to 3 percent of the population, and they're usually <u>male.</u>

Sociopathy is believed to be caused by a combination of biological and environmental factors. Sociopathic persons may have a poor integration of the factual and emotional components of speech, and because of this, they use language freely and loosely. For the psychopath, lying is just a matter of altering the way he communicates.

Honest people, says Dr. Dimitrius, will usually present themselves to others as relaxed and open, and indeed, they actually feel that way in their dealings. However, a sociopath exhibits an exception to this normal behavior. His lack of empathy with others makes him think of people as mere objects to be manipulated.

Interestingly, because the sociopath feels little or no guilt in connection with lying, he has fewer physical reactions that will indicate deceit. He may thus find it easier to fool both other people and the polygraph (lie detector) than those who experience feelings of guilt or anxiety when they lie. However, with such a person, you may get a feeling that something he's saying isn't right. This is because your subconscious analysis is kicking in, and it's time to pay extra attention with your conscious abilities in order to detect signals that the man is lying.

People with hysterical or histrionic *theatrical* personalities (usually women), says Dr. Ford, are most likely to be dishonest when seeking attention or feeling threatened by rejection. Histrionic women are suggestible, and they experience trouble distinguishing between their wishful fantasies and the hard realities of life. They present an "affective truth" (if it feels right, it must be true), allowing it to overcome logic or the actual truth.

Women with histrionic personalities are often seductive in dealing with men, and they use their sexiness for manipulation. They can have an alluring personality, and they dress provocatively, enjoying the attention they receive. They're dramatic and emotional, with little regard for logical reasoning.

A person who exhibits an obsessive-compulsive personality disorder is likely to have had a strict and controlling parent. He will thereafter imagine all authority figures to be restrictive and intrusive to his purposes, and he'll therefore keep secrets or tell lies to stay in control. He will often exhibit inflexible behavior, and he sometimes tends toward being a perfectionist. He focuses on small details in life, and because of his rigidity, he can't feel or exhibit warmth toward other individuals.

Oddly, this type of person often takes pride in his honesty, although he will usually provide an incomplete picture of the real situation in his statements. He will often feel angry when he senses he's not in complete control of a set of circumstances, but he will seek to hide this reaction. He tends to operate with indecisiveness and stubbornness.

Pathological lying refers to lying that is compulsive or impulsive and happens regularly. It doesn't appear to advance the material welfare of the liar, indeed, it often acts as a self-defeating condition. *Pseudologia fantastica*, which was mentioned earlier, is a version of this kind of lying. One purpose of this fabrication of wild tales is to avoid focusing on painful past experiences.

In the movie, *Girl, Interrupted,* set in the late nineteen-sixties, one of the inmates at the mental asylum where the author of the novel on which the film was based spent eighteen months of her life, said she was being kept there because she suffered from *pseudologia fantastica*. She explained that it meant she was a pathological liar. It seems these conditions were dealt with more harshly in the past.

For habitual or compulsive liars, there could be some hostility in their lying. They may be trying to manipulate or distract someone in order to take advantage of them. These people have low self-esteem, and their stories are likely a way for them to feel better about themselves.

I might add that dishonest people often exhibit tenseness and secretiveness in their manner. These nervous types may also show a degree of sneakiness or guile. And you might notice that they seem suspicious of you, because they well know that some people can't be trusted.

➢ **It's the booze talking.**

Most people who abuse alcohol or drugs use deception of themselves and others as a means to cover up their activities or to explain away their behavior. They also deny having any problems with being addicted, often thinking that they are in control of their substance of abuse. Often, they'll involve their entire family in providing a deceptive cover for their alcoholism to the rest of the world. After all, as Tom Wilson noted in *Ziggy* (comics), "Honesty is the best image."

➤ **Sickness and lying.**

Some people have the odd behavior pattern know as the Munchausen syndrome. They are usually from families in which they received little attention or affection, or their parents were simply cold and distant. These individuals develop an attention-getting behavior of pretending to have a serious illness which needs to be treated.

They often pick a rare and critical disease, or one that requires constant care and watchfulness by health givers. Thus, they're the center of a lot of attention, as well as being the manipulator in their own little play. And they enjoy being so clever as to have fooled the doctors and nurses into believing their charade. Some individuals study and know how to display various symptoms, and a few will even submit themselves to surgery in order to prolong the attention and care they receive.

And there's another odd twist in the pretended illness category of lying. In the Munchausen-by-proxy syndrome, a person will actually make someone else sick (usually her child) in order to get attention. She'll have the child convinced that he feels certain symptoms, or she'll even give the kid drugs that will bring about the symptoms of a disease. Then both she and the kid will receive a good deal of attention and sympathy.

➤ **Okay, copper, you got me.**

It seems that violent crimes have a certain fascination for many people. Some will even falsely confess to heinous crimes. Such people tend to be of below average intelligence, have low self-esteem or weak personalities, or just be hungry for attention. Some of them even get to be regulars at the police station, making their appearance to give themselves up each time a terrible crime is splashed in the headlines or becomes the lead story on the evening television news.

Many people tried to collect money through charity confidence schemes or by cheating insurance companies by claiming that they or a relative was injured in the 9/11/01 attacks on the World Trade Center Towers in New York. One woman told her horrific story about making her way down from the 78th floor to safety. Her apparent reason for concocting the tale was so she'd receive personal attention (which she did, even from Rudolph Guiliani). She became the head of a survivors' support group related to the tragedy. It was subsequently discovered that she had never worked in the building and had not been a victim in the attack.

➤ **The <u>narcissist</u> and lying.**

A person with a narcissistic personality disorder may be insecure, sensitive to criticism, vain, self-preoccupied, and one who uses people rather than appreciating their help and good qualities. He will probably <u>not follow through on the grandiose plans he concocts.</u> He exaggerates his past accomplishments. His insensitivity to the feelings of others tends to cause interpersonal strife, leaving him alienated from others.

Despite their apparent grandiosity and arrogant self-confidence, these types of people have low self-esteem. Their difficulties with regulating self-esteem make them sensitive to failures and slights (often imagined), to which they often react with depression or anger. They are so preoccupied with themselves that they feel entitled to special consideration. They often exploit other people for their own benefit.

Narcissistic individuals tend to see the world only from their own perspective and are thus prone to lying. They have the need to observe and define the world according to their own internal states. They often have poor reality testing; the outside world is perceived in personal terms, and the internal world is contaminated with grandiosity. Narcissistic individuals aspire to power and <u>frequently hold positions of authority</u>.

Narcissists who become politicians often state how things should be, and people will elect them because they need to hear those comments and believe that they are true and that the politician will do something to effect them. Neither the politician nor his constituency really wants to look at what the truth of the situation is and how little the man or woman will actually be able to accomplish as far as solving society's problems.

➢ **That's what I thought.**

Dr. Ford emphasizes that one of the basic skills in lying is for the liar to tell people what they want to hear. Thus, salespeople and politicians become experts in doing this, making their lying abilities well-honed. The power-hungry and attention-seeking politician is often narcissistic and will lack the ability to evaluate information very well. The end effect is that he will lie to himself to maintain his own self-esteem, and he'll lie to others to aid him in maintaining his image.

Reactive narcissists have experienced poor parenting which involves either rejection or non-responsiveness, or both, to them as individuals. This type of person is often ruthless in his use of power. He will tolerate no disagreement, and he crushes dissension. His distorted reality (including his self-deception and overt lies) must be accepted by underlings if the latter wish to survive in the organization this person runs.

On the other hand, self-deceptive narcissists, who as children were told by their parents that they were lovable and perfect, are often manipulative leaders. Such a person frequently has interpersonal difficulties because of his emotional superficiality and his lack of genuine empathy for others. He will cruise through life with a silver spoon in his mouth, oblivious to the needs of others.

Constructive narcissists are ambitious, manipulative, and occasionally opportunistic. They generally get along well with subordinates because they have self-confidence, adaptability, humor, and the capacity to recognize the strengths and needs of other people. As a result, they are often able to energize subordinates and achieve genuine accomplishments.

Narcissists can be spotted by their glib manipulation and sense of self-importance. They have a lack of empathy for others, a deficiency of apparent guilt, and they exhibit deceitful behavior. I have known several narcissistic people, and I can relate to the fact that they're extremely hard to deal with on a personal level. Worst of all, you can't really know when you can trust what they tell you.

➢ **Who are you?**

Another type of liar, or perhaps "pretender" would be a more apt phrase, is a rare bird that you might not ever run across. Such a person is what lay people refer to as one exhibiting multiple personalities, while psychiatrists refer to such patients as suffering a "dissociative identity disorder." Dr. Richard Baer of Chicago, Illinois, describes his seventeen-year-stint of therapy sessions with a woman who was diagnosed as having seventeen distinct personalities. The woman is called, pseudonymously, Karen Overhill.

Karen apparently developed the multiple personalities because of horrific abuses she suffered as a child, inflicted by her father and grandfather, who told her that "God wanted her to suffer." So, the little girl would dissociate from her body and personality in order to survive the ordeals without going crazy. Fascinatingly, each of the alter egos had its own character traits and mental problems.

Dr. Baer's task was to confront each separate personality and to convince it to integrate with Karen's basic personality. As you can imagine, that's a lot of confrontation. He eventually was able to integrate all of the various personalities into one entity which Karen enjoys today as a warm and open person.

Who knows what things Karen might have said to other people during those years? And was she even lying? After all, the personality that was speaking was talking from its own frame of reference. Karen told Dr. Baer that she couldn't recall having had sex with her husband, though she must have, as she had two children. So, you'd be apt to get one story or another (up to seventeen varieties) from Karen on any given topic at any given time in any given situation.

> **Everyday garden-variety lying.**

On a more pedestrian note, have you ever been late for a meeting or appointment? And if the reason was something embarrassing or likely unacceptable in the eyes of the others gathered there, might you have fabricated an excuse that sounded good? Oversleeping or getting caught up in a sexual encounter or lollygagging too long in Macy's won't fly as being good excuses for tardiness in most people's eyes. They might accept that you were caught in heavy traffic, had a flat tire, or received an emergency telephone call. Wouldn't you be tempted to use those or similar fabrications?

> **Attitudes toward truth.**

I've noticed that the truth was not all that highly respected by some of the great thinkers of history. George Bernard Shaw wrote, "Truth telling is not compatible with the defence (sp) of the realm." Robert Burton noted, "For fools and mad men tell commonly truth." Another slight of the worth of truth came when Alfred North Whitehead wrote, "There are no whole truths: all truths are half-truths." And William Shakespeare added a comical twist in his play *Much Ado about Nothing* when he wrote, "I thank God I am as honest as any man living that is an old man and no honester than I."

> **Be on the lookout.**

In my line of work, I knew there would often be an incentive to prevaricate among the suspected criminals I'd interview. So, I was predisposed to watch for verbal clues of deception, as well as for body language that suggested stress or unease with what the suspect was telling me. Also important to notice were lines of reasoning that simply didn't add up or make sense with the facts as I knew them to be.

We'll get into the above means of detecting deception or evasion in later chapters. But the point I want to make here is that you must be aware of situations when you should have your guard up and your lie catching antennae deployed. We've discussed some of them: purchasing anything, having services performed, getting repairs done, discussing contracts or business deals, and listening to politicians or advertisers or salesmen. Unfortunately, we must also be alert when talking with neighbors, friends, and relatives.

Writers often remind us to be wary of falsehoods and things that are not as they seem. Charles McCarry wrote, "The goal of politics is to alter human nature, and often politics substitutes a system of delusion for reality." Henry Brooks Adams noted that, "Practical politics consists in ignoring facts." And in *Measure for Measure,* Shakespeare posed a query, "O, what may man within him hide, though angel on the outward side!"

But even so, do we want to confront people close to us on their white or even black lies? That may depend on how important the truth is to you in the particular situation. Also, it could hinge on the expected amount of damage that the resulting altercation might do to the relationship. And always be aware that the truth can be a complex and slippery commodity. As Oscar Wilde put it, "The truth is rarely pure and never simple."

In addition, people don't always act consistently. Dr. Dimitrius says sometimes "good" people do bad things, and that "bad" people can occasionally behave as if they were pure of heart. Irregular feelings and behavior should be differentiated from set personality traits or more ingrained personal behavior.

We can always turn down salesmen, repairmen, or deals with questionable businessmen. But we usually must go on living and getting along with our immediate family, other relatives, neighbors, co-workers, close friends, and some additional associates. In those situations, it may be to the advantage of everyone involved to simply overlook the deception or evasion you've noted. In fact, I believe it's probably for the best that you don't let anyone know about your new knowledge of detecting misleading or untrue comments.

Just let it be your secret. It's another arrow in your quiver that helps you get through life with the confidence and aplomb of a Robin Hood. It's a skill that should help you better navigate the tricky shoals and hidden reefs in the ocean of life. Just remember, everyone runs aground every once-in-a-while. You may want to be a generous soul and toss an occasional life preserver to another person, even though they haven't earned the privilege. I'm sure that Mother Teresa heard a few whoppers in her day, and yet she most likely let them slide.

Of course, we're not all saint-like. We want to be good-hearted and generous, but we're also interested in protecting our rights, our money, and our relationships. Those are huge and highly important undertakings. And we want to do it right.

> **Role of the unconscious.**

Many psychologists agree that our unconscious mind has developed as a means for handling our interactions with other people. The subconscious doesn't let our conscious mind know this is happening. Freud postulated a theory of defense mechanisms in which he said that people will keep information about their real underlying desires from their conscious minds in order to avoid psychological conflicts.

Freud's theory, Dr. Smith tells us, is probably the most influential explanation of self-deception ever proposed. He questions how self-deception can be beneficial to humans, but he acknowledges that it certainly has been established in the history of psychological symptoms. Thus, there must be some psychological perk involved in the process.

Smith also posits that humans are much better at reading the significant signals given by other people through the unconscious than they are by using the conscious intellect. Natural selection, perhaps as a reaction to handling complex social interactions, has developed our minds in this way. The conscious mind, clouded by self-deception, has a very limited grasp of the nuances and complexities of the social world.

S.A. McCornack and T.R. Levine did a study entitled, "When lies are uncovered: emotional and relational outcomes of discovered deception." They wrote that deception in a relationship is a powerful force that can produce mostly negative emotional reactions in the person being lied to. And, unless the person is a sociopath, there will be strong feelings of guilt in the liar.

In her article "Of Love and Lies," Bella DePaulo, Ph.D., iterated that romantic partners were worse than strangers at detecting each other's lies. In a test where one partner was caught staring at someone and the other partner asked whether they found the person attractive, the romantic partner only guessed correctly whether the partner doing the ogling was lying or telling the truth 52 percent of the time. Strangers were able to discern the lies from truths with 58 percent accuracy. Once again, overall, the <u>unschooled are poor lie detectors.</u> And romantic connections can give us additional blinders.

➤ **Detection of falsehoods based on relationships.**

Psychological studies involving deceptive statements used in relationships have shown consistently that strangers and spouses are not as good at detecting deception by a person as are friends. One theory is that "perhaps marital partners often develop avoidance mechanisms to 'shut out' the possibility that their mates may be deceiving them." And, I'd suggest, there's not that "love bug" situation to affect friends' judgment.

Once again, because the deception between friends and significant others can disrupt the emotional closeness between them, there is a chance that the relationship will be destroyed. In the case of friends, this would not have quite the upheaval factor that would occur between spouses that decide to break up, particularly with children and property interests involved. So, sometimes deception can maintain the constancy of a relationship. Also, it's agreed upon among psychologists and this lay person that when people hear what they want to hear, they don't usually see the comments as being lies.

➤ **The big lies.**

I should emphasize that many serious and evil lies abound in the world. These are the ones that cause starvation, disease, famine, war, and the suffering and death of millions of people. They are usually perpetuated by some organization or government.

Adolf <u>Hitler</u> told many lies, but one he repeated just before the start of World War II was crucial. He met with British Prime Minister Neville Chamberlain, assuring him he had no intent of invading Czechoslovakia. Chamberlain believed him, and at Hitler's request, he worked to convince the Czechs that they need not mobilize their troops in defense. In truth, Hitler needed another couple of weeks to get his forces ready for the planned invasion, and he was trying to buy time and eliminate any strong resistance.

Huge lies can start with one person and, if not found out or debated or stopped, can pick up the force of a tidal wave wreaking destruction across the land. In *Poor Richard's Almanack* (1758), Benjamin Franklin observed, "Half the truth is often a great lie." Indeed, I'd submit that many ugly and onerous lies that start great and powerful movements are just so constructed.

Quite enlightening, I think, is the comment made in *Mein Kampf I* by Adolf Hitler, "The great masses of the people . . . will more easily fall victims to a great lie than to a small one." And we've observed the horrific outcome of the validity of that statement. Lenin made a similar comment: "A lie told often enough becomes the truth." Of course, Franklin D. Roosevelt stated the opposite in a radio address, saying, "Repetition does not transform a lie into a truth." Oscar Wilde added a chilling dimension to this debate when he noted, "A thing is not necessarily true because a man dies for it."

But we might see how such dirty snowballs as those fashioned by Hitler and Lenin started rolling downhill by considering a comment of George Bernard Shaw: "It is not disbelief that is dangerous to our society; it is belief." Shakespeare adds a cautionary note in *King Lear III.vi,* by writing, "He's mad that trusts in the tameness of a wolf, a horse's health, a boy's love, or a whore's oath." Another pertinent statement was made by Henrik Ibsen, who wrote, "It is better never to trust anybody."

In March, 2010, msnbc reported in their online news that a recent study had been conducted by the Columbia Business School entitled, "People with Power are Better Liars." Indeed, their research seemed to indicate that powerful people were not as prone to exhibit the usual behavioral signs of lying. That is because, says Dana Carney, one of the co-authors of the study, "Power enhances the same emotional, cognitive, and physiological systems that lie-telling depletes." Big shots develop a sense of entitlement, imperviousness, and self-satisfaction, all of which enable them to lie without feeling guilty about it.

So, if you agree with me that probably a lot of people will tell you misleading or outright untrue and potentially harmful things during your average day in this lifetime, then come along and let's learn some more ideas for spotting deception. It sure can't hurt you. And I have the feeling that you'll lead a lot happier existence if you'll keep reading and travel a little farther in this quest.

➢ **Tales of untruth.**

Much of literature throughout the ages has dealt with the psychology of lying. Several of Aesop's fables mention aspects of this. In *The Fox and the Mask,* one line says, "Outside show is a poor substitute for inner worth." And how many times have we seen the mighty fall because of a lack of integrity? Aesop noted in *The Wolf in Sheep's Clothing* that "Appearances are deceptive." And, indeed they are.

In *The Shepherd's Boy,* Aesop relates another side effect of constant lying. "The boy called out 'Wolf, wolf!' and the villagers came out to help him. A few days later he tried the same trick, and again they came to his help. Shortly after this a wolf actually came, but this time the villagers thought the boy was deceiving them again, and nobody came to his help. "A liar will not be believed, even when he speaks the truth," wrote Aesop. And it's true that whenever a person is shown to be a liar in a community, he might as well move on down the road. His rep is shot in that town.

There are many interesting facets to the psychology of lying. The literature shows that throughout history an open palm gesture has stood for truth and honesty. This is actually an unconscious gesture that is trusted in this way.

➢ **Summary.**

In further regard to truth, La Rochefoucauld adds a caution in *Maxims* when he states, "Truth does not do so much good in the world as its appearances do evil." Another angle on the matter, pertaining mostly, I'd say, to the category of white lies, is the comment by Alexander Pope, "Blunt truths more mischief than nice falsehoods do."

Agnes Repplier made the remark: "There are few nudities so objectionable as the naked truth." "Truth is beautiful, without doubt," said Ralph Waldo Emerson, "but so are lies." And as a capper, Oscar Wilde used a bit of reverse psychology when he wrote, "If one tells the truth, one is sure, sooner or later, to be found out."

The upshot of all of this is that studies regarding your psychological makeup (which has evolved over millions of years), help you understand some of the reasons that you lie to others and to yourself. It also explains the role of fibbing in your social interactions with others. When you're acutely aware of the omnipresence of people who lie regularly, then you'll be more attuned to the unconscious signals that liars give when they are trying to mislead you. Then you'll know who you can trust and who you should avoid. So, let's go forward in our journey to discover the truth.

4

Detecting the Spoken Lie

When man developed his increasing brainpower, he was better able to analyze the mysteries of the world. Robin Dunbar, professor of evolutionary psychology at the University of Liverpool, believes that early people would likely want to discuss their newly formed observations with others. Language evolved in societies to enable people to better co-exist. And the evolution of language enabled our ancestors to more efficiently work together, relax together, and interrelate as a cohesive social entity. Plus, it was nice to not have to play the pantomime game every time you wanted someone to toss you a banana.

The development of language also brought forth a new dimension in the battle between those who sought to deceive and those who tried to ascertain the truth. The use of language to communicate not only made conveying intentions and messages simpler and more efficient, it also made it much easier to tell lies. There's no doubt that language facilitates the ability of one person to deceive another.

The early females, who were together much of the time because they stayed in the camp area performing tasks, used their language skills to develop closer social contacts with others. And it evolved that they began to gossip about other individuals in the group. The value of gossip, Dr. Smith proposes, is that it's an effective means for determining whom one can trust and not trust in the group. When another individual's conduct is discussed by some members of a group, who then spread the knowledge to other acquaintances, then a person begins to be known by most, if not all, members of the group for the type of behaviors in which they become involved. Everyone soon gets a "rep" among the larger group, and those who belong to the group will treat him accordingly.

And, just as today, people would form cliques among friends and acquaintances. Often, these close-knit smaller groups were kept secret from the larger group. And naturally, various smaller clusters of people would cultivate antipathy toward other cliques. Thus, it developed that one of the best ways to bring disfavor from the larger group for your enemy was to spread gossip that would impugn the worthiness of the other faction.

Rather than gossip for information's sake, the tales spread about others' activities would become fabricated in such a manner as to bring censor on the maligned. Such malicious gossip, which was outright lying, was a means of aggression against one's competing cliques. Individuals and small factions were now able to smear those persons or groups they disliked by stabbing them in the back with verbal slights.

Because gossip is a private endeavor, and quite often unreliable, an element of uncertainty is insinuated into the social milieu that was not present when our ancestors were unable to speak. Of course, I'm sure that deception occurred among the first humans even before they learned to express themselves in words. But the development of speech, which is such an efficient method for spreading true or false information, certainly made it much easier to fool or degrade an enemy.

Thus, we have a long history of people using their facility with words to deceive others, and most people in the society realize that this can and will happen. We've learned that we should be on guard, and that we shouldn't believe everything we hear.

We depend a great deal on what people say to us as to how we react to a situation. It's our principal means of communication, and there are ways we can assess verbal signals for veracity. In daily operation, people will subconsciously process a great deal of material about another person in order to reach an intuitive feel about that individual. This includes deciding whether the person can be trusted and whether he's telling the truth about the matter at hand.

➤ **You don't say.**

Walters says that the content of speech accounts for only 7 percent of the total communication that passes between people. But when you consider the other signals provided by the way people send messages verbally, the output is about 20 percent. And if people are trying to deceive you, they'll likely be aware to keep tight control over their verbal output. More especially, con artists and glib, intelligent people will be able to phrase their messages so they sound believable. This may make it difficult to detect verbal signals of deception.

But luckily for you in your quest to identify deceit, people also reveal their true feelings by the *way* they talk. Their facial expressions and the manner in which they convey a statement can be read by an attentive person. And a person's tone of voice also signals a great deal about the true feelings they're experiencing, as well as the true or false meaning of their comment. Haven't we all noticed the varied messages sent by whether a person's tone of voice is whiny, angry, harsh, pleasant, or morose?

➤ **Watch for verbal and facial clues.**

An astute listener analyzes such items as the volume of a person's voice, the pitch, and the rhythm of his speech. He'll also watch the facial expressions used while the person is speaking. If any of these particular facets of speaking or a person's facial aspects change from his normal speech patterns or expressions, then it's a good signal that he's under stress and possibly lying.

The cranial nerves within the brain control both vocal expressions and facial ones. Thus, a person's true feelings and emotions will be signaled, if only briefly, by both his face and his voice. Dr. Glass calls this "vocal leakage" when it's applied to the voice. The "vocal leakage," together with any facial "microexpression," will reflect a person's true emotions to the observant watcher and listener.

Walters makes the interesting point that in each encounter with another person, the other man or woman will either choose to tell you the truth about a matter, or will make a decision to lie. The person may feel that there is some type of pressure on him not to tell the truth. Maybe he'll be exposing himself to jail time. Perhaps he thinks he'll gain some sort of advantage if he's not completely truthful. Or maybe he's just not sure what the result will be of telling the truth, so he'll conceal as much information as possible.

➢ **It's not *what* she said.**

We should also watch for *how* someone says something. Be aware of whether he sounds sincere or sarcastic. Is he giving you backhanded compliments? Does he seem amiable and pleasant on the surface, but he's making unkind, thoughtless, or cutting remarks? If he's feeding you gossip about someone else, be assured that he'll be gossiping about you with the next person he contacts. And pay attention to what could be considered a person's agenda by studying the manner in which he converses with you.

Be wary of people who constantly talk about themselves and act bored when the subject is changed to something or someone else. Assess their vocabulary and use of grammar to judge their intelligence and insight. Evaluate whether they're on the same page with you in discussing the matter at hand. Are they genuinely trying to arrive at a solution that's beneficial to all parties? Be wary if all the plans seem to benefit them the most, even though they stress how great such arrangements will be for others.

Observe whether someone you're speaking with may be saying something between the lines. Does he seem to be leaving out some information, or is he being evasive? Does he hesitate to answer a particular question? These types of reactions were common when I interviewed suspects in criminal matters, and you'll definitely be confronted with such unresponsive chatter when you're dealing with a person who's done something wrong and wants to keep it from you. Incomplete answers are signals that you're going to be on the receiving end of some real whoppers.

Psychologists agree that we should pay attention to the tone of voice when someone is speaking to us. A harsh tone can signal anger, a hoarse one may mean the person is feeling nervous, and a lifeless tone could be a sign she's depressed or simply doesn't feel confident or sincere in what she's telling you. If a person mumbles or trails off at the end of her sentences, she is probably very unsure of herself or of what she's saying, or both. If she's speaking at a certain volume level, and the level diminishes when she answers a certain question, that answer is probably not true or not complete.

Sometimes a person will even, says Dr. Dimitrius, attempt to transmit her true feelings by the way she speaks. Dimitrius suggests we should be aware of the words spoken, the tone of her voice, and her body language as she speaks in order to understand the true feelings and meanings being sent. I'd recommend that you listen closely to what the other person says and concentrate on the actual meaning of the words she's saying. Watch how the things being said seem to affect the person who's delivering them. Don't think about what your response is going to be until after you've thoroughly analyzed what the person has said.

Some red flags to watch for are when a suspected fibber prefaces statements with phrases like, "To be honest . . ." or "You may not believe this, but . . ." or "To be perfectly frank with you . . ." or the like. The person speaking these or similar comments is telegraphing that a lie, or at best a partial truth, is about to be told. Be wary if the suspect says, "I swear on my mother's grave . . ." or "You know I'd never do something like that . . ." He's likely setting you up for deception. These remarks and similar ones should set off warning alarms in your head. Pay attention to them, and fully analyze the statements that follow them.

"Believe me, I'd never do that."

I've always been most successful in interviewing a suspect when I wasn't judgmental or condemning of him. The suspect is in a precarious position, and he's looking for any escape route he can find. If he believes you're part of the solution rather than part of the problem, he'll be more likely to tell you the truth. Don't use any approach that could create resentment between the two of you.

I've seen law enforcement people take a hard-line attitude when interviewing a criminal. They can't help condemning the person for their often heinous and desperate acts. But you won't often get the truth by being hateful or mean-spirited.

Dr. Dimitrius says that people slip up, and they'll often relate inconsistencies when they describe an occurrence. All trips of the tongue are not Freudian slips. And all discrepancies in a story someone tells are not necessarily bald-faced lies. I've seen many times where an interviewee may make small mistakes in relating the facts, or he may say something in a way an interviewer fails to fully comprehend. You should not get hung up on thinking you've caught someone in a lie just because there are small variations in the way they relate their story.

"No, I called him *before* I got dressed."

When trying to get to the truth of a matter, Dr. Lieberman says, the interviewer can mention rewards that the interviewee will receive if he's truthful. It would be like the carrot held before the donkey to get him to move. It should be a type of reward that's real, honest, and advantageous to the interviewee.

The questioner should illustrate to the subject what the positives and negatives of his being truthful or not being truthful will be. Let him see, feel, and taste the good experiences he will enjoy when he tells (as Lieberman suggests that you say) the "whole story." I agree that this is a useful phrase, as it indicates that the subject of the interview has been truthful and cooperative up to a point, and he just needs to go a little further with you. I've often discussed with suspects how they can possibly help themselves by co-operating and telling where the stolen money or goods are hidden or by explaining how their cohorts acted during the crime in question.

❖ **The duffer and the "gimme."**

In my world of crime and punishment, the enticement for truth-telling was often a chance to do less prison time, or perhaps get probation. And if a minor player could help us out in a case by describing how the scheme in which they were involved worked, and by testifying against the major player or players, then they might strike a good bargain, maybe even having all charges against them dropped.

In one case I worked, the prosecuting attorney was offering such a "get out of jail free" card to a co-defendant, but he was still hesitant and unsure what to do. I knew the man was a golfer, so I characterized the decision he faced in this manner: "Let's say you hit out of a sand trap to within four feet of the pin. If you make the putt, you win the hole. But it's a fast green, and there's a tricky break to it that you're not sure how to read."

The guy was listening intently as he imagined the scene. "So, now your opponent says, 'Hey, Phil, that's a "gimme" (golf term for counting the putt as made without having to knock it in). Go ahead and pick up your ball.' Aren't you going to take that gimmee? Sure, you will. And that's just what the attorney's offering you here."

His lips tightened, and he nodded. He agreed to the deal, which was advantageous to him. And we won the case against his co-defendant, who faced a hefty fine and ten years in prison.

❖ **Play your cards close to the vest.**

Walters reasons that an interviewer needs to learn how to challenge someone when he feels the man's lying to him or not giving complete answers on a subject. And to do this, he's obliged to learn ways to be able to identify when someone's trying to deceive him. Or, as I put it, he must be able to spot a lie when it rears its ugly head.

When questioning someone, says Dr. Dimitrius, you are more apt to get straight information from him by asking open-ended questions. The person may tend to ramble too much sometimes, but that also gives you a chance to evaluate how he may feel about the situation in which you're interested. She suggests not interrupting the interviewee, as he may say something of value when you are not expecting it.

I've found that when law enforcement officers ask leading or too-specific questions, this tends to inform the interviewee what the officer's agenda is, and this may contaminate the answer that's provided. It's far better to ask general questions and get the interviewee talking in a relaxed manner than it is to pepper him with specific (and sometimes accusatory) questions.

This makes for good TV drama, but it doesn't always play well in real life. You should work in concentric circles, moving from the general issues of interest to the particular details you need answered in order to solve the problem at hand.

A good way to approach someone about whether he committed an act would be to discuss his behavior, but not to directly accuse him of anything. That way, you're not putting him on the defensive. If you say, "Did you cheat on me with Tawney?" or "Did you steal that jewelry?" you have let the old cat come screaming and clawing out of your limited bag of tricks. The man will then be alert and ready to practice some clever and imaginative deceptive techniques.

It's best not to tip your hand. If you lay your cards on the table by telling a person what you know and/or suspect he did, then he may be able to tailor a story that will fit the circumstances that you know about, but it still won't be the truth of the matter. As long as his tale keeps him out of trouble, that's going to please him immensely. So never start out your questioning by presenting the evidence you have against a suspect, or by being specific as to what you want to ask him about. Be general in your comments about what you want to discuss.

Nance states that people tend to admit just enough of what they did to satisfy the current line of questioning. That's been my experience in interviewing suspects in criminal matters. So, it's best to take it slow and easy with the person you're interviewing. Lead him into the admission trap a little at a time. Have him concur that he was in the area where the crime was committed, that he had access to a car (which you know was used to make a getaway), and that he was alone during the time of the murder.

In a relationship matter, this could mean you'd have him admit that he got off work on time, and he did happen to stop for a drink before coming home, and that he may have run into some people he knew while he was there. How cozy he got with one of them may be harder to wrangle out of him. But by leading him into giving rather innocent admissions, he sure can't argue at that point that he wasn't at the scene of the crime (or the tryst you suspect).

A person will be much more apt to agree to peripheral issues than to answer forthrightly that he murdered the victim in cold blood because the guy owed him money and wouldn't pay up. And as you ease closer to the heart of the matter in your interview or conversation, remember to be alert for those questions that he avoids answering. That's a good sign that the man's being deceptive or at least evasive with you about some of the points in question.

Also be suspicious when his <u>answers</u> to your questions come forth <u>too</u> cleanly, <u>quickly,</u> and smoothly. That could signal that he's been preparing for your interview or conversation, and that he's guessed what questions you planned to ask. So, <u>query</u> him along <u>different lines</u> for a few minutes, and then come back to the initial mode of questioning. This may throw him off his rhythm and confuse him as to where he was in the process of relating his canned response.

Try to ask him questions about the infractions he's committed in oblique or backhanded ways. If this fails, or in order to flesh out what admissions he's already made, begin questioning him as to extensions of <u>what happened after</u> or as a result of the actions he's already told you about. He probably will not have thought out his story to that extent or in that much detail, and you'll be putting him in a vise with no escape. When he shows signs of nervousness or stress, and he's not able to give logical answers to your additional queries, you'll know you're getting close to the information you want to learn.

➤ **Other ways to skin a cat.**

I've always thought that the "water around a rock" method works much better than trying to push that stubborn boulder down the creek bed by force and strength of will and bullying. That is, you can use some subtlety and indirectness in asking questions, sort of a connect-the-dots approach to gathering information. Lieberman points out that you can get an initial indication of whether a person may have done the act in question by the way he responds to your query.

For instance, he says you should frame the question so that the person might find it a bit odd, but not challenging. He will either laugh it off or give a reply that answers the gist of the inquiry. I think that a question that might suffice could be something like: "Jack, did you run into anyone unusual downtown last night?"

If Jack didn't encounter or meet Tawney, and have drinks with her at the Lush Losers Lounge, as someone mentioned to you they believe they saw, he'll say something like, "No, just the typical weirdoes you find downtown at night." Or he may reply, "No, just the usual suspects. I saw Bill and John heading into the bowling alley."

However, if the person is guilty of what you're vaguely implying, he'll immediately get suspicious. He'll want to know, and will probably query you about why you've asked the question. He'll be curious as to where you got the information that you're asking him about. If he acts concerned that you asked such a question, there's probably a good reason that he's being apprehensive. He may even start making up a story that, as you just look at him in silence, will turn into a long, convoluted, and rambling piece of fiction.

When a person doesn't answer the question you asked him, but wants to know why you wish to know, then you have a clue that he's withholding information. He may get angry and start to argue about small details or minor points of what you've said. Also, he may try to berate the worth of the facts as you've laid them out. That way, he's not denying that he did something. What he is saying, in effect, is that you can't prove that he did what you suspect, because your facts are not specific or strong enough. In such a situation, you're right to be suspicious that he probably did perform the action in question.

Other tactics a person put on the spot may attempt are to attack you with comments such as, "Who do you think you are?" or "I don't think that's any of your business," or "You're just jealous." What he's really doing is deflecting the thrust of your inquisition. He wants to change the topic from what he did to what you're doing to him. And some people will try to control the conversation by being boisterous and bullying you and using a loud and dominating voice.

In verbalizing a response, a person who's being deceptive will often repeat your question in his answer, especially when just denying the truth of the matter at hand. Say you ask him, "Have you been cheating on me?" He will probably be caught off-guard, and if he's guilty of what you suspect, he'll be frantically trying to think of an answer that will sound plausible and truthful, but he will feel a bit stunned at that particular moment. He will also sense that he shouldn't hesitate too long before answering, so he has to spit something out.

"No, I'm not cheating on you," he'll say, with his false statement parroting your question. And if he doesn't use a contraction, but he says, "No, I am *not* cheating on you," then Dr. Lieberman claims there's a 60 percent chance that he's making a deceptive comment. (For instance, as in the infamous quote, "I did *not* have sexual relations with that woman.")

➤ **Slip-ups and other clues.**

Another behavior to watch for is an attempt by the person being questioned to suddenly change the subject of the discussion. This means your quarry is uncomfortable with the topic you've raised, and he wants to alter the course of the conversation. If the person finds your comment interesting or provocative, he'll want to discuss it in more depth. This is a good indication that he's being honest with you. A dishonest person would likely be wary of continuing the discussion about that subject, afraid that he might slip up and say something that will suggest he's guilty of being a bad actor.

Sometimes a person will exhibit a definite pause when answering your inquiries. Dr. Dimitrius says this is sometimes accompanied by a "deer in the headlights" look, and one should be alert to assess what the interviewee may be feeling. Is he offended by what you asked? Have you made him angry? Or could it be that you've caught him in a lie or posed a question to which he feels inclined to lie? Watch for his body language as well as listening closely to what he's saying. You may spot some type of corroboration that he's trying to sell you a pack of malignant, misleading lies.

Often when people are lying, they'll have slips of the tongue including stuttering, mumbling, using incorrect grammar, and making errors in syntax. They may also exhibit halting or uneven speech. Their voice pitch may rise, and they may speak at a slower pace than normal, with hesitations. They may use faulty rhythm in expressing a thought, as though they're confused. Often liars will use shorter answers than normal, pause before speaking, and make general statements rather than give specific answers.

A liar might repeat his comments, as though he's a stuck record (or CD). And you should watch for answers that don't really match the questions you asked. Don't be afraid to pursue the avenues leading to the questions you want answered until the subject responds adequately. Also, watch for the other signs of lying, such as making grammatical errors or suffering slips of the tongue. Other signals include stammering, muttering, or making speech errors.

At a loss for words; hesitating.

➢ **The Jokester.**

Has someone ever said something sarcastic or mean-spirited to you, then said, "Hey, I was just kidding." Then they'll usually laugh or smile or pat you on the arm. Dr. Glass tells us such a person is revealing that he's jealous of you or feels <u>hostility</u> toward you.

What he's said to you is probably the way he <u>really feels</u>. The <u>lie</u> is that he's "<u>kidding</u>." He may not like you, but his relationship with you is such that he can't let you know this in a forthright manner.

Often such people feel insecure about themselves, and they feel competitive toward you because they think you may be superior to them in some way, or just a lucky son-of-a-gun. But they're leaking information about just what they think of you. And, I'd suspect that such a person wouldn't hesitate to fib to you under the right circumstances. If they don't like you and don't respect you, why would they feel that they owe you the truth?

I've learned through experience as an FBI agent that you should also watch for soft phrases used prior to a person's telling their story. If she uses such preambles as: "Well, I think that . . ." or "As I recall . . ." or "It seems to me . . . ," then she's tipping you off that she's about to serve up some untruthful answers. An exception would be that some people are basically unsure of themselves, and they'll tend to use these phrases frequently. So, you'll need to notice whether she happens to talk this way in her normal speech patterns. If not, watch for such non-committal phrases and consider them to be tip-offs.

We've all observed occasions when someone has suffered what Walters calls unexplained "memory lapses." These occur in situations where the person would often be expected to recall the circumstances being asked about. People claiming such lapses will use phrases such as, "I <u>can't recall</u>," "Not that I can remember," or "To the best of my memory . . ." These phrases are often made by criminals and politicians when they're asked the thorny questions. We've even seen such phrases come up in Senate hearings involving CEOs of large companies who have received and possibly misspent huge bailout payments from the U.S. government.

When an interviewee minimizes the severity of the crime in question, says Nance, we should pay close attention. This is an indication that he probably did it. And always be aware that avoidance is the most common form of lying. Thus, you should be very suspicious when the questioned person can recall some points of the activity in question, such as those that don't damage him or put him in jeopardy, but, conveniently, can't seem to remember other details of the circumstances when it might tend to incriminate him.

➤ **Verbal maneuvers.**

If someone is telling you a story that you don't have enough information about to know whether it's true or false, Dr. Lieberman suggests four methods to use to help you analyze the situation. The first one he calls Ask-a-Fact. This involves asking a person a direct, clear and simple question about the subject you want to explore. If the person is telling the truth, he'll answer quickly and easily, without having to hesitate to conjure up a good story. If the suspect pauses or goes off on a tangent, not answering your direct question, you can be suspicious that he's hiding something.

The next method is to Add-a-False-Fact. Dr. Lieberman says if someone is telling a story about his recent trip, and you suspect he may be embellishing it or downright concocting the information to sound exotic, then you should ask him a question that you know to be false but that sounds plausible in the context of the conversation. It should be detailed and something that you made up yourself. Throw in something like, "My uncle supervises the baggage handlers there, and he says that they're using color-coded ties on the luggage now to indicate whether someone should be stopped for Customs inspection. Did you notice a tie on your bag? What color was it, and did the Customs Inspectors ask to open your bag?"

If the interviewee goes along with the made up "fact" that you thought of on the fly, you'll know to be suspicious about what the person's telling you. There's no plausible reason for his agreement. However, if he says, "I don't know what you're talking about, I didn't see anything like that," then you can be more confident that he's probably telling you a straight story.

Another approach is to Support-a-Fact, where you'll politely ask the person to give some proof of his adventure by showing pictures or souvenirs or other documents. A simple example might be, "I'm sure it's hard to keep your money straight in another country. And I'll bet the bills are really different from our money. Do you have some Italian lira with you? I'd love to see what it looks like."

And with the Expand-a-Fact technique, you take a statement or assertion the person has made, such as she's sick and can't go out with you, and you add details to it that she didn't say. For instance, "I'm sorry you can't make it to the movies. I'm sure a migraine headache must be painful. What do you take for it?" If she goes along with your comments and doesn't correct you, then you're right to be suspicious as to whether she's really sick or she just doesn't dig how cool you are.

> **Keep your yap shut.**

If you ask someone a question and he answers it, but you don't respond to his answer, and you don't ask a follow-up question, then the ensuing period of silence will make him think he hasn't sold you on the truth of what he said. So, he'll often feel compelled to add something to his previous statement. This may provide extra information that will plug up some gaps in the story. In addition, this need to fill an uncomfortable silence will sometimes pressure the interviewee to provide hints that indicate the direction that further questioning should take. It would pay to be alert for such critical comments.

The more you can get someone talking about the subject in which you have an interest, the better your chances that he'll slip up and say something that will indicate that he did what you suspect. Law enforcement officers realize the value of asking a suspect a question, jotting down his answer, then just looking at the person and not saying anything further. This pause, especially when the officer seems to be studying the suspect, can be rather unnerving to someone who may be feeling a bit tense already.

Often, the suspect will feel obligated and subconsciously under pressure to add something to the answer he's just given. And many times, the additional information he provides will be harmful to him and helpful to the questioner. This technique can work for anyone in any situation.

These periods of silence during a conversation seem to weigh heavily upon someone who's trying to lie their way out of trouble. Dr. Lieberman refers to this phenomenon by the phrase "Silence is gold-plated." By this, he means that a questioner should watch for a person who seems to be uncomfortable during these spaces of quietude. Wait him out. It might be of value to you.

> **Let me help you out.**

Some phrases that can be effective in encouraging a person to tell you the truth about a certain matter include, "Can we be perfectly honest about this?" or "Let's get to this bottom of this," or "Just between you and me, what really happened?" This gives the person a chance to come clean after he's been working hard to keep up a deception, and it could well be that he's tired of the strain and the guilty feelings he's been experiencing. Sometimes it does feel good to really "get something off one's chest."

Or, if several people have been involved in a deception, you can appeal to one of them as a confidante. You might say something like, "I know this wasn't your idea. You probably just got sucked into this thing. You're not like them. I know I can trust you to tell me what really happened." Often, he'll take this life preserver you're tossing him and snitch on the other involved parties. Once again, offering him some type of incentive as a bit of a bribe to open up wouldn't hurt your chances to learn the truth.

> **Watch for slippery answers.**

Then there are what Walters calls "modifiers," which he equates with escape clauses in contracts. "At this time, I don't intend to raise taxes." (What about after the election?) "I was basically at home all night." (Except when you slipped out to shoot the victim?) "Essentially, that's all that happened." (But what about the part when you ditched the getaway car you were driving?)

Another form of response is the "blocking statement." A blocking statement would be one such as, "If I were going to do it, it wouldn't be like that." (Wasn't there a book something like that?)

Or the person might say, "Why would I do something like that?" Or "Why would I lie about something like that?" (Well, I don't know, why don't you tell me, buddy? Perhaps in order to avoid a divorce, or losing your job, or maybe getting a lethal injection?)

➢ **Why would I lie to you?**

Another signal noted often would be the use of "bridging phrases." These would include ones that skip over pertinent information in the interviewee's story. "Later on that day . . ." or "After a while . . ." or "The next thing I knew . . ." In these cases, you would naturally want to backtrack and have the person fill in the "unimportant part" of the story that he left out. It might prove illuminating to the question in point.

➢ **And that's the damn truth.**

Oftentimes a liar, says Dr. Lieberman, will be more insistent and adamant in his responses than a person who's telling the truth. He just doesn't wish to be questioned further on the matter, and he wants to make a strong statement that you'll have to accept unless you want a fight on your hands. Whereas a person who is truthful doesn't mind if you misunderstand him or want further clarification about whatever comments he makes. Lieberman also mentions what he calls globalizing and depersonalizing the question. Instead of someone saying that he's not lying to you, he'll hit you with some statement like, "I'm totally against lying." He's hiding behind a code of morality that he doesn't even subscribe to.

➢ **And then I said . . .**

Nance says that a liar may leave out an important detail

when she's telling her story, then go back and insert it later in the tale, saying she forgot about that particular point. I'd compare her to a poor joke teller who doesn't give all the necessary specifics in the first telling of the story. Nance also says you should ask an interviewee what someone said to her during the incident in question. That's because it's more difficult for a deceiver to make up comments from another person than it is to tell the story in her own words. I'd expect that this would be a good time to watch for hesitation, stuttering, and poor syntax from the person being questioned.

When an interviewee tends to ramble in his answers to your questions, Dr. Dimitrius believes that he's insecure or confused. However, I'd say that it could be because he's nervous or just not focused mentally. This is a difficult situation for the questioner. I've interviewed many suspects who were not very intelligent and were not articulate in the least. It was hard to know if they were being evasive or they just couldn't track my questions and respond appropriately and effectively. It becomes a matter of evaluating the person's native intelligence and his ability to express himself cogently. And, of course, his nervousness does tend to affect those elements.

But it can be a significant signal when an interviewee has previously been unruffled and coherent in his answers to your questions, and then he suddenly becomes rattled and somewhat inarticulate in his responses. That's when you may well have hit upon a subject that's very sensitive to him. Suddenly, the interviewee fears it might be detrimental to his well-being to answer the questions completely and with total candor. Another sign may be when you try to guide the interviewee back from his ramblings to the matter at hand, but the man resists returning to that area of questioning. Any time a person changes their demeanor, and especially when they exhibit a sign we know is connected with lying, it's best to pay close attention to what they're saying and not saying in response to your questions. You've hit on a touchy area.

Rambling: But I didn't . . . no, see, I . . ."

> ➤ **Not playing with a full deck.**

Dr. Lieberman points out that some people can't provide a straight or truthful answer because they have some type of mental disorder. I've found that it usually becomes clear when you start questioning a person that he may be suffering from such a problem. Also, the person can be impaired by heavy drinking or drug use or abuse. But sometimes you have to hear a person out to determine their mental state and/or any other problem they may have. I've listened to some people who looked completely normal, and told a story logically and fully for some minutes, then drifted off with their narrative into never-neverland. Most often, the people who live even more than most of us in their own crazy worlds, whether schizophrenic, paranoid, or simply delusional, will exhibit obvious symptoms of their affliction in their physical mien and their behavior.

> ➤ **Oops, I didn't mean that.**

You'll sometimes notice that a person will use a politically incorrect and offensive term in speaking with you. Dr. Glass notes that these people are sometimes just unaware of how situations have changed in the world. Or they may not care about the sensitivity and dignity of others. I believe that often these verbal "slips" by intelligent people are similar to those who say "just kidding," in that they're giving away how they actually feel about certain racial or religious or cultural groups.

We've seen many instances of celebrities and politicians being thrust into the headlines for using offensive comments that they later try to publicly retract. It seems to me that their true feelings may have been enunciated on the first go-around.

➤ **In other words . . .**

A good way to elicit the true response to a question that you need answered is to rephrase the question. If you watch reporters trying to eke answers from politicians during press conferences, or as they walk to their limousines or helicopters afterwards, you'll note they use this tactic quite often, and sometimes with good results. It's a strong sign when the person you're questioning becomes uncharacteristically defensive. This usually signals the person is upset, or embarrassed, or possibly trying to avoid having to lie, or to cover up a lie previously told.

➤ **Those little things that you do.**

Some physical problems a liar may experience are coughing, mumbling, licking his lips, swallowing several times, and clearing his throat. If a person speaks very softly, almost inaudibly, it could signal that he doesn't believe what he's telling you. I've observed all of these features in people I've interviewed on occasions when I thought they were guilty of violating a federal crime. And yet, I've run across a few who remained calm and intelligible during questioning. In those cases, you have to work harder at thinking up questions that will put the person into the penalty box. Listen carefully to his answers, and be quick to follow up on any seeming discrepancies that you note in his stories.

If slow and hesitant speech by a suspect is accompanied by body language such as shifting in his chair, fidgeting with his hands, or failure to maintain appropriate eye contact, the person is exhibiting nervousness and may well be lying. These manifestations may stem from the fact the person is trying to avoid answering a question or has just given a phony answer to one. This is the time to pursue your line of questioning with gusto, pressing the person to give you some type of straightforward and definite answers. Don't allow him to waffle and vacillate and slip out of the noose of your specific queries.

Watch for what Walters terms "displacement" comments, which are constant references to others in order to take the spotlight off the person being questioned. Such comments would include, "All the other guys were doing it," or "Anyone would have done the same thing." In short, be suspicious when someone talks about "they" or "everybody," because he's trying to deflect attention from what he has done.

>   **I just wondered.**

Another good interview technique is one in which you ask a leading question that the interviewee will perceive as innocent and be willing to answer. You might ask, "Did you do any Christmas shopping during lunchtime?" Then the person, whom you saw having lunch with a co-worker that seemed far too chummy, might see this as a nice alibi for his possible indiscretion and answer in the affirmative. You can follow up with querying him as to what stores he visited and asking whether he found any good bargains. You can tell by the lack of detail or the insincerity in his tone that he's making up the supposed shopping spree you've led him into having to describe. And it will show you that he's very uncomfortable about having you know anything about his lunch partner.

An example given by Dr. Lieberman has to do with a woman who discovers that she has herpes. She's been with two men during the pertinent time frame, and she wants to know which one gave her the disease. Instead of calling them both up and asking if they have herpes and gave it to her (which they'll both deny) or calling them to accuse them of giving it to her (which they'll deny even more strongly), she tries a tactic he calls, "I'm just letting you know."

In this method, she'll call each of her suitors and let them know that she's just found out that she has herpes. Imagine that suitor number one says, "Well, don't look at me. I didn't give it to you! I'm clean." Suitor number two says, "You *what*? How long have you had it? You may have given it to me." Can you guess which one passed the malady along to her? If you thought that suitor one was acting rather <u>defensively</u>, you're right. And think about how suitor two was concerned that she may have given him the disease, while suitor one kept denying he could be the source, not worrying about catching the disease, because he already has it.

> **That's not right.**

Sometimes a person seems to <u>contradict everything you say.</u> This can be very frustrating and emotionally charged. You feel as though you always have to explain or defend your remarks. Many times, says Dr. Glass, such an individual is trying to compete with you. He may be jealous of you, and he's often insecure. Plus, he's exhibiting his disrespect for you and your comments.

Along the same lines is the person who is <u>always</u> making <u>cutting remarks about other people.</u> She may do this directly to you, as well, but she will most certainly do this when you're not present. She doesn't have much self-respect, so she attempts to make herself feel better by belittling everyone around her. She won't give your opinions any credence, and she'll feel compelled to offer a "better" solution or to degrade what you've said. Of the people I've run across who do this, I've noticed that they won't hesitate to exaggerate, stretch the truth, or just plain lie to make their points seem more valid.

> **To trust or not to trust.**

Ongoing medical studies, first revealed publicly in April of 2010, reflect that some folks are more trusting of strangers than is the norm. I suspect part of this situation can be accounted for by their upbringing and the sanguine examples of their caregivers. However, an interesting side issue has been identified by scientists. It seems that the hormone oxitocin is not produced in adequate amounts in some individuals.

Interestingly, oxitocin aids humans in sizing up other people (from their looks and actions), as to whether they should be trusted. Those with an insufficient production of oxitocin tend to be less suspicious and more trusting of people, whether it's warranted by circumstances or not. And we've learned that this can be dangerous in our deceptive society.

> **How's that again?**

Liars have a difficult time constructing a story that has all the components of what a true story will contain. First of all, the stories they tell will convey a feeling of implausibility. Then, fibbers won't include the details that are contained in a true story. They won't be able to concoct and describe their supposedly personal experiences in a believable way. A liar won't tell such things as what the weather was like, how he felt during the situation, what he thought about, what peculiar actions took place, and what the participants in the activity said while it was occurring.

On the other hand, some con men become so practiced at telling lies that naïve, trusting, or unsuspecting people will accept them, to their detriment. I once dealt with such a fellow. He had a record of being able to con young women into believing his hard-to-swallow patter, and to grant him dispensations, including sexual favors. I'll describe one of his escapades.

❖ **It pays to be dubious of others.**

Most con artists are smart and have people skills. They can read people well, and they often try to establish some type of connection with the mark they're addressing so as to allay any suspicions the person may have concerning their veracity. In one case I had in Emporia, Kansas, a man who had been imprisoned more than once for his con games was up to his usual pastime of trying to hook up with a young woman. He was in his sixties, and he preferred women of about twenty.

In this instance, he affiliated himself with a local church, playing the part of the affable Christian. He befriended a nineteen-year-old girl and conned her by claiming to be a CIA operative who had to accomplish a covert operation. The naïve young woman was taken in by his blandishments and agreed to go on a trip with him to help him complete his mission.

Along the way, he even demonstrated some phony karate moves he claimed the Agency had taught him, and he would occasionally stop at pay phones to make "confidential" calls.

Plus, he had a device he stated was a radio transmitter that he could use to send messages to his supervisor to keep him posted on their progress. As we tracked his travels around the country through credit card purchases and subsequent interviews of people in the stores where he bought items, we learned that he traversed about a dozen states before arriving back in Kansas to refill a necessary prescription for the young lady.

FBI agents were able to stop him and to rescue the kidnapping victim. I spent a couple of long sessions with the victim, explaining to her what had happened. She slowly realized that she'd been under the spell of a consummate con man. Hopefully, she'll remember the lesson and be more careful and clever in the future. As to the con man, I next interviewed him in Leavenworth Prison.

➢ **Signals.**

Other observable forms of communication include whether the person being analyzed clears his throat too often. Walters terms this a "stalling mechanism," which the person is using to buy time to think of a good (i.e., passable) lie. This person may ask you to repeat the question, answer the question with a question, repeat the question as he's denying it, make a comment which doesn't really answer the question, or pretend he didn't hear the question. (Have you ever seen the montage of Ronald Reagan with a hand cupping his ear and a puzzled look on his face as he was walking away from reporters who were vainly shouting questions at him?)

Most people are watching for such signals automatically, without consciously noticing the various components that they're studying or knowing exactly what they're basing their ultimate "gut reaction" upon. Those of you who study this book will have the advantage of knowing precisely what you're looking for, and how you should analyze and evaluate the various comments, expressions, and body language. You'll have your emotions and intellect under control, and you'll be in charge of the conversation.

➢ **Stay cool.**

Another point to consider is to be amenable to the suspect, make it seem as though you're not condemning him, and allow yourself to be receptive to hearing his side of the story. Hopefully, this will make him more relaxed and forthcoming, and you'll be able to get to the truth of the matter. Sometimes, interviewers get angry, and they'll lash out at the suspect. They feel that they want to punish whoever is responsible for having done the terrible act in question. But be aware that there is little incentive for the wrongdoer to tell the truth when he knows he'll automatically receive punishment for doing so. You need to offer him an element of hope that he'll get some type of reward if he comes clean and tells the real story. It may only be the relief of confessing and not having to worry about being caught in a lie anymore. Or he may want to make a deal that will benefit him in a tangible manner.

I've seen FBI agents and police officers try to browbeat someone into confessing to the commission of a crime. It doesn't usually work. I believe in the old saying that you'll catch more flies with honey than with vinegar. I always attempted to make the suspect feel relaxed, and I tried to make him believe that I was on his side to the extent that I would do what I could to help him out of the jam he was in. For instance, if he was co-operative in providing information, I said I'd make that clear to the judge, to be considered in regard to any possible sentence he might later receive. And I'd be sure to do so. Believe me, the suspect can tell when you're being sincere with him or just trying to play him to improve your conviction rate.

➢ **Too good to be true.**

Remember to beware of the situation where a person answers a question too fully and easily. Dr. Lieberman says that if an answer sounds too perfect, it's probably been rehearsed. Someone who doesn't want you to find out what he really did will have taken care to construct a comprehensive and detailed story that seems plausible and reasonable. Most people don't speak in a complete text sort of way. They'll furnish various parts of an answer, and then sort of tack it all together. For instance, if a detective asks someone <u>what they were doing</u> the night of a <u>certain date about two months previously,</u> unless it was Christmas or some special occasion, the person who's being <u>truthful</u> will say they have <u>no idea.</u> The <u>suspect,</u> possibly expecting that you would ask him some day, will have a <u>ready-made story</u> concocted with many particulars.

➢ **Circumlocution.**

Those who seem to speak indirectly, <u>not</u> using plain language or <u>direct statements,</u> says Dr. Glass, may be avoiding telling you the truth. If someone seems to be wandering in her comments, not getting to the point about what you've asked her, she's probably trying to talk her way out of telling the truth about something. Also, if a person gives <u>too much information</u> that's <u>extraneous</u> to the subject at hand, this may be a smoke screen to hide what she's actually not telling you.

Several items to watch for that are couched in what Glass terms the "liars' syndrome" are using a lot of pauses and saying "er" and "um" often. She adds that a person may repeat words or partial words as he mentally tries to work out an answer (not a truthful one) to an unexpected question. He'll say, "So, then I went . . . I went by the convenience store." Or, "I real—I really thought I'd done that." Such people often lie to make themselves feel more important and to control or tear down others. They will also offer effusive, but not heartfelt compliments, and sometimes they'll be flirtatious to attract people as a way of inflating their egos.

Watch for <u>"surgical denial,"</u> Walters warns us. "No, I <u>didn't use hard drugs.</u>" (So, did you use any kind of drugs?) "Well, the guys passed around a joint." (And did you partake of it?) "I <u>took a puff, but I didn't inhale.</u>" (Once again, there's a familiar ring to the story.)

People will <u>ordinarily</u> answer what you asked, <u>without volunteering extra information,</u> especially at the first of the conversation when they may not know what the thrust of the questioning is about. Watch for a situation where a suspect will offer you information he wants you to know, even if it's not in direct response to your question. Of course, in a law enforcement interview, the subject of what you're interviewing the person about will be made clear. But if you ask someone a question that seems innocuous and general, and he responds with a <u>detailed answer</u> that makes you realize he knows where you're headed and what you might suspect him of doing, you can be sure that he's probably committed the questioned act.

Other verbal clues to possible deception are fuzzy answers which show that a person's thinking is not organized and engaged and spontaneous. The subject may repeat your question almost word-for-word before replying. This is probably a stalling technique, allowing him to think of a plausible response. He also may express himself in incomplete sentences. His words may sound clipped and his sentences incoherent, needing further explanation. He may exhibit a halting manner of speech. And he may repeat himself.

A number of phrases used for stalling and gaining time to think of a credible answer when a person doesn't want to tell the truth are listed by Dr. Lieberman. Some of them are:

"Where did you hear that?"

"It depends on how you look at it."

"What's your point, exactly?"

"Why would you ask something like that?"

"Well, it's not as simple as yes or no."

It will be easier for the interviewee to lie to you, says Lieberman, if he thinks he's justified in lying. That is, he'll be more comfortable and capable of lying if he believes in the general purpose and worth of what he's saying, even if he doesn't believe in the actual words he's telling you. I've had that happen where people are dedicated to a <u>religious or political cause,</u> and if they tell the complete <u>truth</u> it will be <u>damaging</u> to those causes. I suppose such a person is subconsciously weighing the lesser of two evils according to his system of value judgment.

> **Discomfort.**

When a person who is <u>normally fluent</u> in her speech begins to exhibit pauses, repetition of words in a sentence, and stuttering and <u>stammering</u>, Dr. Glass says it may well indicate that she's lying to you. Of course, some people have a stutter when they're talking normally or when they're under pressure, so you should be aware of the person's usual speech patterns before drawing any conclusions based on this particular phenomenon. Besides, we all have moments when we're caught at a loss as to what to say. But a long hesitation can be an indicator that the person is trying desperately to formulate a believable-sounding answer to a question that she doesn't feel she can answer honestly.

This would also be a good time to watch her face for that flash of an expression that signals her true feelings at the moment. Does she look scared, stunned, and surprised by your question? Does she have that startled animal look? Watch for that quick and honest reaction. Then pay close attention to her answer, and analyze it carefully.

➢ **Tell me more.**

A good way to get more information, and perhaps a more truthful version of something you've just been told, is to <u>ask</u> for <u>more details</u> about what the person said. Don't just ask the man to give you more particulars of the story. Instead, use leading phrases like, "And so . . ." or "So, then . . ." or "Meaning . . .?" The person will usually offer something more about what they've already stated in order to satisfy your curiosity or interest, perhaps slipping up and giving away more than he meant to, or maybe just making a comment that he hadn't thought out thoroughly enough, and which you can easily disprove.

➢ **Assessing veracity.**

One method of evaluating verbal responses for truthfulness is known as the Statement Validity Assessment (SVA). In this model, seven verbal characteristics are given consideration. These include negative statements, plausible answers, irrelevant information (outside the topic being discussed), overly generalized statements (use of words such as never, always, nobody, etc.), self-references, direct answers, and response length.

Psychologist Vrij examined the studies conducted using

these criteria. He found they showed that liars tend to make short statements. This is possibly because they have to invent an answer on the spot. They also tend to give answers that are indirect. I've seen this many times both on television discussions and in my interviews where a suspect won't say, "I didn't rob the bank." They'll say something like, "I wouldn't rob a bank." Or maybe they'll comment that, "I'm sure I was across town when the bank was robbed." They could say something like, "Do you see any money around here?" (Or your significant other might say, "I wouldn't have a drink with another girl." They might even phrase it, "You know I don't go out for drinks after work.")

> **Incomplete stories.**

When someone is making up a story, he'll likely fail to mention two elements that are usually present in truthful stories. That is, the liar won't talk about the reactions and the apparent feelings of the people he interacted with. An honest man will say something like, "When John spotted his dented car, his mouth fell open and his eyes got as big as saucers. I'm sure it was a big shock to him." The fibber will leave out such commonly related details.

Also, a prevaricator won't tell what went wrong during the interaction. As Murphy tells us in his famous law, if something can go wrong, it will. But in the liar's story, the car never fails to start or has a flat tire. No one is late, throwing off the timing in going somewhere. It never rains at the worst possible moment. If all goes beautifully in a tale, it's probably manufactured. If someone is telling you a story that's fraught with perils, it's probably true.

Vrij reported that there was no indication in the studies he examined that deceitful suspects gave more general type statements or provided more irrelevant information than truth tellers. They did make more negative statements and fewer self-references than those providing true accounts. And another clue to their deception was the obvious perception that their answers sounded less plausible. It's a good time for the questioner to hit the narrator with some laser-guided queries. Pick out weaknesses in the story and attack them, like when you're trying to break a chain, you hammer on the weakest link.

However, it's not a good idea to confront a person the moment you realize you're being lied to. It's better to string out the questioning a bit longer, to see what other lies the person may tell that you can disprove. And you should try to determine as much information as you can from the person, because once you let him know that you've caught him in a lie, the tenor of the conversation will probably change.

If the story-teller realizes you suspect he's lying, he'll be hesitant to answer any more questions, and he may clam up for good. You may even decide to end the questioning before you reveal that you suspect he's lying. You can always check out other things he's told you and then confront him later with all of the lies you've caught him in.

> **Protect your knowledge.**

Walters says you should never reveal to anyone what signals you noticed that told you he was lying. It could be tempting as a way to put pressure on him to reveal the whole story, but it's not a good idea. That's sort of like a magician telling how he did the trick. Now the person will know to avoid such behavior the next time. On the television show *Lie to Me*, some of the actors who can detect falsehoods will mention the techniques they used when they accuse someone of lying. But that's more for drama and to inform the audience how they noted the fibs. It doesn't work well in real life.

A liar, says Lieberman, won't ask the right questions. He's often unaware that a true conversation involves both answering and asking questions. He's focused on whether you are convinced by the answers he gives to your questions. Beyond that, it's not a real conversation to him. He's not interested in learning anything from you. He just wants to pass the "truth" test.

> **Voice pitch and volume.**

The voice has three characteristics, including the pitch, volume, and rate of speech. Stress or anxiety, such as that felt by a liar who's on the spot, should affect one or more of these three characteristics. A raised vocal pitch was demonstrated by Deputy Sheriff Barney Fife on the sitcom *The Andy Griffith Show.* When he got excited or scared or agitated, you'd believe that as a kid he'd had a terrible accident with his bicycle seat.

High voice volume can indicate a person is angry or upset. But if it lowers to a barely discernible level, the person may be trying to minimize what he's saying to you or to disguise his words or meaning. He's uncomfortable with the questions you're asking, and he's seeking a means of avoiding them.

If the person starts talking faster than normal, he may be getting excited or angry. A decrease in pace may show his difficulty in discussing the particular subject. Always pay attention to what a person's normal speech rate is before you ask him any questions he may find disturbing.

Remember that pauses before answering questions indicate that the person you're talking with may be trying to compose deceptive answers. And keep in mind that people who are being devious will also exhibit "speech dysfunctions" more than the norm, which could include muttering, mumbling, stammering, stuttering, or slurring their speech. Also, in this regard, be aware to watch for people who have been drinking too much alcohol or using drugs, as they may also have slurred and dysfunctional speech.

Of course, in any discussion, you must be aware of the personality of the particular person with whom you're dealing in your line of questioning. It's thought by some psychologists that intelligent people will be more often believed than people of lesser acumen. Perhaps this is because they can think of more plausible answers quicker and better.

Or maybe smarter people just present a better impression. Also, they could be more fluent with language and tend to give a smoother presentation of their lies. For instance, studies have shown that sales people tend to give no verbal indicators of deception, perhaps because they're used to presenting things in a positive manner, or maybe because they don't feel much unease in stretching the truth, just as they must do in their jobs.

> **I'm not saying that.**

If someone tells you what they're not doing, says Dr. Lieberman, such as making a statement like, "I don't want you to take this the wrong way," or "It's not that I don't want to go out with you sometime," or "I hope it won't hurt your feelings," then she's doing exactly what she's implying that she's not. And there's a clever way of lying through implying that some people use, such as when Richard Nixon said, "I don't want anyone not to vote for John Kennedy because he is a Catholic." Or maybe someone saying, "I saw your girlfriend with this cute football player at the movies last night, but I'm sure they're just friends." The people who make such statements definitely have an agenda in getting you to believe something by stating it in a manner that suggests they're denying it could happen.

> **That's not what I asked.**

Something you'll note quite often in any political discussion, and which is an indicator of lying by means of evasion, is the answer that doesn't really respond to the heart and soul of the question. For instance, if someone is trying to set me up on a blind date, I may ask whether the woman is attractive. When the answer is something like, "She goes to yoga classes all the time, she's really smart, and everyone loves her," then the implication that she has many virtues and good habits doesn't really answer my initial question about her looks.

> **I'm just like you.**

To help establish rapport with a person you're questioning, Dr. Lieberman suggests trying to match his posture and movements. If someone is standing with his hand in his pocket, with his weight mostly on one leg, then do the same, without being obvious about it. Try to use a similar rate of speech as the person you're interviewing. Use some of the same words he does when he's talking. This should put the man at ease and perhaps get him to open up a bit.

Be sure not to interrupt what he's telling you. Be polite and respectful, unless he makes it necessary to get more forceful with him. Ask questions that can't be answered with just a "yes" or a "no," but must be explained more fully. You want to be able to hear and judge longer sentences, so always ask open-ended questions.

> **Assessing content.**

Another important part of the SVA is what is termed the criteria-based content analysis (CBCA). There are nineteen points in this evaluation. However, the assessment process was originally developed to determine the validity of statements made by children in abuse cases. So, I think some of the criteria are not especially relevant in conversations between adults.

I've extracted the nine points that I think could be useful in detecting whether verbal statements are true. These are:
1. logical structure
2. unstructured production
3. quantity of details
4. contextual embedding
5. descriptions of interactions
6. reproduction of speech
7. unusual details
8. superfluous details
9. accounts of subjective mental state.

All of the above elements seem to me to be ones you should watch for in assessing the verbal content of a man's comments.

With the logical structure criteria, you're naturally looking for whether the person's comments make sense. Do the statements hold together as a coherent whole? I've noticed in interviewing people that they'll often say something which doesn't quite hang together with the rest of their story. Oftentimes, if you'll pursue that particular trail, you'll come up with the story behind the story, or perhaps even get to the core of the truth. Then it happens that some people just can't tell a lie very well, and their account is so full of holes it's hard to know where to begin. In such a case, be patient and question them until you find out why their comments are so scattered.

> **But before that happened . . .**

Unstructured production is a term that refers to the method of telling a story. Often, when a person is upset about something, they'll tell their tale beginning in the middle or near the place where they felt they were wronged by someone. It's sometimes difficult to get them settled down and be able to get them to start at the inception. You may have to just let them tell their tale in whatever order they want, then go over it with them to reconstruct the proper sequence of events.

However, just because a story is structured well, you can't count on it being true. Often when people tell a lie, they'll present the anecdote in a strictly chronological fashion. This can be a signal that they've made up at least part of the tale, or that they're leaving something out. It's easier to remember a false story and tell it correctly when a person tells it from first to last. Jumping around to different parts of the story is difficult to manufacture, as well as to keep straight for the deceiver. So, be sure to be aware of signals of prevarication if someone starts telling you a tale that seems too pat. It might be a manufactured and well-rehearsed attempt to bamboozle you.

Quantity of details refers to a story that's related to the listener with a number of descriptions of actions that happened, such as quotes of comments by the participants, and reports of reactions by the other people involved to things that happened to them during the situation. A truth teller will include statements about the place, time, ambience, weather, and his feelings when actions occurred. A liar can seldom tell a story that's as richly detailed as that of a person who actually lived through a stressful event.

After all, someone who is telling the truth as he knows or recalls it is merely searching his memory and then relating what is there. The deceiver will have to make it up out of whole cloth. Except, of course, the liar could use the framework of what actually happened, but then leave out parts or change the parts of the story that would incriminate him. But this becomes a delicate and difficult balancing act, as well.

Contextual embedding means that someone who is telling

the truth about a situation will often make references to details that relate to him. She might say, "I was watching *Oprah*, and it was about halfway over, when I heard someone breaking the glass on a kitchen window." Maybe she'll be out for her regular walk in the park, and she'll get to a certain point in her walk when something happens. The person will be aware of and mention that it was hot, and she was getting sweaty, and she'd just passed under a shade tree when a man jumped out of the bushes. Liars will try to concoct their stories in their heads, and they often just think of the actions involved, without being aware that they should mention the ambience of the location and how the activity fits in with their regular routine.

The descriptions of interactions among the people present at the scene will be more realistically presented by a truthful person than by a liar. There will be a sense that she's giving you the story in scenes, not just stating rhetorical pronouncements. A truthful person might say something like, "I yelled 'Stop!' at him and held out my hand, because that's what I learned to do in this self-defense class I took, but he kept coming toward me, and he grabbed my arm, so I tried to pull away, but even though he looks kind of skinny and wasted, he was strong, and he yanked me up against him. And then he just kind of overpowered me. And that's how it happened."

Reproductions of speech are just a continuation of the above descriptions. But it's something that a liar won't usually relate to you. Truth tellers often quote what was said by the participants in the actions in question. Phonies are more likely to report what someone supposedly said in a narrative form. An honest account of a situation might include, "So, I said I don't have much money in my account. But then he said, 'Well, if you have even a thousand dollars, that will show good faith on your part, and I'll feel okay about sharing this money I found with you.' So I looked at the cash he showed me in the duffel bag, and I said, Okay, I'll get out a thousand if that's what you want. And he just smiled and said, 'Great. Let's go.' So then we drove to the bank and I withdrew the money from my savings."

Unusual details may be given by someone who is relating a true story. A liar will not usually include them in her false statement. For instance, the person may say, "I didn't really trust him at first, because he had long black hair in a pony tail, a three-day beard, and a tattoo of a skull on his right shoulder. But he seemed nice enough, and I needed to get to my music lesson, so I got into his Volkswagen bug. Besides, the car was kinda cute, bright red and shiny, you know?"

Superfluous details are icing on the cake which probably indicate that a person is telling a true story. She may say something that is not really on target as far as the situation you're discussing. Such an instance would include something like the person saying, "We drove along Main Street for about fifteen minutes. We were just chatting, and everything seemed okay. I noticed that Macy's was having a sale on jackets on Saturday, and I told him I might go to that. Then he told me he really liked me and he wanted to go have a drink with me somewhere. That's when I said that I needed to get to my lesson right away."

➤ **You're kidding me.**

If you're asking someone a serious question, watch closely if he tries to make light of it or use humor to defuse the importance of the query. I've even had people sitting in jail try to use this particular diversion on me. It's not an appropriate response. The man who had snuck money out of the other teller's locker tried his best to manipulate the interview by using this tactic. He was a glib and intelligent young man, so I'm sure he'd been successful with his charm, good looks, and practiced patter in most of the dealings in his life. But I was there to question him and other workers about a serious offense—stealing money from a bank vault. I like a good joke or a clever turn of phrase as well as anyone, but that wasn't the time or place.

➤ **That's how I felt.**

Accounts of one's subjective mental state will often be given by a person actually relating a true story or incident. He may say, "I got kind of nervous when she said her boyfriend might be at the bar, and he'd probably get pissed at me. So I started thinking maybe I shouldn't go inside with her. And I said, do we have to go to that particular bar? And she said, 'Yes, I have to pick up my paycheck.' So, I decided that we'd have to go, and maybe I could do it without getting into trouble." Notice that the witness not only mentioned how he felt about something that was said, but he told what he was thinking in relation to the situation. He also related comments by another person. Most liars won't be able to conjure up such intricately detailed comments about the circumstances they're relating.

Also, liars may not realize that such details will be evaluated by the person to whom they're relating their story. Another factor may be that the person making up a tale won't provide too many details because he's just not imaginative enough to mentally put himself into a scene and then to relate everything about it. I've written mystery novels, and I know this type of fiction production is difficult to do.

Besides that, the liar is faced with the worrisome problem that if he gives too many details he won't be able to remember all of them. This is a valid concern, especially if the questioner asks him to repeat his story or even parts of it. The prevaricator may also be anxious that if he tells an overly intricate story, then the person he's trying to fool will check out the particulars and find at least some of them to be false. If he's talking with an FBI agent or a jealous girlfriend, he may well be right to be concerned about that particular point.

➤ **He said *what*?**

Be suspicious of someone whose reaction is exaggerated for the question or comment made to them. Dr. Lieberman refers to this type of response as "compensation." He gives the Shakespearian quote: "Methinks the lady doth protest too much." As usual, Shakespeare's line encapsulates the situation. For instance, you may ask someone why they didn't pick up milk that evening. A truthful answer would probably be, "Oh, I completely forgot. I ran into Marcie at the store, and she told me about Jan and Mike breaking up." Whereas someone who is guilty of something, such as running into an old boyfriend before she got to the store and having drinks with him might go something like, "Hey, I've had a hard day. I can't remember everything, you know. Maybe you could pick up things on your way home some time. Why does it always have to be me?"

Also, beware the person who tries to make light of something that deserves more serious consideration. Perhaps a woman might take the option of saying, "Oh, sorry I'm late. On the way to the store I ran into Phil Johnson. You remember, we had a couple of dates a long time ago. He wanted to catch up, so we had a cup of coffee. But I did get the milk. And I'm famished, how about you?" If she's not the type to stop on the way home to have coffee (or the probably slightly harder libation that she shared with Phil), you might want to examine a little more closely what their exact relationship was and may once again become.

A person who's feeling guilty about not getting the milk because she ran into Phil, had a drink, and chatted for a while, might also take a more defensive position about this question. For instance, her answer might be more along the lines of, "I can't remember everything. I was really busy, and I was thinking about this project we have to finish at work, and I didn't recall about the milk. You know, you forget things sometimes, too."

If a comment leaves you wondering: *What got into her?* then the answer may well be that the devil is forcing her to tell a fib. And remember, if you catch a person in one lie, then press to find out what other falsehoods she's been telling you. Lies prefer to travel in packs. They don't usually like to go out alone.

We've all heard and used the elongation of words as a playful or demonstrative strategy when talking with someone. Dr. Lieberman notes that someone speaking truthfully may use such elongated words as, "Yeeesss," followed by an explanation. A liar won't use such a method of speaking. He'll offer more bland and straightforward answers, and responses that are less playful. Someone might say, "The party was g-r-e-e-e-a-t!" This is probably exactly how they feel. If they say, "Oh, the party was good," then you can definitely question their sincerity.

Aldert Vrij says that liars will often use an abundance of speech hesitations while answering a question. Such hesitations include use of the sounds of "er," "um," "uh," "ah," and the like. They will often have a lengthy latency period when answering questions. That is, the period of silence between a question being posed and an answer being given will be overly long. It's rather like the hesitation between a question being asked by a reporter in the U.S. of another reporter in Italy, with the delay in transmission and reception over the satellite hookup.

Both the manifestations of speech hesitations and periods of latency probably occur because the liar has to think harder and longer to manufacture a plausible answer that will hang together with whatever lies he's previously told. It's complicated to produce fibs with good structure and consistency. Nobody ever said that lying was easy.

➤ **Stress test.**

Another reaction to watch for is the stress level of the person being interviewed. If you change from questioning him about the suspected wrongdoing to asking about another subject matter altogether, and he then becomes more relaxed and talkative, you could make a mental note to yourself that he's probably been lying to you previously. The person who's trying to convince you of his innocence won't want the subject under discussion dropped until you've settled the matter. As Dr. Lieberman states, "Remember, the guilty wants the subject changed; the innocent always wants a further exchange of information."

When I mentioned watching for signs of stress, of course the principal displays indicating that will be from facial expressions and body language. We've discussed expressions, and we'll soon talk about body movements and postures. You'll have to be aware of and able to notice various signals from all of these different sources in order to keep on top of the situation in which you're involved.

In further regard to interview techniques, you should ask questions that will add information to what you already know about the situation in question. Determine whether the person's answers are consistent with the truth with which you're familiar. And once you catch someone lying in regard to a part of the story that you know about, then you'll feel confident about pressing forward to determine what else he's lying about, or what else he knows and isn't telling you.

In the movie, *Presumed Innocent,* Harrison Ford in his part as a prosecuting attorney who's suspected of murder says, "You lie to your lawyer. You lie to the investigator. You lie to the jury. That's the way the game's played." And, I'd suggest, life itself is merely an extension of the criminal justice system. So, watch yourself out there in the courtroom of daily living.

➤ **Boo boos, et cetera.**

Other suspicious vocal features are recurrent speech errors, hesitation in speaking, and a slower than normal speech rate. If these activities are observed, they could be considered indicators of deception. These mannerisms are a type of delaying tactic, and they signal that the person is uneasy, and that he's probably being deceptive.

I've found that you'll usually notice this type of behavior in a person with more limited education and intelligence. He will look as though he's thinking hard to come up with some answers that will get him off the hook. And when you've nailed him with a question that he really doesn't want to answer, he'll pause a beat or two with a stunned look on his face. At this point, he may also stutter and stumble over his words.

A person who's more educated, intelligent, and articulate will have fewer problems with awkward pauses or with stammering when speaking. He'll be able to think fast enough and to speak smoothly enough that there will be little opportunity to observe such aberrant speech behaviors. But even with a more sophisticated and clever person, when you hit him with a particularly incisive question, he'll react with a longer period of silence and sometimes with a look of surprise. It's as if he's suddenly been mentally stunned and can't respond fluidly and without hesitation.

The type of question that will elicit that response is one that you've been holding like an ace in the hole. It can be formulated from some knowledge you've developed about the person prior to questioning him. And often the question can be sharpened and refined in your mind by things the person says or doesn't say during the interview. Then when you judge the time is right, you can spring it on him. You can even throw the query in at a time that seems out-of-sync with your other questions. This might provide more of a shock factor.

Also, never forget that someone can deceive you by not speaking. That is, an interviewee can fail to mention or bring up a particular subject, or he can make evasive or incomplete statements about it. If you don't question him thoroughly about a vital part of the story, he sure isn't going to bring it up. He can't be tripped up by something he didn't say, and he doesn't have to remember it as part of his story that you may be able to prove wrong. Also, he's not going to fill in any gaps in the inci-dent that you don't query him about. So, always try to be very scrupulous in your line of questioning. Follow all the branches that emanate from the tree trunk of the matter at hand.

The person who's being evasive will always try to give you just enough information to satisfy you, but not enough for you to figure out the whole truth of the situation. And he'll certainly not tell you enough to implicate himself in anything. In fact, he may try to send you off in another direction to chase down some tricky rabbit holes.

Walters says that the way to counteract this type of person is to rely on logic. That is, make sure that the person's story is complete and coherent. You might not be able to catch him by observing signals of lying. He's not actually lying, in his mind, he's just not telling you everything. And it definitely helps if you know some facts about what happened in the circumstances in question. Then you can better detect the part of the story that he doesn't seem to want to discuss.

Say you find a credit card receipt in your significant other's pocket (not snooping, just doing the laundry, of course). It shows a charge for a meal at a nice restaurant the day before that seems more than what one person would likely spend. And you know that you were busy working at your job, watching the kids, or scrubbing floors at home. (I'm just posing a hypothetical situation, okay?)

You definitely shouldn't take the receipt and confront your boyfriend or husband with it early in the conversation, asking for an explanation. He'll likely give you one that's fairly plausible. He might say something like, "I had lunch with Bill, and he hadn't cashed his check yet, so I covered it. He'll pay me back." Now, are you going to telephone or go talk with Bill to verify the story? Odds are, that would prove too awkward and embarrassing, so you'll drop the matter. But still, you'll wonder about the whole situation, won't you?

Now consider if you'd said something to the effect of, "It surely was a nice day yesterday, wasn't it? I took a walk at lunchtime and really enjoyed it. Did you have a chance to get out of your office?"

If he says he had to stay in his office to get prepared for a meeting, and he just ate a sandwich, you'll begin to wonder what he's trying to hide. Then you can ask a few more seemingly innocent follow-up questions such as, "Oh, that sounds awful. You didn't even get to duck out a few minutes for some fresh air?"

Once you have him locked into his story, the lunch receipt will be more damning evidence and impossible to explain away with some glib, but plausible answer. Before showing the receipt to him, however, you might throw him off balance a bit by making some comment like, "Honey, I don't think you're being completely truthful with me. A friend of mine told me they saw you driving on Lincoln Avenue at lunchtime."

Now you'll likely receive an astonished look from him. And his sudden recollection that he had to run an errand will sound lame under the circumstances. Plus, it still won't jibe with the receipt in your pocket that you're ready to spring on him at the right moment. By planning your questioning in a strategic manner, you've put yourself in a position to control the discussion and to have a good idea of whether your mate is telling you the real 4-1-1 on the situation, or whether he's giving you the runaround while he runs around.

➢ **Indicators of lying.**

And the Freudian "slip of the tongue" still indicates the person has had a "brain farc" that gives away what he's thinking, but what he's not saying out loud to you. Dr. Lieberman agrees with the validity of the Freudian slip as a revelation of a person's true thoughts, feelings, or intentions. He gives the example of a student who meant to say, "I spent all night completing that project," but instead says, "I spent all night *copying* that project."

Also, remember to watch the person's body language when you're speaking to him. If he shifts his head away from you as you question him, he's trying to stay away from the uncomfortable pressure you've put him under. And if you hit him with a difficult question, his head may jerk away. Or he may turn away more slowly, but deliberately.

Turn the head away; a lie will follow.

Beware when someone won't face you directly, but she turns sideways to you. When anyone twists her body or chair away from you, she's avoiding your questions. And when she turns and points her feet toward an exit, she is definitely sub-consciously signaling that she wants to get out of the situation she's in.

Turning away from your questions.

When you're talking with someone, and you want to determine the truth about a matter under discussion, remember to be alert for any speech errors the person may make. Vrij says you should consider such items as word or even sentence repetition. This would conceivably be caused by nervousness, and would be a form of stammer or stutter. Also, this would likely be an unusual speech pattern for the person you're questioning. And be alert to watch for incomplete sentences. This could well indicate that his brain has suddenly told him: *Wait a minute, that last comment won't wash.*

So, he may make a sentence change after a pause, or even during the sentence. This is a strong indicator that his brain is working harder than should be necessary to answer a simple question. Sometimes, I've noticed, you can almost see the wheels spinning in someone's head when you've asked a particularly incisive question. He senses that if he gets this one wrong, the whole house of cards he's been constructing during the interview may just collapse around his ears, and he may soon be playing strip poker with some hard-bitten dudes in the Big House.

And the other signs we've mentioned may provide signals that come into play when someone is flustered by your questions. When a person is taken aback and can't answer your question in the normal flow of the conversation, he may do some things to fill the lapse. Needing extra time to think up a believable answer, he'll hesitate before he speaks. He may also clear his throat or cough before he actually answers.

A person being interviewed may try to block you psychologically or, in effect, shield himself from you and your questions by using inanimate objects. He may place a drink or a pack of cigarettes between you and him. He may pick up a pen and fiddle with it or chew on it. He's protecting himself from a perceived verbal assault by you. He will also try to avoid answering the questions that will incriminate him. He may try to deflect the interview in another direction or to end it altogether with some comment like: "Well, that's about all I know regarding that matter. Now, I really need to get back to work."

Blocking you with an object.

Then there's the basic symptom of nervousness on the part of an interviewee when he's placed in a confrontational situation. People may indeed be somewhat nervous or edgy when approached by a law enforcement officer or a jealous mate, but extreme nervousness suggests that the person is probably guilty of whatever he's being accused of. You might see such manifestations as trembling hands, rapid breathing, or profuse sweating. Some people get flushed, some turn pale.

In addition, some individuals will chew on their lips, have trouble swallowing, or have to clear the mucous from their throat that forms because of their high state of anxiety. They may cough several times because of their nervousness and from the tickle that comes from draining mucous..

People will also wring their hands, or smooth their clothing, or pick at imaginary lint. And they'll toy with their rings, bracelets, or necklaces. Any type of repetitive and usually unnecessary motion a person seems to perform automatically and without consciously giving it thought, can signal that the individual is reacting to stress. Perhaps you've induced that stress by the questions you've asked him.

Licks of the lips means you could get gypped.

Also, a person under pressure, who is feeling stressed, will often have trouble concentrating on what you're asking him. He'll appear distracted or zoned out. This is almost like going into shock.

I've seen people who look as though they're willing themselves to disappear from the uncomfortable situation in which they're trapped, and then possibly reappear in another more favorable and pleasant location. They'd probably be delighted to enter a wormhole and be transported to another time and place altogether.

Dr. Lieberman suggests another clue to deception is when someone uses a fact you've just stated to make the case that what she's saying must be true. However, if you analyze the lack of a true connection or any plausibility in the resultant explanation, you'll discover that it's only a clever ruse to get you to connect a truth with a falsehood. This can be a tricky area. But as in most dealings with liars, when you take the time to question thoroughly and to analyze the answers you get from the person, you'll clearly notice at what point she tried to throw you off.

And beware of anyone trying to assert a moral high ground. When she brings out, however subtly, her good character or moral strength, she's probably trying to set you up to believe that she couldn't have done some act you suspect her of performing. I suggest you don't fall for it, but that you make a thorough investigation of the actual facts in the circumstances in question.

There have been a good many televangelists and others of the "Lord's servants" who have been found guilty of various criminal charges. It's easier to tell others not to sin than not to do it yourself. And some people get away with a great deal of skullduggery by wearing a cloak of piety to hide their true selves.

Two suggestions made by Dr. Lieberman seem to make sense. During questioning, when the interviewee has finished answering an important question, look directly at him and say, "Really?" You're not actually calling him a liar, but it may seem to him that he needs to explain or expand or at least repeat his answer. While he does so, it will give you a chance to further evaluate his response and his behavior patterns as he talks.

I observed a detective do a version of this tactic in a bank burglary interview I was sitting in on. When the interviewee would lie about an important matter, the detective would put down the pen he'd been assiduously taking notes with, and he'd simply look directly at the subject in a calm manner with just a hint of reproach in his expression. He wouldn't say anything, or glare at the man in a threatening manner, but the "Really?" question was strongly implied by his demeanor. Usually, the subject would qualify or expand or even change the answer he'd just given. It was as if a lie detector had just beeped that the fellow was trying to put something over on us.

> **Truth can be stranger . . .**

If a story is very detailed and somewhat strange, it's usually true. We've all heard the phrase, "You're not going to believe what happened to me." When this comment is followed by a bizarre story, you must ask yourself: Why would someone go to the trouble to make up all those crazy details? Most people don't think that someone would, and they're usually right. Unless the storyteller is a pathological liar, they're not going to start telling an odd tale just to see if you'll believe it. Lies are more often used as defensive mechanisms to keep a person from getting implicated in wrongdoing. The normal fibber is not going to put himself unnecessarily out on a limb and have to keep lying in order to keep it from being sawed off.

However, if a person is smart and eloquent and imaginative, he may know you'll think that way, and so he'll concoct an outrageous but detailed and somewhat plausible story to convince you to believe a bald-faced lie. In the Beverly Hills cop movies, Eddie Murphy plays a Detroit detective who's traveled to California to "help out" on a case. Each time Detective Axel Foley needs to get into someplace, or get by with something, he concocts the wildest imaginable tales, all told with bravado, flourish, and high volume. He overwhelms the person he's trying to deceive, disabling the poor man's bullshit detectors with a high velocity barrage of lies. And then he gets what he wants. Of course, this is mostly show biz stuff, but it could conceivably happen in everyday life.

> **It was all a big mistake.**

As a savvy interviewer, you shouldn't concentrate on trying to shame the suspect into admitting he performed a horrible act.

Instead, you might consider changing the emphasis and the slant of your interview to inquiring what his intentions may have been before the awful event happened. You should approach the person with the attitude that he probably didn't have a choice, or he was forced to do certain things, and then the overall situation somehow got out of hand. You can tell him you want to understand what happened that changed the circumstances and made things go wrong.

In your questions and comments, you'll suggest exculpatory reasons for the person's behavior, such as that you realize it may have been unintentional, a slip, a mistake, an accident, or an unlucky event that the person got involved in. You'll act as though the focus of your concern is not *what* the man did, but *why* he may have done it. You're helping him realize that these unforeseen circumstances "make it okay" that he made a mistake in his actions. You convey that you understand how such things could have happened even when he didn't intend for his actions to cause such terrible consequences.

Other examples of situations in which you may find yourself questioning someone are when money is missing from your business, your significant other has been gone somewhere for a lengthy time on several occasions with no explanation, or you're reviewing a resume that just seems too good to be true. Dr. Lieberman suggests you use some line of questioning such as, "Everybody pads his resume just a bit. I think it shows guts. So, tell me, which parts were you the most creative with on your resume?"

He also mentions a tactic of saying that you want to hear exactly what happened from the person you're interviewing. You can live with what happened, but not with the person lying about it to you. I would often tell an interviewee that I wanted to hear his side of the story, and then we could work something out on how to best resolve the situation. People seem to like it when another person will actually listen to their version of events.

Another ploy to use when questioning someone is to suggest that now is the time that they can tell you what really happened. Tell them that after this particular time, you'll have to report what they said, and if it's not correct, you'll be forced to do what you have to do to them. Don't be specific. Let their imagination run with the situation. This may play out in their head as something much worse than the punishment they might receive under the law.

Then give them one last chance to tell their side of the story about what happened. If what they say next shows that they're mostly concerned about what you can do to them, they're probably guilty of what you think they did. If they return to the assertion that they're innocent of what you suspect them of doing, they may well be.

In an online msnbc article dated May 8, 2010, titled *7 Signs Your Honey May Cheat,* by Dr. Hilda Carle, Ph.D., she says that one strong signal that your partner may lie to you about critical matters is that he or she tends to fib about small, unimportant items. He may not be truthful about such matters as where he ate lunch, or who he ran into at the mall (and had a couple of drinks with). Dr. Carle makes the salient point that cheaters (and I'd add habitual liars), will often tell falsehoods about many of their activities even where there's no reason to do so to save face or stay out of trouble. I've run into people like this, and I agree that such constant fibbing is a strong indicator that you can't trust much of what the person tells you. As I mentioned elsewhere in this book, lies seem to run in packs.

It's important to note that people are very aware of what they're saying, and they've practiced conveying meaning through language all their lives. So, it is sometimes difficult to note clues in the spoken language that indicate prevarication. It would clearly be daunting to try to sift through the rapid-fire statements that Eddie Murphy spews like verbal machinegun bursts in his movies.

However, the suggestions I've offered to you in this chapter should give you an advantage in spotting verbal clues to deception. Use these methods, together with the later suggestions on how to detect hints from body language, and I believe you'll be able to spot incidences of lying when they're directed at you.

5

Lying in Our Society

> ## Are deceivers universal?

You may be getting the uneasy impression that lies and the lying liars who tell them (courtesy of Al Franken) are everywhere in our society and throughout the world. Could it truly be that lying permeates our planet to such a degree? I'm afraid I'll have to be the bearer of bad news by saying, "Yes, Dorothy, there are liars far and wide, even in Kansas." I've served in the FBI in Alabama, New York, Washington, D.C., Chicago, Puerto Rico, Texas, California, and Kansas, and I've found a good many honorable people, as well as deceivers, in every place I've been.

As I mentioned briefly earlier, non-fiction authors James Patterson and Peter Kim wrote that over two thousand people were interviewed about their truthfulness, and 91 percent admitted to lying regularly both at home and at work. In short, prevarication served as a normal part of their social repertoire. It was the way they chose to deal with life and everyone with whom they came in contact. And when you think about it, can we trust that the other 9 percent told the interviewers the truth about not lying? I wonder.

Lying was mentioned in the Bible when Jesus said, "Ye are of your Father, the devil . . . there is no truth in him. When he speaketh a lie, he speaketh of his own: for he is a liar, and the father of it." *John* 8:44. As you might suspect, Jesus seemed not to be a fan of deceit. And he even told the Jews who believed in him, "If ye continue in my word, then are ye my disciples, indeed; and ye shall know the truth, and the truth shall make you free." *John* 8:31, 32.

Aldert Vrij suggests that there are various reasons that men and women lie. They will exaggerate or outright fib concerning matters about themselves so that they will better impress others or better protect themselves from embarrassment in certain situations. They also lie in order to grab an advantage for themselves in a bargaining circumstance. And from the time we were kids, we've all lied to elude punishment for our transgressions. These lies are classified as self-oriented, as they are extended in order to benefit the liar himself.

> **Social lying.**

Then there are lies that everyone tells to get along better in social situations. These are other-oriented comments that mostly serve to make people to whom they're communicated feel better about themselves. These might include complementing someone on their new moustache, blouse, or the way they play the piano, when one is not necessarily that taken with those particular things. In this same vein, people tell social lies in order to maintain the closeness or workability of relationships. The actor Hugh Laurie, who plays the lead role of Dr. House in a series by that name, put it well in a segment titled, "It's a Wonderful Lie." He made the observation, "There's a reason why everyone lies. It works."

And in the above situations, people may tend to believe the liar simply because they would rather go along with the statement than test its validity. After all, few of us would want to know that others really don't like the way we dress or tell jokes or sing. We know we're not the handsomest or prettiest or best-dressed individuals around, we're not professional comedians, and we don't play our musical instrument of choice well enough to be accepted into a symphony orchestra or the Rock 'n' Roll Hall of Fame. A testament to this universal psychological reaction seems to be intimated by Sir Winston Churchill when he said, "Men occasionally stumble over the truth, but most of them pick themselves up and hurry off as if nothing ever happened."

So there are numerous relationships, many alliances, and many foes developed within groups. And when you think about it, do you want your enemies knowing everything about you? Don't we even hide bits of information from our friends and relatives? Mark Twain said, "Every one is a moon, and has a dark side which he never shows to anybody."

Take, for example, the time that you broke the cookie jar or lamp or whatever, and mom and dad really didn't know if it was you or your siblings. Did you 'fess up and face the music? Some of you did, but many didn't. It's always a little easier to avoid blame when possible. Who wants to be grounded or to miss a favorite movie or get a spanking? Of course, there can be eventual consequences that we didn't anticipate. Scottish poet Sir Walter Scott suggested those potential problems when he wrote, "O what a tangled web we weave when first we practice to deceive."

And as we proceed through our lives, do we often try to avoid punishment for infractions of society's "rules" by making excuses, blaming fate or others, or by disavowing knowledge of the trespass altogether? Do we sometimes tell our spouse that someone must have hit our bumper in the parking lot, not that we accidentally backed into a stupid pole that shouldn't have been there in the first place?

It's no wonder that we guard our own information that might be disapproved of by the group, and we won't normally tell the whole truth and nothing but when dealing with others. The movie *Liar, Liar,* starring Jim Carrey, showed this concept in spades. He was a lawyer, whom many tend to think of as a sneaky, two-faced type person, anyway. But the truth is, he could have been in any profession and the principle would have held just as strongly.

When Carrey was compelled by some unknown force to tell nothing but the truth for an entire day, including a hilarious

stint in a courtroom scene, chaos broke out. He couldn't prop-
erly question his own voluptuous and scheming client. He had
terrible problems dealing with the judge. In short, we could
readily see, from the fabricated circumstances, that if someone
told no fibs, exaggerations, evasive comments, half-truths, or
lies for a period of time, he'd be unable to function in our society. I expect that this was true even in cave-dwelling days.

So, we tell white lies to get along in our workplace. We
don't tell the boss he's too demanding, gruff, out-of-touch with
reality, crass, and ignorant. We don't let slip to our secretary
that she's shallow, dumb, incompetent, uninspired, and almost
worthless. Our co-workers and supposed equals are spared our
knowledge that we're superior to them in intellect, emotional
stability, imagination, determination, and the coolness factor.
Allan and Barbara Pease assert that lying is the oil that greases
our interactions with others and lets us maintain friendly social
relationships. And so it may well be.

➤ **Take the truth for a spin.**

In an online msnbc article by Eve Tahmincioglu, dated December 10, 2007, titled "Don't Lie, But Don't Be Afraid to
Spin," she suggests that, "some resume gaps can be plugged,
others should best be avoided." She goes on to say that on a job
resume and in your interview, it's okay not to tell the whole
truth. Don't put dates on your resume, she advises, in order to
avoid having to talk about embarrassing gaps (including, I suppose, a stretch in prison or that stint in an asylum for the crimi-
nally insane).

She adds that sometimes you don't want to share every intimate detail with a prospective boss. I think we can see where
we're going with that. But she does add that she doesn't think
one should blatantly lie on a resume or in the job interview, noting that when you lie, you can expect it to come back to haunt
you.

In keeping with this idea, recently on the radio there have
been advertisements about preparing a resume, and they matter-
of-factly suggest that the applicant should not include abilities

or strengths that they don't possess, as this could result in later embarrassment if they're found not to be true, and they might not get the position they seek. The commercial also suggests that this practice (lying on the resume) could also affect the applicant's ability to perform the job if they don't really have the qualifications they claimed. Gee, good point.

Did we shoot straight with our teachers and professors in school? Did we ever polish the apple to give them the impression that we thought they were great? Did we try to figure out how to sneak the answers into the test room when we hadn't studied as much as we should have? (Incidentally, I never did this, and my grades will attest to it.)

Then there's the matter of income tax. To think, our forefathers fought and died to avoid "taxation without representation." At any rate, are we all perfectly honest when we add up those cash payments we received, those deductions we're taking, and those expenses we supposedly shelled out in our business dealings? Sadly, for the economic fitness of our country, I think not. There are statistics on the billions of dollars owed (that the government knows about), but I won't delve into those. You get the point.

Walters mentions that, "We are faced with deception all around us." He says we're either lying to someone or being lied to much of the time. And it's not just criminals who are guilty of doing so. He gives the examples of "fudging a little on job or loan applications." He also notes that we might not be technically honest when asked to evaluate someone's oral presentation at work or his ability to play bridge.

Another example with which we're all familiar is the posturing and little fibs or embellishments or avoidances we use on our first date with someone. There were a lot of amusing situations brought out on the sitcom *Friends*, when the character Ross had to divulge that although he was only about thirty, he'd been married and divorced three times, and that he had a son with one ex-wife (who was a lesbian), and a daughter with another of his (twice married to) ex-wives. Somehow, the facts didn't flow smoothly in normal, get-to-know-you conversation.

Dr. Ford makes the point that people use rationalization to explain their behavior or responsibility for certain outcomes, thus disguising from themselves and others the true nature of their underlying drives, needs, and abilities. And Dr. Smith says, "The conscious mind, clouded by self-deception, has a very limited grasp of the nuances and complexities of the social world." He adds that if we somehow became transparent to another's gaze (as in the movie *What Women Want,* in which Mel Gibson can read women's minds), then social life as we know it would unravel.

The power to deceive, says Dr. Smith, is our "main weapon in the struggle for social survival." He comments that without that power, we'd be like sheep among wolves. And he asserts that our ability to read others' intentions from their nonverbal behavior is our strongest protection against becoming hapless victims. That's why I'm providing you with methods for spotting lies, so that you'll be better able to protect yourself, your family members, and your friends through the new-found, or improved, abilities that you'll derive from reading this book.

Another facet of being able to detect lies, says Walters, is that every day we gather information from different people and various sources, and we make decisions that affect our livelihood, our health, and the best interests of our close relations and associates. When we can't depend on what people are telling us, we can be adversely affected in one or more of those areas. I'd have to conclude it would be to our benefit to be as positive as we can be about the honesty or lack thereof of those we deal with. We should learn and practice the techniques set forth in this book, and we should always be alert to what's being said and how it's delivered.

In an article in *The New York Times* newspaper of November 21, 2007, entitled "Denial Makes the World Go Round," by Benedict Carey, he states that studies in psychology and anthropology have shown that people need to ignore some bad behavior by others in order to get along with them. He says, "The psychological tricks that people use to ignore a festering problem in their own households are the same ones that they need to live with everyday human dishonesty and betrayal, their own and others'."

Carey goes on to suggest that denial in a relationship with one's significant other can make that relationship stronger. He mentions a series of studies done by Sandra Murray of the University of Buffalo, and John Holmes of the University of Waterloo in Ontario. They showed that some people idealize their partners by emphasizing (and often exaggerating) their strengths and downplaying (or ignoring) their flaws. It was found that people who idealized their partners in this manner were more likely to remain in the relationship and to report a satisfactory union than those partners who did not. Self-deception, it would seem to me, is a strong elixir for maintaining the bonds of a romantic relationship.

In a *Scrubs* episode, the doctors were discussing whether one of them should tell his new girlfriend some peculiar things about himself. Some favored telling, others suggested it might be better not to, and one said to let the craziness out in small doses. Then the head of the hospital said, "Go ahead and lie. It's a time-honored tradition in relationships between men and women." So, there you have it.

On the television sitcom, *Will and Grace,* the main characters are having a problem in their relationship because Will's ex-boyfriend is back in town, and Grace knew about it but didn't tell him. Naturally, Will runs into him unexpectedly. Then Will asks Grace something about the ex-boyfriend, and Grace says she can't tell him because he might get upset. Will persists, saying he's over the boyfriend and he won't be bothered by the information. So, Grace tells him what he wants to know, and Will predictably goes ballistic. She reminds him that he said he wouldn't be bothered by the knowledge, to which he responds, huffily, "Well, excuse me, I lied."

And even the anti-hero (later to become a decent cyborg) played by Arnold Swartzenegger in *Terminator III: The Rise of the Machines,* made his position about lying evident. After the soon-to-be wife of the leader of the counterrevolution of mankind against the machines controlling Earth provides some information to the Terminator, he then starts to close her back inside a panel truck.

She pleads, "But you said if I told you, you'd let me go."

Arnold coolly responds, "I lied," then slams the door closed, trapping her inside, and with one hand bends a tire iron around the door handles.

The novel, *Swimming in the Volcano,* by Bob Shacochis, addresses social lying in relationships between men and women by using the thoughts of the main character, Mitchell Wilson: *What good is truth, she had asked him, if it can't provide at least some small happiness? Then she had lied to him later that same night, making promises about love. Proving perhaps that falsehood could bring its own joy however temporarily into the world.*

William Shakespeare wrote the line in his play, *All's Well That Ends Well,* Act 3, Scene 5, "No legacy is so rich as honesty." But I think he was a little more honest about the real human condition when he wrote in the play *Timon of Athens,* Act 3, Scene 1, "Every man has his fault, and honesty is his."

> **Omissions.**

As to a more specific type of lie, Madison Smartt Bell writes about a character in his novel, *Straight Cut,* saying, "And he never did answer the question. Kevin was never very much for direct lying. He always just sort of omitted things." Don't we all?

Lies, deception and omissions are at the forefront of the 2008 movie, *Body of Lies.* This political thriller, replete with action, shows characters played by Leonardo DiCaprio and Russell Crowe who, though both working for the CIA, can't seem to tell each other a straight story. DiCaprio plays a CIA operative who's tracking a high-ranking terrorist in Jordan. Crowe is the CIA head of operations in Jordan who misleads DiCaprio and aids the terrorist. Then DiCaprio starts playing the lying game to survive. The tagline for the movie: *Trust no one. Deceive everyone.* No one ever said that international spy games were a bundle of laughs.

In a *Seinfeld* sitcom episode, Elaine realizes belatedly that she was supposed to be an alibi for a woman with whom George was having an affair. When she's telling George that she was caught off guard by the husband's telephone call, she says, "What was I supposed to do?" George predictably says, "You lie. How hard is it to lie?" Jerry walks by just then, having had a lying experience recently, and says, "It's not that hard." Then we get to the consequence part where George asks what the husband threatened to do to him. It's rather severe, and Elaine has to sheepishly tell him, "He said he was going to sew your ass to your face."

➤ **Subconscious lie detection.**

Some psychologists believe that humans have evolved an unconscious mind that's devoted to our dealings with other people that never divulges its secrets to our conscious awareness. Psychoanalyst Robert J. Langs states that the "deep unconscious system" was designed by natural selection to quickly and accurately size up other people. This evolution of the unconscious, perhaps as a reaction to handling complex social interactions, has developed our minds in this way.

In a study done by S.A. McCornack and T.R. Levine entitled, "When lies are uncovered: emotional and relational outcomes of discovered deception," they determined that deceit in a relationship is a powerful force that can produce mostly negative emotional reactions in the person being lied to and (unless the person is a sociopath), strong feelings of guilt in the liar. We're all familiar with these feelings, and one reason you're reading this book is to avoid the gut-wrenching realization that you've been deceived about an important matter. You can also eliminate much of the worry and many of the feelings of insecurity created by your doubts as to whether someone important to you personally, or vital to your career or finances, is actually telling the truth about a situation.

In 1986, G.R. Miller and associates did a review of information about deceptive statements used in relationships, and they determined that from the few studies done, a consistent result was that strangers and spouses are not as good at detecting deception by a person as are friends. Miller states that "perhaps marital partners often develop avoidance mechanisms to 'shut out' the possibility that their mates may be deceiving them." This seems to be a good self-protection method.

Once again, because the deception between friends and significant others can disrupt the emotional closeness between them, there is a chance that the relationship will be destroyed. In the case of friends, this would not have quite the upheaval factor that would occur between spouses that decide to break up, particularly with children and property interests involved. So, sometimes deception can maintain the constancy of a relationship. Also, it's agreed upon among psychologists and this lay person that when people hear what they want to hear, they don't usually see the comments as being lies. And I'd suggest that they're not going to go digging further in an effort to bring up a truth that would be damaging to their ego and possibly their emotional connection with the other person.

> **Does the government lie?**

Harkening back to the field of politics, on the November 4, 2007, show of *60 Minutes,* Bob Simon reported that one of the main pieces of intelligence information that the Bush administration built its case upon for invading Iraq in late 2001 consisted of false statements gathered by German Intelligence from Rafed Alwan, an Iraqi defector that the CIA code-named Curve Ball. The man insisted that he was a chemical engineer who had worked in an Iraqi facility they called a seed purification plant, at which they were actually making deadly biological agents. He stated that trucks would drive into the site alongside a warehouse to be loaded with these deadly agents, some of which had killed twelve workers in an accident at the plant. The trucks thus became mobile biological weapons that could move around the country and avoid detection by weapons inspectors.

Strangely, aerial photos of the facility revealed that there was a wall constructed in the location where Curve Ball insisted the trucks pulled up beside the warehouse, making his story logistically impossible. This information was confirmed by United Nations weapons inspectors during an onsite inspection. They also tested for any traces of biological agents and found nothing.

Although this information was furnished to the White House three weeks before the American attack on Iraq began, it had no effect on the inhabitants therein. Also, George Tenet, the CIA Chief, assured the members of the administration that the case for the invasion of Iraq by America (which included Curve Ball's pitch) could be presented to the American public as a "slam dunk" argument. Secretary of State Colin Powell then presented this "solid intelligence information" to the world as proof that Saddam Hussein was in possession of deadly mobile biological weapons trucks.

And when FBI agent Georg Piro interviewed Saddam Hussein for seven months following his capture, it was his steadfast opinion that Hussein had possessed no weapons of mass destruction (WMD). Either the United Nations weapons inspectors had found and dismantled any facilities that could work on such development, or Hussein had dismantled the others himself. His supposed main reason for suggesting to the world that he had WMD was his fear of Iran and their power to possibly overthrow him. However, Hussein did claim that he still had the people who were capable of developing WMD, and that he would probably have put them to work once all sanctions were lifted. Also, Hussein stated he miscalculated the fierceness of the attack that Bush would level at Iraq.

At any rate, the invasion began. And in the years following that fateful action, thousands of American troops and Iraqis have died in pitched battle or from RPG's or roadside IED's. Hundreds of billions of dollars have been drained from the U.S. Treasury. And the con man known as Curve Ball attained his goal of being admitted to live in Germany as a legal immigrant.

Another facet of the importance of dishonesty in the field of politics usually becomes apparent as the political race for the party nominations for presidential candidates gets heated. It appears that all the candidates simply must exhibit how obsessed they are with truthfulness. However, the slant which they seem to take is one claiming that all of the other candidates are profound liars and just basically dishonest curs, while, in contrast, they are a pillar of honesty and purity. Senator John Edwards came up with a new way of expressing this sentiment when, during the 2007 Democratic primaries, he accused Senator Hillary Clinton of "not being in a truth-telling-mode." I suppose that gets the point across.

Then there was a gripping movie in 2007 named *Shooter,* starring Mark Wahlberg, in which he, a former Marine Recon sniper, was framed by members of the U.S. government for a supposed assassination attempt on the President, in which a leader of another country that the powers that be wanted out of the way was "accidentally" shot instead. One of the higher-ups in the conspiracy against Wahlberg's character was a U.S. Senator, played by Ned Beatty. Near the end of the film, just before Wahlberg gets his revenge against the conspirators, the Senator is talking and drinking with some of his cronies in the plot. He delivers the memorable line, "Fuck you. The truth is what I say it is." Then Wahlberg conveys his own brand of truth and justice with his sniper rifle and numerous explosives. Still, as an audience, we're not that thrilled with the suggested revelations about how our government gets things done.

> ➤ **The dadgummed guvament ain't fair.**

Many people are less than smitten with the morality, ethics, and truthfulness of the federal government. This distrust was brought to bear one August morning in 1993. A man named Gary McKnight was due to be sentenced that afternoon in a federal courtroom in the Frank Carlson Federal Building in Topeka, Kansas, for conspiracy to possess with intent to sell 104 marijuana plants he grew on his small acreage. There was a bit of a technicality involved in the charges against him that stuck in his craw. Such a case could only be handled by the feds if the guilty party was growing more than one hundred plants. So, McKnight felt that he was being harassed because of the fertility of a few extra marijuana seeds.

He thought the government was using a big lie to convict him under the letter, but not the spirit of the law, which was intended to clamp down on big, commercial pot growers and sellers. He just wanted the weed for personal consumption and maybe some for a few close friends. The reason he was not willing to serve the probable seven to nine years he would have received as a sentence was a strange and chilling one which I'll reveal later.

The FBI Resident Agency (RA) office in Topeka, which consisted of five agents, was located on the third floor of the Carlson building. On that fateful morning, McKnight entered the building and began an all-out assault on the people inside. Two of our agents were out-of-town, and one was on the street. Another agent and I were at our desks doing paperwork. It was about ten o'clock in the morning when I heard the first shot.

Actually, it was a string of gunfire. Seven or eight shots were fired one right after the other. For a moment I was stunned by the surreal quality of the event. The other agent came out of his office asking if I thought that was gunshots.

"I think so," I said. "We'd better check it out." I pulled my pistol from my desk drawer and holstered it. The other agent grabbed his weapon, and we met in front of the bulletproof door to our office, opened it, and moved into the hallway.

Now there were more loud cracks of gunfire coming from the floor above us. They were ear-splitting, because the building had a large open atrium from the first floor to the fourth, and the sounds ricocheted off the brown brick walls. The other agent ran down the hallway straight ahead of us. I jogged along the one to our right. I could tell that the shooter was just above me on the hallway of the fourth floor. I stopped at the end of the hall and opened the door about a foot, bracing it open with my shoe, thinking the man would soon be coming down those stairs.

And then, there was a huge boom. Around the inside perimeter of the open atrium was wrapped a shield of ¾-inch Plexiglas™. Whatever made the noise shattered a hole in the clear material, and some pieces of it hit the far wall. Many other bits rained down on the brick flooring four stories below. Then a strange few moments of silence filled the building, only to be followed by another loud blast.

This time, the noise was directly over my head, and I felt a tremor reverberate through the wall. At that moment, I realized the man was detonating bombs. I hoped he didn't have anything stronger than what he'd already used, or I was sure the wall would collapse, and we'd go with it.

I maintained my position at the door, but no one came down the stairs. I could hear more shots, and it seemed that the man or men must have gone into one of the office spaces. At this time, I saw the other FBI agent run back into our office. I hustled down there to regroup. He grabbed the M-16 from our gun room. And we picked up some hand-held radios for communication.

We hurried back to the spot where the other agent had been. It was behind a brick wall beside an elevator, diagonally across the atrium from the corner office where the shooter had entered. We knew he was in there, because another bomb went off. And he was still shooting. At this point, we'd been advised over our handie talkies that several SWAT teams were on their way to the building.

But we thought the shooter would probably leave the office at any time. We could see about ten feet inside the door, so we knew we'd see him when he started to leave. We had a clear shot at the doorway. We wondered if he'd have hostages in front of him. But we decided that if it looked as if we could hit him, we'd try to take him down.

The assault went on for a while longer, and then another bomb exploded in the office where the guy was holed up. This was followed by another gunshot, and then, oddly, complete silence. It was an unsettling quietude. Something had happened. I had an idea about what, but at that moment, there was no way to know.

The police SWAT team arrived and set up in positions down the hallway from the office where the shooter was located. There were also snipers on the rooftop of the U.S. Post Office across the street. Occasionally, one of them would radio that they'd seen the attacker through the window moving around inside the office. I saw no motion, and it was still silent.

The FBI SWAT team arrived from Kansas City. They began clearing each room of the office building, making sure there were no more guys with guns and no more bombs planted elsewhere. They finally got to the office where the shooter was, and I could see them enter from a side door, three of them with large Kevlar shields in front of them. There was no gunfire. And then there was an "all clear" signal. The report was radioed that the attacker was dead.

I took the elevator upstairs. The security guard who had been hit with the first string of shots lay lifeless on the floor. The man who had been talking with him had also been wounded, and he'd been taken to the hospital. I walked down the hallway, noting holes from gunshots and rips in the wall from shrapnel from the pipe bombs the guy had tossed. Several other people were wounded that day from bullets or pipe bombs or from trying to escape the deadly onslaught.

I ran into my supervisor, who asked me to secure the crime scene. As I started to enter the office where the attacker had been, a SWAT team member asked me what I was doing. I told him I was going to secure the scene for evidence. He said, "You might want to go around some other way. That's a live bomb on the floor there." It was in the doorway, about five feet from each of us. "I think I will," I said.

When I entered the office from another door, I saw the gunman lying on the floor. One of his pipe bombs had exploded while he was holding it. It had ripped a hole in his abdomen and almost blown off one of his legs. Then he had shot himself with one of his three pistols. A briefcase lay beside him. He'd had twenty-one pipe bombs in it. Five had detonated in the building. Three that he threw down failed to explode. Four others had gone off in the car that he'd parked beside the building, sending up a towering cloud of pitch black smoke.

The strange feature of the whole scenario was that the man came from a family in which all the men had congenital heart defects. He left a video behind telling about it. One of his uncles, the oldest one in the family when he died, passed away at age forty-six. The attacker was thirty-seven years old. He figured the likely sentence he'd receive from the federal government would be a life sentence for him, and he thought it was unfair. But then, he made his own life a lot shorter, didn't he? And he killed, injured, and terrorized innocent people in the doing. Lies, real or perceived, can infuriate and lead to terrible damage.

> **The whole truth.**

In less spectacular ways, the propensity for deception of many of our citizens affects the American Justice system in a negative way. I mentioned earlier that people often lie on the stand in court. This apparently has being going on for a long time, as the Bible mentions the situation where the high priest and the chief priests and the elders were gathered together as a council to seek testimony against Jesus so they could put him to death. In *Mark* 14:56, in the King James version, it is said: "For many bare false witness against him, but their witness agreed not together." But of course, why let facts stand in the way of accomplishing whatever the Powers That Be wanted?

> **The sanctity of sports.**

Even sports seem to be tainted with deceptive practices. The winner of the Tour de France bicycle race in 2007 got dethroned and kicked out of the sport for blood doping. Barry Bonds' record-setting home run hit number 756 was questioned by many. The ball was purchased for more than $750,000 by a private citizen who had an asterisk branded on it prior to sending it to the Baseball Hall of Fame. The use of steroids by

Bonds and other high profile players has sullied the good name of baseball in America. Even Alex Rodriguez, the highest-paid player in baseball, was alleged to have tested positive for the use of steroids in 2003. He later admitted he'd done so, claiming he was immature and stupid at the time. Mark McGuire basically did the same. Pitching great Roger Clemens was indicted in August, 2010, for lying to Congress about his alleged use of steroids. Also dishonoring the sport's sanctity was the revelation of gambling by former baseball icon Charley Rose, who admitted gambling on the outcome of baseball games.

Could officiating in pro sports be questioned? An official of the National Basketball Association (NBA) was charged with making improper calls during games in order to affect the outcome and better his betting results, as well as those of some of his acquaintances who were members of Organized Crime. And don't we all wonder just a little bit more than before how those referees can make such obviously terrible calls?

Professional football is wracked with players who lie and use drugs and smash up vehicles or other citizens. Bill Bellachek, coach of the fabulously successful New England Patriots football team, was determined during the 2007 season to be videotaping rival teams' coaches in order to steal their signals. He and the team were fined heavily for their attempt at deception. Players are always being fined or suspended for their outrageous conduct. Maybe it should be that way for politicians, businessmen, and salesmen, too.

Michael Vick, quarterback for the Atlanta Falcons, was found to be involved in an interstate dog fighting ring. He was later charged with abuse of some of the dogs. He was found to have kept over sixty dogs in a mansion he owned. And he participated in gambling on the dog fights that were held. For a time, he was evasive about his connections with dog fighting. But more information surfaced, co-defendants agreed to testify against him, and he served nineteen months in Leavenworth Penitentiary before moving to a halfway house. He was also adjudged by an arbitrator to be liable to return about twenty million dollars to the Falcons which he received as a bonus when he signed with them.

Then there was the situation involving Plaxico Burress, a talented receiver for the New York Giants football team who figured prominently in the Giants' win of Superbowl XVIII. He unwisely carried a pistol tucked into his waistband, gangster style, into a New York nightclub. He had not obtained a license to carry the weapon. Of course, the infraction became much worse and much more widely known when he managed to discharge the pistol, shooting himself in the thigh.

A friend who was with Burress in the nightclub tried to find out from a trainer on the team how best to handle (cover up) the circumstance. Then a doctor in the hospital where Plaxico was treated failed to report the gunshot wound to the police, contrary to criminal law statutes. Then the word got out to the media. And so Plaxico was left facing a New York state law which stipulated that for carrying an unlicensed firearm in public, a convicted person would receive a sentence of three-and-a-half years' incarceration.

In early 2010, we heard the frightening news of a car crash involving Tiger Woods. As not only a golf star, but a sort of icon for many people because of his dedication and success in a sport largely populated by whites, though he is of mixed race, there was concern among a large portion of the population. But Tiger seemed to be all right, and when I heard the story about his wife bashing in the back window with a golf iron in an attempt to rescue him, I said, "Oh, oh, it sounds like a marital dispute." (See what I mean about fibs not making much sense?)

And, indeed, there was reason for the unhappiness on the part of Tiger's wife. As fourteen women came to the forefront to claim their portion of the notoriety involved in the tawdry scenario, the clouds of unpopularity began gathering over the star of golfdom. Although adultery is unlawful in many states, he was not charged as of the date of publication of this book. But some sponsors and fans defected, and Tiger was out of golf for about five months. As of the 2010 PGA tournament, it seemed he was not yet back on his game. Lying and cheating and deception can cause great distress to a person, particularly when it's discovered and publicized to the hilt.

➤ **Nothing new under the sun.**

In an article dated December 22, 2008, entitled "A Highly Evolved Propensity for Deceit," Natalie Angier discussed how fraudulent behavior has been a part of developing societies throughout history. Indeed, the more advanced the intelligence of the animal (including Man), the greater seems the penchant for twisting the truth and trying to deceive his fellows. She gives examples of how a baboon fooled his angry mother by pretending to spot danger on the horizon; chimpanzees in zoos have tricked visitors by looking pleasant and holding out a straw to them, luring them close enough to grab them and bite their ankles; and Rhesus monkeys have cleverly stolen items from humans.

➤ **Our distant cousins.**

Another incident at the Gorilla Foundation in California indicates that lying has been a part of our society and our heritage for a very long time. Koko, a lowland gorilla handled by Dr. Francine "Penny" Patterson of Stanford University for many years, has learned how to make over 1,000 hand signs from the American Sign Language repertoire. Koko understands not only the signs, but also about 2,000 words in the spoken English language. In addition, Koko is one of the few non-human species known to have cared for a pet of another species. She's taken care of several cats during her lifetime.

At one time, when one of her pets was a tiny kitten, Koko got upset about something and threw a temper tantrum. As you might imagine, it's no small matter when a 500-pound-gorilla gets enraged. During her hissy fit, Koko tore a sink from the wall. Later, after she'd calmed down, her handlers confronted her about the churlish behavior and resultant broken sink. But Koko acted as one of us might have done in similar circumstances. She looked at her handlers, pointed at her innocent companion, and signed the words, "Cat did it."

➢ **Lies in literature.**

Not as far back as the primates, but still hundreds of years ago, William Shakespeare commented on veracity in his play *Measure for Measure,* by saying, "Truth is truth to the end of reckoning." So, if all of our lies are accounted for, judgment day might become a lengthy process. Voltaire was sanguine about the situation (and hopefully the Lord would be as well), when the author penned the statement, "Love truth, and pardon error."

Once again, Shacochis speaks convincingly about lying in his novel, saying: *Kneeling now at his bedside, in her guilt, she lied and found relief, seeing her husband believe her tale . . . In the darkness, she sensed her husband's sad acceptance of the act, and when his hand searched out hers in comfort for this loss . . . she herself was half convinced that her story was true, and nothing could be done to change its consequences; nothing would ever make it different.*

A comment on literature in our society was made in the December, 2007, issue of *Atlantic* magazine, in a review of Dennis Johnson's novel, *Tree of Smoke,* which won the National Book Award. The review was written by B.R. Myers, and it had the transparent title of "A Bright Shining Lie." The long and short of it was that Myers disliked the book a lot, and he was shocked by the many effusive comments about it by such literati as Philip Roth and Jonathan Franzen. He suggests that by their gratuitous remarks they must be trying "to preserve a writer's reputation, to stimulate the book market, or simply to go with the flow."

When Myers presents such examples from the novel as this: ". . . . he could hear also the pulse snickering in the heat of his flesh, and the creak of sweat in his ears," I have to give credence to his assessment. His concern is that perhaps, ". . . once we Americans have ushered a writer into the contemporary pantheon, we will lie to ourselves to keep him there."

➢ **Relationships.**

However we might feel about lying moralistically, as a

practical matter, fibbing does seem to keep our society humming along with the least amount of friction. In a *Redbook* magazine article, 1993, the author and editor Pamela Redmond Satran wrote about lies that married women told their husbands. She mentioned that one woman said if she told her husband the truth for a month, they'd be divorced by the end of it. Another woman made the sage comment that what people really want when they ask for the truth is "all good news." Once again, we find the suggestion that many lies are directed toward preserving a relationship.

Satran and Kimberly Bonnell wrote for *Glamour* magazine a bit called "New Glamour List, Unedited, 30 Things He's Not Telling You," some of which I thought fitting to include in this book. One is that the "Great Moments in Brewing" folder on his computer actually contains links to his 47 favorite porn sites. Another is that he does wish your ass were smaller and your boobs were bigger. And lastly, he never separates his whites and darks in the washing machine (but I'll bet a lot of you experienced and perceptive women readers already knew that).

When Annie Murphy Paul wrote an article called "Mind Reading" in the September/October 2007 issue of *Psychology Today* magazine, she interviewed Ross Buck, a professor of communication sciences at the University of Connecticut. He stated that humans' communication abilities have grown more sophisticated over the thousands and thousands of years they've been developing. And he believes that a form of mind reading helps us to "create and maintain the social order." He thinks a degree of "mindsight" is necessary for the smooth operation of a society in which people are civil to one another.

Josh Billings spoke to the paucity of truth in our society when he said: "As scarce as truth is, the supply has always been in excess of the demand." Herbert Agar concurred with this view when he said, "The truth that makes men free is for the most part the truth which men prefer not to hear." And Mark Twain put it this way: "The history of our race, and each individual's experience, are sown thick with evidence that a truth is

not hard to kill and that a lie told well is immortal."
> **Wall Street wizards.**

And how often do we hear about stock market scandals? There's an area of our financial concerns that we'd certainly like to think was stable and honest and above reproach. But, sadly, greed quite often makes men lie and cheat and steal. On the msnbc news page for November 7, 2007, (a day when the DJI plunged 360 points), Michael Brush wrote an article entitled "Preying on Investor's Subprime Fears." He commented that insiders make money by manipulating stock, particularly when there is fear about some particular sector, and/or the market as a whole is shaky. (This even paled to the September 29, 2008, Dow Jones Industrials drop of 777 points, the largest ever, thought to have been fomented by the endangerment of brokerage firms, banks, and mortgage lending companies owing to the ridiculously risky, but high interest and profitable, mortgage loans they'd been making.)

At any rate, Brush believes that scam artists made over half a million dollars one day by manipulating the stock of Lehman Brothers at a time when it was susceptible to doubt due to the subprime mortgage problems affecting the economy in general and them, among others, in particular. It seems there were a couple of suspicious large purchases of short deadline put options. These options give the buyer the right to sell a stock at a certain price that's slightly under the current market price. Then the rumors hit that Lehman's was about to announce a seven billion dollar write-off due to loans made on subprime mortgages. The stock declined, the put options were exercised, and some fraudulent traders made off with a pile of cash.

The same scheme was pulled with the stock of the American International Group (AIG). Large blocks of put options were purchased, and then rumors surfaced about a pending enormous write-down because of losses by AIG in the subprime mortgage loan area. The stock dropped in value, the put options were exercised, and the investors who had bought them made about 2.5 million dollars. When AIG refuted the rumors, its stock price recovered. Of course, now the government—which means we taxpayers—has bailed out Lehman's, AIG, General Motors, and other corporations, plus a number of banks.

Brush interviewed Jon Najarian of OptionMonster, which tracks unusual stock movements as a means of deciding on making trades of their own. Najarian commented that the large size of the put option purchases, and the ease with which they were handled on the market, both in the buying and selling of them, suggested that perhaps a "well-heeled hedge fund" or some similar type investor had made the transactions. He stated that they called this type of move a "reverse pump and dump" maneuver. In a straightforward "pump and dump," someone will purchase a stock in advance of an announcement of positive news, or put out their own positive rumors, then sell when the stock advances. The reverse situation, as was used in this instance, is to buy put options and then start or merely take advantage of negative rumors or news.

Brush went on to mention that a similar occurrence had happened with the stock of Countrywide Financial in advance of negative rumors. And with Washington Mutual, the same type of transactions happened just in advance of a press conference by New York Attorney General Andrew Cuomo, in which he announced a lawsuit against Washington Mutual which negatively affected its stock prices. Just watch the headlines for future examples of this type of lying and immoral chicanery.

> **Pssst. Want a house?**

Subprime mortgage loans were a doozy of a scam on numerous people in America. Lenders were extending mortgages to anyone who walked in the door wanting a house. No matter that a good number of the people were not financially able to purchase one. The mortgage companies were giving them the loans, many at very high interest rates (or more generally, ones that started low and then went higher as variable rates rose, or ones with balloon payments due later down the road), and the people were happy. They stayed happy until the interest rates on variable loans started to edge up, and until they ran into a job layoff, and until they had some form of financial hardship that made them unable to sustain payment on their home mortgage loans, which they really couldn't afford in the first place.

And now, with homes foreclosed on across the country, the housing market as a whole is in the doldrums. New home construction is down. New home sales have plummeted. Existing home sales are stagnant, with values slipping as much as 15 percent, or even much more. People are losing money when they sell their homes. Many people are "upside down" on their house mortgages, meaning that they owe more on the mortgage than the house is worth on the open real estate market. So there's another unneeded anchor slowing our economy's ship.

> **A Huge Scam.**

In December, 2008, Bernard Madoff, the founder of Bernard L. Madoff Investment Securities, LLC, was arrested and charged with running what amounted to a Ponzi scheme through a hedge fund he operated. The scheme involved investors receiving payouts (characterized as interest) from money provided to the fund by later investors. The losses to about 13,000 investors in the hedge fund amounted to an estimated $65 billion, making it one of the biggest scams in dollar value of all time. For his indiscretions, Madoff was sentenced to serve 150 years in a federal penitentiary. And other "business partners" of his were put under the government microscope.

> **Religion and morality.**

There have been crises in many religious groups throughout history. The Muslims, through Ayatollah Ruhollah Khomeini, the Supreme Leader of Iran, issued a fatwa (religious edict calling for his death) on Salman Rushdie for writing *The Satanic Verses.* They also violently protested the drawing and publishing of twelve cartoons by a Danish cartoonist that showed an image of the prophet Mohammed, which they believed was sacrilegious. (Although, it turns out that depictions of the Prophet have been sketched and painted by artists from the mid-twelfth century to the present.)

Baptist preachers have been accused of adultery, lechery,

and drunkenness. Snake handling cults appear in the press from time-to-time when one of their followers ends up on the wrong end of some poisonous fangs. My point being that religious sects throughout history have had problems that came to light because (big surprise) the people in them are possessed of human qualities and frailties.

So, I'm not singling out the Catholic Church for any other reason except that there have been some big headlines in the past few years, from 2002 when the sex abuse of young boys and girls by priests in the Boston archdiocese first became publicized, to 2007, when the Los Angeles archdiocese paid $660 million dollars to over 500 participants in a lawsuit claiming abuse there. In short, priests, bishops, and possibly some cardinals have had guilty knowledge of such indiscretions over the past 40 years, and yet none of them came forward to tell the truth about what was happening, even within the hallowed walls of the church or cathedral itself. As late as 2010, the Pope and the church were still trying to quiet the outrage.

The upshot of this is that we must be vigilant, even with those we think we can trust, to make sure that their illicit behavior doesn't harm us or our family. Teachers are in the headlines from time-to-time because they're madly in love with some teenage student. On occasion, they even jump in a car with their young paramour and head for Mexico.

And we sometimes hear of pedophiles who have been working in child protection agencies of one type or another. Sometimes we learn that a former sex offender has moved into our neighborhood either because he has registered, as the law requires him to do, or because he has failed to register and has been caught trying to molest some child. It's well know in law enforcement circles that sex offenders often have a hundred or more victims before they're caught. And there seems to be no known method of rehabilitating them.

> **Sex practices in polite society.**

Of course, when it comes to sexual preferences and practices, there are more varieties than I'm aware of or can imagine.

Some people are drawn to elderly folks, some to young ones, some to purses, feet, shoes, latex, leather, sadistic and/or masochistic practices. Others favor auto-erotic behavior, where they hang themselves or use some type of ligature to choke themselves until they're about to pass out, while masturbating. Their ejaculation is reputed to be extremely satisfying. But then, they sometimes do pass out and are found hanging by the ligature in a state that's extremely dead. About ten percent of the population prefers gay sex. Some are bisexual.

Other preferences include fantasies about having sex with nurses, schoolgirls, cheerleaders, babysitters, and gymnasts. A few people enjoy being whipped or spanked or otherwise mistreated. Some are into bondage and flagellation. Others like a "golden shower," where someone urinates on them, or what I'll call a Number Two cascade upon their person. Bestiality is a common practice. Horses, donkeys, chickens, sheep, cows, and dogs are often sought after as partners. Some people actually like to wear diapers and be treated like babies, including going potty in their didies, and having someone change them and powder their big chafed bums.

At any rate, you can imagine the amount of lying, evasiveness, and avoidance that goes on in the worlds of these people. They have problems to hide from polite society. And just like serial killers, they live next door to someone who will someday tell a member of the press that, "He was real nice and quiet. I'd talk to him sometimes out in the yard. He seemed friendly enough and never caused any problems around here."

Not to say that you have to distrust everyone you meet. But you do have to be aware that there's a lot going on in the world that could someday affect you or yours. You should be alert to spot when something or someone doesn't seem right. Your mind-reading and lie-detecting antennae may be trying to warn you of something. And that something could be a malevolent, damaging lie. So, always remember your strategies for detecting deception, and stay prepared.

6

Let the Buyer Beware

➢ Lies in the Marketplace

In the October, 2007, issue of the *AARP Bulletin,* an article by Patricia Barry discussed the various scams being perpetrated on people of retirement age concerning insurance plans to supplement Medicare. One Bobby Box, 76, had to pay a $16,000 medical bill even though he had Medicare insurance and had also purchased a Medicare Advantage plan. He was quoted as saying, "The saleswoman said it was a supplementary insurance that paid what Medicare didn't. She lied."

In the same issue of the *AARP Bulletin,* an article by Sid Kirchheimer reviewed door-to-door scams being pulled across America. He noted that a favorite one involved people selling magazines, often at a highly inflated price. A variation would be the suggestion by the salesperson that the money was being solicited for a worthy charity, but whatever the approach, the buyer would end up with subscriptions to magazines that he didn't want. Also, people were being burglarized when they would allow these magazine "sales representatives" to enter their house.

So, what is your best protection? You must be aware that lies are ubiquitous. They're out there everywhere, and they can hurt you if you don't learn to spot them and develop methods to deal with them.

How to Spot Lies

Fortunately, everyone, from noting life's experiences alone, has developed at least some techniques for detecting lies and handling the information accordingly. You know the burgers shown on fast food commercials will never appear on your plate exactly as they look on TV. Consider the comment by F. Scott Fitzgerald in *The Crack-Up*: "Advertising is a racket . . . its constructive contribution to humanity is exactly minus zero."

Anyone knows that commercials exaggerate, extol, and embellish the qualities of the product. Also, they excuse any deficiencies the item may possess. Have you ever listened to the possible side-effects of drugs the spokespersons are trying to get you to take, all delivered with a light-hearted smile on their faces? It'll scare the bejesus out of you.

> **Get your red hot whatzits right here.**

Of course, there's the bait-and-switch promotion where the company will advertise a bargain price for a certain item, say a lawnmower. When the customer shows up looking for the mower at the advertised price, he's told by a salesman that the mower is sold out, or that the advertised price is good for a very basic model, but that he'd recommend one with better features on it that sells for just a little higher price. The customer, being no fool, can see that the mower the salesperson recommends is superior in several ways, so he'll want to buy that one. And once the person gets home with the mower, he'll want to believe that he made the right choice, so he'll continually remind himself that the mower he bought is clearly better than the "stripped down" version that was on sale.

Another saying by Vauvenargues in *Reflexions* tells us: "Commerce is the school of cheating." That's a strong statement, but with a definite core of truth. For instance, most of us are aware of a type of advertising called "puffery." We see it constantly in newspapers, radio advertising, and especially on television. Puffery can be used exceptionally well on TV, because they can not only spiff up the product where it looks terrific (umm, those gorgeous, steaming, butter-drenched lobsters), but they can also use implication concerning the value of the product.

That is, the item will be surrounded by beautiful people, fancy cars, and images of sandy white beaches or breathtaking mountains or spacious lawns of huge mansions, all to implant favorable ideas in your brainpan in association with the product. Have you ever seen whiter teeth than on toothpaste ads? Do you notice any overweight fellows showing us exercise equipment? Are the folks drinking beer ever morose, dejected, or depressed?

In short, they lie about the product. Dare I say that drinking beer won't give you an amazing physique and entice bikini-clad chicks to drape themselves all over you? Sadly, it won't, and you can believe me on that one. I've tried it many times, with abject failure every time out of the gate. Wearing cheap clothes bought from large distributors won't make you look like a model. Hair won't magically grow on your bald, barren noggin.

Part of this is attributable to the fact that, to some extent, we're all gullible. There's an old Spanish proverb that says, "If fools went not to market, bad wares would not be sold." This, of course, relates to the old caveat (*Caveat emptor,* actually): "Let the buyer beware." And the theme is reiterated by Edith Sitwell, who postulated that, "The public will believe anything, so long as it is not founded on truth." The effect of all this being, I suggest, that we should arm ourselves with the knowledge to be able to detect and defuse any deceptions with which we're assailed.

Or would it be possible to just avoid the liars, deceivers, and exaggerators? Could we seek out only honest businessmen and workmen and salesmen with whom to conduct our affairs? In a way, that's what we all do attempt to do. But doesn't it sometimes seem an impossible task? Thomas Fuller noted in *Gnomologia* that, "He that resolves to deal with none but honest men must leave off dealing." Perhaps you don't want to be that disillusioned and distrustful. Maybe you have more faith in mankind. In a way, that's good, because it indicates you're probably honest and expect others to be.

However, there are even differences of opinion on that matter. An old proverb states: "You can't cheat an honest man." While Gracian says in *Oraculo Manual,* "Nothing is easier to cheat than an honest man." My own experiences in the FBI are that con men are successful with both extremely honest folks and with those with a little larceny in their hearts. When someone thinks he may get a "really good deal" on a product if he doesn't ask too many questions about it, he may end up feeling very chagrined when he finds he's been "scammed."

Sometimes those who don't have a dishonest bone in their bodies are prone to believe that they can trust everyone else, thinking that those fine people will be totally honest, as well. Fortunately, this is true much of the time, probably because most of the people they know socially and in business are ones they grew up with or met in church or know from a civic service club. But when a duplicitous person comes along wanting to part this type of honest soul from his funds, he'll do it in a heartbeat.

On the other hand, many schemes are based upon the fact that we all want to get something for nothing, or at least a good deal of something for very little. Thus, we see the cons that are based on "found money" that will be split with the mark if he will put up some "good faith" money of his own. Or the trickery where the con man promises to give a person an unbelievably large percentage return on his money in a "can't miss" type of investment. The key word there is "unbelievable." If it sounds too good to be true, it probably is. But I'd suggest that you consider some of the following situations before making up your mind.

Salesmen seem to know all the tricks. That's because they must either learn them or take up another line of work. Some folks seem to "know" many sales methods instinctively. We call them "born salesmen." At any rate, it's good to be aware of some common practices of the universal sales force, as we all must deal with them. Let's say the salesperson helping us in the furniture store just happens to ask, "Say, where are you folks from? Oh, Cleveland? I used to live there before I moved here.

Great place, huh? I really hated to leave there." And now you and the former Ohioan have a bond that somehow assures you that he'll probably cut you a good deal and treat you right. He'll also determine other bonding activities: hobbies, sports teams, golf, preference in cars, and clothing tastes.

People promoting items tend to give away other things for free. It doesn't cost them much, it psychologically puts you in their debt, and it also makes you think that they're really nice guys who would probably be willing to give you a bargain price on what they're selling. And who doesn't like to get a free pen, T-shirt, ball cap, calendar, or coffee mug?

Another ploy we all fall for is the half-price sale. Hey, how can you go wrong? Get two for the price of one. One item is actually free. You can't beat it. But you'd better be aware of whether the actual price they quote is what the item was really selling for. Perhaps they just marked the item up for a half hour, then marked it down to get you to react. Everyone loves to get a bargain. But not everyone proves to be a good bargain hunter.

You should always know the going market price for whatever item you're seeking. This goes for shopping in pawn shops, too. I've gone to them, thinking to find a guitar for a cheaper price, and found they were trying to sell used ones for the same retail price as the new guitars I'd just seen in other stores. And don't ever be suckered in by a "today only" price. Or the ploy that someone else was just in looking at that item and is due back soon.

Dr. Lieberman also mentions the "bandwagon effect." Will we buy something if it's a bestseller? Absolutely. Have you ever read some bestselling book and wondered what all the hype was about? It was about getting you and others to believe that you'd be missing the bandwagon if you didn't buy the book. And then there were the Snuggies, the blankets with sleeves that millions of people saw on television and rushed to buy. Was there a bit of mass hysteria there? Or was the product something that was necessary and highly functional? I couldn't say, I somehow managed to live without one.

The laugh tracks on sitcoms are meant to make us chortle at a joke or situation because others apparently think it's funny, so we should, too. Have you ever seen a show that you found not funny or clever in the least? And doesn't the laugh track seem grating and ridiculous during those scenes? Don't be a person who has to have the best-selling, hottest, latest, most advanced technologically, and coolest new product on the market. It's all hype, my friend. Just buy what you want and need when you want and need it. Don't let slick commercials and marketing suggestions of not "fitting in" if you don't have the new item affect your purchasing habits.

Another trick cited by Dr. Lieberman as being employed in the sales game is the "rarity" effect. Car salesmen love it when a new model car comes on the market that people like, but not enough are being produced to meet the sudden demand. Can we be patient and wait until they are making enough of them that they'll give us the usual discounts on the car? Or do we feel compelled to pay the exorbitant sticker price in order to have the coveted item? What do *you* think? And man, don't a lot of poor parents get stuck badly at Christmas when their little darlings just can't live without the "hot" new toy of the season?

Always be sure you ask yourself why a person may be selling their used house, car, horse, television, boat, or motorcycle. Make sure that their reason passes the common sense test. Don't buy at a "fire sale" price until you've researched the market value, availability, and estimated future worth of the item in question. I've noticed that recently there's been a commercial on television about how you can help a coin collector that you know by buying him a certain freshly minted memorial coin. But you'd better talk with the coin collector himself to see if he really wants such a coin, which seldom, if ever, appreciates in value.

I'm constantly amazed that brokers who sell stock and commodity futures continue to do well in their business ventures when 90 percent of their clients lose most or even all of the money they invest with them. Were they really upfront about how risky that market is when describing it to their new customers? Or did they stress the leverage they'd have on their investment money and the potential for making huge gains from small moves in the market? And did they mention that the leverage principle could work against the potential client when the market was moving opposite to their expectations?

Benjamin Disraeli, a legendary statesman, once said, "There are three kinds of lies: lies, damned lies and statistics." Lieberman makes the assertion that just because someone shows us a handsome color chart or graph showing fantastic gains in a certain business or stock, that we shouldn't be swayed by the implications. Without very thorough analysis by knowledgeable people, we're not well-advised to interpret statistical data ourselves. And you should never let yourself be convinced to project any type of future movements in the price or value of the item in question based on past performance.

Now let's talk about car salesmen. One time I was investigating a used car sales lot in Texas to see if they were re-titling stolen cars and selling them. There were eight salesmen working on the lot. As a matter of course, I ran criminal checks on them. Seven of the eight had criminal records including crimes much more serious than jaywalking, speeding, or shoplifting. So, be forewarned. You're seldom going to be dealing with any saintly folks in the "tin pushers" world. And that includes the ones advertising "Christian Car Sales," or some such pitch. Just because there's a Bible verse over the door doesn't mean the salesman's office or the person within is sanctified.

Try to recall the last time you bought a new car. Even if the salesmen are all basically honest, let's face it, there are tricks and techniques that have been developed over the years by dealers and salesmen that serve to give the dealership the highest margin of profit on each car and to give the salesman the highest possible commission on every sale. Sorry, but they're not in business to give any widows, orphans, or wounded war vets a great deal on their shiny new rides.

Will some of them give you a good price? Yes, if they figure that you know the tricks they use and they're just wasting their time in trying to jack up the price on you. (They say that you "have all your ducks in a row.") Then they'll settle quickly for a reasonable profit and save themselves and you the hours' long process of "sweating you." As you probably know from experience, this procedure will get you so frustrated and impatient with the situation that you'll sign just about anything that looks somewhat reasonable in order to get out of that small, airless office in the dealership.

There are good books about buying cars, and I'd suggest you read one or two before buying your next dream vehicle. I won't go into detail here trying to say what those books can tell you, but they do outline the many ploys used by car salesmen. Also, there are books and magazines which list prices for new and used cars, as well as online sites about pricing and whether a particular vehicle has been in an accident or flood or hailstorm.

One thing to be aware of, though, is that when trying to trade in or sell your vehicle to a dealership or used car lot, they won't be willing to deal with you on the "blue book" prices which supposedly represent a fair value for your used car depending on condition and mileage and add-ons. They have their own "black book" with prices that are considerably lower which they will stick to (while sticking it to you), and all the used car salespeople will have these books (why not, if it will help them make more money).

Anyway, just be aware that car salesmen will be trying to derive a profit from you on three fronts: keeping the sales price as high as possible; keeping your trade-in allowance as low as possible; and making money from financing your vehicle. Some tricks to watch for are "preparation charges," which may be listed as high as $1500 on a new vehicle, and which are pure baloney. A charge for undercoating is a scam. Buying at dealer's invoice, which sounds like a good deal for the buyer, is actually a good deal for the dealership and salesman. There are thousands of dollars of profit for the dealer built into that price.

In fact, the dealership owners have a built-in per unit incentive that is not enumerated anywhere, and that even many of the salespeople are not aware of. This will amount to over a thousand dollars in itself.

The best method for buying a car is to find out the actual dealer price for the car as it's equipped, subtract the delivery charge, add about 10 to 15 percent (less for SUVs or other unpopular vehicles), add back in the delivery charge, and try not to pay more than that for the car. It will take some patience and talking and avoiding distractions that the salesman will try to throw at you. One favorite is, "What kind of payments do you want to make?" Oh, they'll see to it that you'll come out with that figure (plus about fifty dollars per month wiggle room), but watch out for the number of months you'll be paying that figure. It might stretch out far beyond the reasonable useful life of the vehicle and end up as an exorbitant price for it.

Also, be sure to get your financing from some other competitive place. Know the real value of your trade-in, and if you can't get that amount, sell the vehicle yourself. And don't fall for the "I'll have to talk to the sales manager to see if I can get you that price" gambit. If he needs to talk to the sales manager more than one time, he's just "sweating you." Be willing to say, "I'll have to think about that price and check with some other dealerships," and then walk out and do just that.

Just remember that they need to sell those cars much worse than you need to buy one. Especially in the current economy, with car sales down precipitously and dealerships (not to mention entire corporations) fighting for their economic lives, you should be able to wrangle a bargain price just by being willing to purchase a vehicle. And toward the end of the sales year, when the new models are looming to be shipped to the dealerships' lots *en masse,* they'll desire even more fervently to evacuate the year-end models. Also be aware that often "program vehicles" or "demonstrators," which have only been driven a few thousand miles, can be purchased for an especially good price, with their warranties intact.

Then how about those "Scientific tests show . . ." comments we're continually seeing? Does it ever give you pause to find out that <u>tests</u> on certain types of arthritis or pain or heart <u>medications are funded by the corporations</u> who manufacture and <u>sell the products tested</u>? How many "scientific" tests do you suppose were performed concerning the health risks of cigarettes? Do you feel safer in your vehicle because a test dummy "survived" a crash test?

According to D. J. Miller and Hersen, even audits of scientific studies by the U.S. Food and Drug Administration (FDA) have shown critical deficiencies in the manner in which the studies were done or the way the results were reported. And we're all aware of the massive toy recalls throughout the United States because of the paint containing lead that was used on them. This was no oversight. The Chinese manufacturers chose to use the lead-based paint because it was cheaper than the safer type. They also endangered many lives by producing home-building materials that contained an unacceptable level of formaldehyde. Lies create dangerous circumstances for everyone.

Beware of salesmen who want to be your buddy. Dr. Lieberman cites versions of the bait-and-switch trick that they'll use. This will range from getting you to buy a more costly item because the <u>item you wanted "Just ran out," "Went like hot-cakes,"</u> "Has some drawbacks that you should consider in your situation," or "Just isn't for you." This salesperson will likely be able to offer you some nice discounts if you buy a certain dollar value of goods from him. And be sure that you get the details (brand name of product, percentage of discount, guaranteed delivery date, free home delivery) put on the written contract. Get what you pay for. Develop an eye for value. Do your research about products and their price ranges when you're in the market for a certain purchase.

Don't be swayed by snooty salesmen in fancy and expensive stores. If you wander in one of these elite emporiums some day, as I once did because my significant other liked a blouse that was displayed in the window, you'll be confronted by someone who may expressly or implicitly suggest that they might have some other products in a different part of the store that wouldn't be so pricey. They're intimating that you don't have the wherewithal to buy regular items there.

They may be right, but their use of reverse psychology ignites a burning feeling of "I'll show them" in your chest. In my case, the blouse cost over $200, and this was a number of years ago. It was way out of my price range, and in my opinion, overpriced. I didn't go so far as to buy it, but I felt compelled to buy a tie that was also priced too high just because of the logo imprinted thereon. The only time anyone ever noticed the shiny tie was once when I talked with a representative of the company that made it when a trailer full of their goods had been hijacked, and another time when a prisoner at the Leavenworth Penitentiary commented on it as I walked by his cell. Ah, well.

> **Give 'em that old razzle dazzle.**

Going beyond the salesman's tricks delivers us into the territory of the con man. There are some standard confidence games or "cons" that have been worked on the public for years. These are also called scams, grifts, swindles, flim flam, and bunko games. There are new variations from time-to-time, but I think if you're aware of the usual patterns of these basic cons, you'll be able to detect when someone is about to pull your chain and snatch the contents of your wallet or purse.

The badger game is basically a type of extortion swindle in which a man, usually married, is lured into a sexual encounter with a hot woman. In the more sophisticated version, the con men will videotape the tryst. Another method is to have someone burst into the room and snap photos. Or sometimes two guys will come in claiming to be detectives who are going to arrest the man for having sex with a known prostitute. The gist of the trick is to catch the "mark" or object of the con in a compromising position which he doesn't want revealed to his wife and family and/or the community. The detectives or photographers will offer to destroy the evidence if the man will pay them some money. The poor guy with his pants down is in a tricky position, eh?

Another common swindle is the bank examiner scheme. Someone will telephone or appear at the door in person, claiming to be a bank officer or a security officer of a large bank. He'll be dressed in business attire and will usually have some type of badge. The questioned bank will be the one where the person keeps his accounts. The scam artist will claim that a teller or other employee of the bank is suspected of stealing money from customers' accounts, and he wants the person's help in identifying the thief and bringing her to justice. Then he'll ask the person to go to the bank and withdraw a large amount of money, with the somewhat preposterous story that they want to see what the suspected teller will do when someone makes such a withdrawal. They assure the mark that he can redeposit the money soon.

Next, the con artist will claim he needs to take the money long enough to record the serial numbers of the bills or to mark it with invisible ink. Or, he may, once he has the money, later tell the mark that the money that was withdrawn was all counterfeit bills, and that he'll have to keep it for evidence in the case against the teller. And often, in this situation or similar ones, the con artist won't even need to have the mark voluntarily turn the money over to him. He'll take a quick look at it, and then hand the envelope back to the mark. But when the victim looks in it later to retrieve his money, he'll find a bunch of cut up paper, as the con man has smoothly switched his substitute envelope for the mark's. Needless to say, the grifter will disappear, and so will the victim's money.

One sunny morning long ago I was walking along the streets of Brownsville, Texas, on my way to the office. I didn't bump into Delta Dawn, but I did spot a car with an out-of-state license plate and four men sitting inside it. There was something fishy-looking about those guys, and I had the thought, "Oh, oh. There's trouble." They seemed to be looking for something as they rolled down the street. But their expressions were not relaxed, inquisitive, or appreciative as those of tourists would have been. Their demeanor seemed inhospitable and predatory.

I learned the next day that the men had tricked a local citizen into paying $10,000 for a supposedly very valuable diamond ring which turned out to be a fake. Then they disappeared from town as suddenly as they appeared. Unfortunately, when I observed them in their auto, I wasn't in a position to see the numbers on their license tag, or I could have helped provide some suspects for that particular scam.

Many people are taken in by the "get-rich-quick" schemes. Most of these fraudulent plans are a form of Ponzi or pyramid scheme. Multi-level-marketing is a similar type of business arrangement, but it is considered, for the most part, to be legitimate. The difference is basically in whether the company has an actual product that one or more of the participants can sell and make money with. In the Ponzi scheme and the pyramid scheme, the return on investment for the earlier investors comes from the money put into the scheme by subsequent new investors or from the funds reinvested by more senior investors.

Carlo "Charles" Ponzi was an Italian immigrant who set up his money-making scheme in the Boston area in late 1919 as an investment broker. He sold bonds which supposedly made money from fluctuations in trading prices in international reply postal coupons. He promised the bonds would earn a return of fifty percent in forty-five days or one hundred percent of the original investment in ninety days. In truth, the fluctuations in trading in foreign postal coupons provided little or no money. But investment money started pouring in when Ponzi paid off the initial investors, as promised, and word quickly began to spread about the fantastic deal. Subsequent investors were paid their returns by even later investors buying into the scam. Ponzi garnered about forty thousand investors and made a stated fifteen million dollars ($150 million at 2006 dollar values) before the scheme was investigated and shut down by federal agents and the Commonwealth of Massachusetts. Ponzi was convicted of mail fraud and state fraud charges.

Pyramid schemes are based on this same principle, where

the initial investors in an undertaking receive a good return on their money because their profits are paid from money put into the scheme by later investors. The product is non-existent or non-profitable. The whole idea is based on a "bubble" theory, or the investment of money by "later fools" who keep the scheme afloat.

Looked at statistically, the pyramid scheme can't be sustained for more than a few rounds. Wikipedia gives an example that if six people are on the first level of the pyramid, the subsequent purchasers needed to sustain making money would increase geometrically and quickly. By the fifth tier of the pyramid, there would need to be 7776 new investors paying in to prolong payments being made to the people above them. By round eleven, 362,797,056 people would need to join and invest. That's about the population of the United States. By round thirteen, more than twice the population of the world would need to get invested. Perhaps aliens would be interested?

Often the originators of the pyramid schemes will rig the odds even further by making up names in the first tier, so that they will receive all of the payments for those slots. And, it should be noted, they don't have to put in any money. About 88 percent of those who invest in pyramid schemes will lose all their investment. About 94 percent lose some money on the deal. Those who start the schemes are the ones who make money. By the time you hear about a scheme where someone you know has made a profit, it's too late to get in and make any money from it. And it's illegal in the United States, Great Britain, and other countries.

Chain letter arrangements are based on the same illegal and unprofitable models. And there are internet versions of these schemes, as well. Similar setups include "8-ball," one in which the top tiers consist of one, two, four and eight members. Thus, fifteen members are included in the top tiers. And the top seven may be the same person, who has not had to pay in any money. If everyone below him puts in $1,000, the top man (who holds the top seven spots) will make $56,000. A few people below him may make $8,000 each. After that, the scheme will likely collapse.

In "matrix" or ladder schemes, there are, typically, ten people in a row or ladder. To obtain a spot on the matrix, you must buy a product (let's say an e-book at an inflated price). Then, when you move to the top spot on the matrix, you'll receive a nice prize such as a color television. But take a look at the math involved. For the first person in the line of ten spots to win the main prize, there will have to be nine more people sign up. But for the second person in the line of ten spots, there will have to be eighteen people sign up behind him in order for him to receive his prize. That is, there will need to be the eight people that signed up behind him in order for the first person to win, then an additional ten people to advance him off the line so that he can win.

As you can see, the number of people needed to sign up becomes quite large for those who weren't in on the game early. So, people will quit signing up, and those above them will lose. The man at the top will receive the difference in the cost of the product from the amount paid, buy a few nice prizes for the lucky winners, and then pocket the rest of the payments from those who will never move forward in line.

➤ **You need investment capital? No problem.**

Another type of situation I often ran across in my FBI work was the "advance fee" scheme. Usually, someone would offer to broker a loan (act as the finder of the funds and as a go-between for the lender and the borrower) for a person wanting funding to start a business venture. Of course, the person would have to provide the facilitator some up-front money for any of a number of reasons, such as having to provide travel funds for the broker to meet the financier, or to otherwise help facilitate the arrangements for the money to be transferred to the eagerly awaiting borrower.

Naturally, these were people who had a good business idea (they thought), but didn't have the collateral or business experience or setup to be able to obtain a loan from a more traditional lender, such as a bank. Typically, the plans for the broker to obtain the funds would almost, just almost, come together, but at the last minute some unforeseen or unfortunate incident would occur that kept the broker from getting the money. This would often be dragged out for months, while the broker was living high off the fees he received and the would-be borrowers were suffering mightily from each new disappointment. But I was able to get many of these types of con men arrested and prosecuted, and some even went to prison.

> **Watch out for these scams**

Beware of anyone who claims to have found money. He may catch you off guard by showing you a backpack or briefcase or a plain paper sack full of enticing twenty- and hundred-dollar-bills, inquiring whether it belongs to you. Then he'll discuss with you that since he could find no owner identification, maybe the two of you should keep the money.

He'll ask you to hold the money while he checks a newspaper for lost and found, or calls the police station about missing money, or some such. But then he'll question whether he should trust you. And he'll decide that he wants you to put up a matching amount of money to show your "good faith" to him. Once you give him your money, he'll depart, never to be seen again. When you later open the bag, you'll either find slips of blank paper, or counterfeit cash, or just some trash, as the con man will have made a quick switch when you weren't focused on the bag.

Odds are about fifteen-million-to-one that you'll win a state lottery. They're even worse when you get an e-mail or a phone call from an unknown person saying that you've won a valuable prize. The basic gimmick in this scam is that you'll need to pay him "shipping costs" or a "handling fee" or whatever in order for him to be able to send you the money. Sometimes he'll con you into providing your bank account numbers and personal information, indicating that he needs someplace to send the monies to. His interest is really to quickly siphon funds from your account. Clearly, don't ever give anyone your credit card numbers, back account numbers, or personal identifying information unless you know them and there's a deal involved about which you're sure of the validity.

> ➢ **Those tricky e-mails.**

Many Nigerian schemes are being sent out by snail mail or e-mail. They'll usually involve unclaimed money for an heir that can't be located, or government funds that are sitting there unused, or some form of lottery winning. A few such scams, copied from my today's e-mail receipts, are substantially as follows:

Following the directives from the Office of the President, Federal Republic of Nigeria, as a result of petitions by Foreign Contractors over non-payment of their contract claims, my office has been appointed to look into all overdue contract payments yet to be released for verification and immediate payment. (I cleaned up most of the inevitable errors in spelling, grammar, and syntax.) The message goes on to say that someone has claimed to be my authorized recipient for these funds, and that if this is not accurate, to contact them immediately.

The upshot is that if I get in touch with them, further methods will be employed to part me from my money by saying they'll send the large sum directly to me. Then they'll either want a fee from me to help facilitate the transfer, or they'll just steal money from the bank account information that I provide them with. And I won't be able to complain to the authorities, as I was originally trying to cheat the Central Bank of Nigeria out of money I wasn't owed.

PayPal™ Alert: Your account access has been limited. You have one new Security Message Alert! Please click here to remove this limitation. Okay, I signed up for and used PayPal™ one time several years ago. It seems rather unlikely to me that they would be contacting me concerning my account. But I clicked on the place to remove my limitation, just to see what it would ask me for. At that time, my competent and alert computer security manager flashed on as a pop-up, warning me that the site contacting me was probably a phishing one. Phishing is a way of obtaining your personal information to use in stealing your money.

Online Cyber Lotto International, Madrid, Spain: This is to inform you that you have been selected for a cash prize of 915,810.00 Euros held on the 17th of November, in Spain. This selection process was carried out through random selection in our computerized e-mail selection system (ess) from our data-base of over 250,000 e-mail addresses drawn from which you were selected. (I didn't change the syntax in this one.) Hmmm. Now I'm thinking that maybe I won't have to finish writing this book after all. And if you find yourself not reading this sentence, I'll probably be sitting on a beach in the South of Spain drinking a Piña colada and watching senoritas frisking in the frothy surf. *Que bueno.*

Notification of Tax Refund on your Visa or MasterCard (from the IRS): After the last annual calculations of your fiscal activity we have determined that you are eligible to receive a tax refund of $329.30. To access the form for your tax refund, please click on the link below.

As a matter of fact, the IRS *has* been interested in my last tax return, as they recently sent me a check for $1.32 as part of a refund they owed me. And now they supposedly want to send me more. It's hard to see how the U.S. government manages to fund the Iraqi war with their scrupulous attention to making small refunds to taxpayers. But hey, it's more Piña colada money.

You have one new message at Mazuma Credit Union. In order to read the message, please click on the link below. The link suggested that the Mazuma Credit Union temporary (I think they meant to say "temporarily") discontinued my account. But when I did click on the link, my computer security company once again advised me that the site may be designed to trick me into submitting my financial or personal information to online scammers. They add that this is a serious security threat which could lead to identity theft, financial losses, or other dissemination of personal information. Gee, that's what I've been trying to tell you good folks reading this book. Besides which, I've never had any dealings with that credit union.

Online-World Cup 2010 Lottery Winnirng (sp) Notification: The Canadian Government sponsors this lottery for the promotion of the 2010 Soccer World cup to be hosted in South Africa. We happily announce to you the draw of the Euro-Afro-American Sweepstake Lottery International Programs held on Thursday 28thDec, held in Essex United Kingdom and Ontario Canada. This lottery scheme (at least they're being honest) was created to bring awareness to the world, being that South Africa is hosting the next world cup in 2010. They go on to say that I've won a cash payout of 2 ½ million dollars. Man, is this my lucky day, or what?

Oh, no, I didn't. The next e-mail from a nice gentleman informs me that I've won another 2 ½ million dollars in a lottery held in Cambridge, United Kingdom. I had no idea there were that many lotteries. But, as they inform me, people like Bill Gates and the Sultan of Brunei promote and support this lottery in order to encourage the use of the internet and computers. So, I suppose it must be on the up-and-up. I don't think Bill Gates would lend his name to anything phony, do you?

Okay, now we're talking. Some fellow who's the Operational Manager of the Intercontinental Security and Delivery Company, United Kingdom, advises me that my funds of eleven million dollars have been approved for immediate delivery to me. He doesn't say to what I owe this great and good fortune, but I guess I won't look a gift horse you-know-where. Although, perhaps if I check the right end, I'll see where this stuff is coming from.

At any rate, do people really fall for these schemes and scams? Yes, and that's why I'm warning you to be alert yourself and also to watch out for your elderly friends and relatives who are the most susceptible group when it comes to being taken advantage of financially. Also, people who don't speak the language in which the communication is issued, or who have a lack of much financial or security knowledge due to limited life experiences, may be scammed by such ruses.

The next e-mail I see is one in which someone from Liberia needs my assistance as a business partner by letting them deposit into my bank account a sum of about five million dollars. I suppose our business arrangement will be sorted out later, but for now the person is in danger from the instability in his country, so the transfer of funds must be made right away. Perhaps I should take a break from my writing to handle this request.

Then there are the schemes where someone wants you to cash a check for them through your bank account. For this small favor, you'll be paid a handsome fee. But even if the check is legitimate (that is, drawn on a good company account, but stolen or forged), the payee's name will often have been changed. The upshot of cashing such a check is that you will have to pay back the bank for the funds stolen from the company, and you'll also be subject to charges for money laundering. Such a deal.

At this point, I skimmed through the remainder of my junk e-mails. And be aware, that sometimes these scammers are able to send you an e-mail directly to your principal e-mail safe list. The remainder of these e-mails gave me the opportunity to be business partners with someone who had a large sum of money at their disposal but didn't have the proper business experience, or U.S. citizenship, or the investment know-how to handle such an amount of money and somehow he was able to intuit that I certainly did. Often, the sums of money will be ones that a rich person intended to go to a relative, but that relative and others have died, and the person writing the message is a lawyer or someone who is somehow in control of the funds of the deceased.

Another popular message is one where government funds have been set aside for a particular purpose, but that purpose is no longer relevant. Now, if the funds are not taken out by this person with the ability to do so, they will revert to the government entity. And no one wants to see a faceless and often evil government get any more money than it already has, do they?

One of my e-mails told the story of a general who had

twenty-four million dollars in the bank. I guess those foreign governments pay their fighting men pretty well. Sadly, the general and his wife and only daughter had been killed in the war in which he was fighting. And now the funds were due to revert to the bank in which they were being held unless a representative of the estate could be found to receive the funds. Fortunately, the person writing to me had a way of legitimizing that I was an heir to the estate if only I would agree to claim to be that heir and subsequently accept the funds into my bank account. Naturally, for this help, I would be given about thirty percent of the money. Shoot, I'd be able to buy straw sombreros and suntan lotion for the rest of my beachcombing days.

At any rate, a thorough discussion of scams, swindles, and cons could easily take a large size book to relate, so I'll stop at this point. Once again, some common sense awareness that there are con men out there, that there's no such thing as something for nothing, or a free meal, and that if something sounds too good to be true, it probably is, should alert you to many of the scams you run across. Then your application of the clues for detecting falsehoods and deception should give you an even greater chance of protecting your assets from theft by trickery. Just keep your head up and your fraud-detecting antennae fully extended, and you'll do well. If in doubt, ask your lawyer, or a knowledgeable relative, or the police what they think of the particular situation in question.

7

Body Language of Liars

➤ **Posture and movements.**

There are many types of moves or postures people use, consciously or unconsciously. When they make certain gestures during a conversation, you can consider them suspicious and as indicators of attempted deception. When the indicator occurs in connection with verbal signals of deception or incongruity, one can be reasonably certain that the subject is offering up some untrue comments, or just "slinging some bull."

There are universal nonverbal behaviors, says Navarro, which most people will exhibit under some circumstances. And then there are what he terms "idiosyncratic nonverbal behaviors," which are bodily movements or postures that are particular to a certain individual. The longer you know a person, and the more closely you observe his actions, the better you'll be able to evaluate what his nonverbal behaviors mean.

It's necessary to establish the way someone acts when he's not under stress. This will give his baseline behavior. Changes in this behavior are what you should watch for when reading him. The more changes he exhibits under questioning, the more certain you can be that he's stressed and possibly being deceptive. With more changes and observations of "tells," you can more confidently make judgments about what his body language means. The greater number of signals you notice, the more certain you can be of your diagnosis.

The Pease's state that, "Observations of gesture clusters and congruence of the verbal and body-language channels are the keys to accurately interpreting attitudes through body language." From my experience as an FBI agent, I'd have to support this concept. I've been alerted many times by various aspects of body language that a suspect might be trying to pull a whole skein of wool over my eyes in claiming he was innocent of a certain crime. Let's examine some of these instances.

Many people can't tell a lie without becoming nervous. There are various signals people exhibit when they're uneasy, a few of which include rocking in their chair or shifting their weight repeatedly, fiddling with objects, wringing their hands, coughing, and perspiring. Their heart rate will increase, and you might be able to see the fast pulsing at their temples. We've all seen such actions in nervous people, so they're easy to spot. The trick is to be sure that such nervousness equates with dishonesty in the particular circumstance at hand.

Clenching or wringing hands = deception.

The limbic portion of the brain, says Navarro, is the hard-wired part that signals us to act reflexively. Millions of years of human development have wired our brains to tell our bodies when to fight, run, duck, block, jump, blink, cover up, or scream, among other reactions to a threatening situation. The limbic part of the brain also houses our emotions, and will decode for us how we should feel in certain situations. For instance, the limbic brain could cause us to startle, blush, or clench our fists, according to the appropriate stimuli, before our conscious brain even has time to register what has happened that we should react to. The freeze response to stimuli is also ordered up by the limbic portion of the brain when it senses danger. Since limbic reactions occur before a person has time to contemplate what is happening, much less do something about the circumstances, it is beneficial to us to learn these various limbic reactions and what they may mean so that we can evaluate what an interviewee is feeling in a given situation.

The neocortex part of the brain, in contrast, is for reasoning what we should do to react in a certain circumstance. It also houses our memories. We use it to mull things over, not for immediate, reflexive action.

When faced with an arrest situation, I'd always watch a subject's body language for any signals of "fight or flight" he demonstrated. Eyes darting around the area, possibly checking for escape routes or weapons, hands twitchy or making nervous gestures, rapid breathing, sweating, and tenseness would all signal that the subject might be ready to break bad. If I noticed a person turn pale and his lips appear thin, I'd know it was because of secretions by his adrenal gland, and it signaled that he'd gone into a mode where he might either attack me or run.

Another sign to be watchful for is a sneer. This happens when a person feels angry at you or with the situation, or he feels threatened physically or emotionally. Nostril flaring by a subject can also be meaningful, as it might indicate that he's taking in extra oxygen prior to performing some act, usually one that will not be beneficial to you.

In addition, it helps to know a person's background so that his eye movements, facial expressions, and other bodily movements can be put into context. For instance, if a person is normally high-strung and jumpy, then he'll be even more nervous and fidgety when he's talking to a law enforcement officer or a person of authority, or even just when he's confronted directly by someone in a tense situation.

When such a nervous person is placed in the context of a possible arrest or confrontation with someone, the signals of the sweaty palms, excessive eye blinking, and fidgety body movements may not be as guilt-reflecting as they'd be if the person were normally a calm, cool, and collected individual. Navarro also says about five percent of people perspire excessively, and that many people who are nervous have sweaty palms, so this indicator is not necessarily a sign of deception. However, I'd say that such signals should alert you to listen carefully to what the person tells you and watch for other body language signs of deception.

As we've touched on earlier in this book, there are many types of movements and attitudes that a nervous person (and often a nervous and guilty person) will exhibit when being questioned or just approached by officers of the law, angry employers, or indignant significant others. We'll examine them singularly. But pay attention to the above suggestion to watch for gesture clusters. Relying on deciding the guilt or innocence of a person on the basis of one type of body movement is not suggested. You should have more pieces of the psychological puzzle in order to make a coherent picture of a person's culpability or guilelessness. Many people who are nervous in a situation will exhibit multiple signals. So don't mistake one habit a person may have, such as playing with their hair, as being proof positive of their guilt or dishonesty.

> **What's normal or baseline?**

When you're trying to elicit information from someone, you'll first need to establish what his normal behavior patterns are when he's stress-free and not under pressure to answer questions. This will be the baseline for his actions. Talk with him in a relaxed way. Ask him a few questions to see how he acts and what mannerisms he uses in normal conversation when he doesn't feel he's being interrogated. Observe which side his eyes move to when he's asked a question that should compel him to access his memory. Then ask him some questions that ought to cause him stress. Watch and compare the difference in his tics, mannerisms, postures, movements, facial expressions, and eye movements. You should have a good idea of what mannerisms could be sending signals that the person is being deceptive.

> **Universal moves?**

Some gestures we recognize as being universal, regardless of a person's nationality, race, sex, culture, or locale. We realize that all people smile when they're happy, scowl when they're sad, angry, or frustrated, and cry when they're feeling sad or depressed or overwhelmed. Almost everyone will nod to signal they mean "yes." Shaking the head from side-to-side indicates the person is saying "no."

> **Fidgeting.**

Fiddling with objects shows tension and insecurity. If it starts when you ask the difficult questions, it's a good indication that the person has previously been or is about to tell a lie. Twisting or curling of the hair around a finger, or playing with a bracelet or ring, or smoothing a tie or skirt will show nervousness. Sometimes a person will bite his fingernails. When a person feels unsure and insecure, says Dr. Glass, he will often feel a need to touch something material in order to soothe his nerves.

I think that fidgeting of some part of the body as well as squirming by a person also illustrates his nervousness. But, of course, even when they're not lying, some ill-at-ease people will act jumpy, play with their hands or objects, and have trouble concentrating on your questions. So these gestures should be considered in the context of whether other signs of deception are also displayed, either verbal or physical.

> **Other gestures of deception.**

Gerald I. Nierenberg and Henry H. Calero advise their research into parents' ability to read the gestures of their children uncovered many "tells" that children use when lying. These movements include averting the eyes, covering their mouths when they speak, licking their lips, looking down, and blinking rapidly. They'll also swallow frequently, shrug their shoulders, and scratch their heads. Suffice it to say that these same gestures, when used by adults, still mean that the person is trying to fool you.

Covering the mouth shows deceit.

Jef Nance gives examples of gestures to watch for which mean that the person you're speaking with is not receptive to what you're saying. Such gesticulations or postures might include turning his body at an angle from you, avoiding eye contact, establishing a physical barrier between the two of you, crossing his arms, and concentrating on some diversion such as taking out a cigarette and lighting it. If the subject is signaling that he's rejecting what you're saying, then you're having little impact on him.

Navarro states you should be aware of pacifying behaviors that a person performs when you're talking with her. These are a reaction to stress or discomfort the person is feeling in the situation. They're meant to comfort the person performing them, and they include such movements as stroking her arms, chewing gum, biting on or fiddling with a pen or pencil, jiggling a foot up and down, or touching her cheek or nose or mouth. Women, specifically, will touch the suprasternal notch (the hollow at the base of the front of the neck) when they feel afraid, uncomfortable or threatened. It's a defensive move that makes them feel protected.

Other gestures that signal when a person feels under stress include exhaling in a puff, rubbing the forehead or temples, and tugging at her collar. People will literally get "hot under the collar" from not only anger but from stress. Another strong sign that someone is being deceitful is if they rub a finger beneath their nose. This is because a release of chemicals called catecholomines in the body will make the nose swell and itch.

That pesky itch when I fib is a pain.

If you've cornered a liar through your skillful questioning, he may feel scared or frustrated or just plain stressed. These sensations can cause a tingling on the back of his neck which he'll notice subconsciously, if not consciously. In addition, his neck (and forehead and other places) will often start to perspire. So, when he scratches or rubs the back of his neck to remedy the itching or the discomfort of the perspiration, you'll have a good clue about his lack of veracity.

A perspiring or itchy neck signals distress.

Other signs to watch for, states Navarro, are when someone adjusts his tie or neck scarf, yawns, rubs his palms on his pants legs, and increases his rate of smoking or gum chewing. These movements indicate the person's discomfort. So watch for which questions elicit the strongest signals of uneasiness in the interviewee, and then shape the interrogation accordingly. When the person's stress level rises, it's time to hone in.

➢ **Watch for small signals.**

Women are more observant of gestures and expressions than men, and thus are more effective in detecting falsehoods. They're better at noticing "microexpressions" that flash across a liar's face in a split second, and contrast with what the person is saying verbally. And they'll notice "microgestures" better than men. These could include unconsciously induced movements or bodily responses such as the face and neck flushing, facial tics, excess sweating, dilation or constriction of the pupils, and rapid blinking. Other movements include fidgeting, shifting of the feet, and running one's tongue over his teeth.

Perhaps because of women's aforementioned observational skills, and their ability to mimic facial expressions and reactions, or maybe simply owing to their greater facility with language, women are more apt at lying than men. They tell more complex lies, adding details that make for verisimilitude. They also tend to avoid the sensitive subject, attempting to talk about other things. And when a woman is <u>attractive,</u> she'll be thought of as even more believable (this actually works in favor of men, too).

> **Physical effects of lying.**

Unless a person is a total sociopath, he will probably experience feelings of anxiety and guilt when he lies to you. These psychological feelings produce physical reactions which can be noted by astute body language watchers. One such movement would be to grab one's ear. This would be the equivalent of the "hear no evil" chimp, where the person is trying to subconsciously block out your dastardly questions.

As we've mentioned, when a person starts touching her mouth, nose, eye, or other parts of her face, it signals that she's getting nervous and stressed. Some people will put a hand on their face, and others will stroke or scratch some part of the face or neck. Some people try to make it look natural or planned, as in the photograph below, but it's caused by the anxious feelings they get from lying and feeling guilty about it.

Trying to look natural under pressure.

Psychologist Desmond Morris discovered that lying causes a tingling in the face. The fibber will react to this feeling with a scratch or firm rub, usually on the cheek, to alleviate the unpleasantness. Much like the rubbing beneath the nose signal, this may be done quickly and without conscious thought. The liar may not even be aware of having performed the movement.

But you'll recognize that he's given a signal, why he's done so, and what it means.

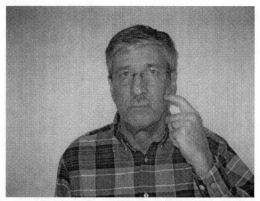

Scratching the cheek signals deceit.

Dr. Smith notes that self-deception (or I might refer to it as convincing oneself) has developed psychologically in our makeup as human beings for the purpose of calming many of the stresses of life. And he adds that this facet of our personality or psyche also aids us in being able to lie to others. He thinks this self-deception is vital for one's psychological equilibrium. Perhaps this is so, and I suspect that everyone does do it until they feel comfortable with the way they handle situations and other people.

➢ **Attitude is important.**

I believe that a person's overall attitude is a relevant feature to observe. Dr. Lieberman makes the point that if someone is <u>accused</u> of a heinous act and <u>fails to respond vigorously</u> and with indignation, it's a good sign that he's <u>guilty</u> of what you're calling him out for. He says to watch for an expressionless look, rather than one of surprise or consternation, when a person is accused of a serious act. If someone of true integrity is told he's suspected of doing something dishonorable, he'll likely be offended and stand ready to defend himself as a natural emotional reaction. There will be no "negative affect," or lack of appropriate response, such as the reaction that O.J. Simpson reportedly displayed when he was told by police that he was a suspect in the slayings of his ex-wife Nicole and her friend, Ron Goldman.

➤ **Chin and head movements.**

Chins may reveal emotions, says Dr. Glass. Someone who's angry will jut the chin forward. You'll probably immediately sense hostility when you perceive this gesture. If he retracts the chin, it means he's concerned about protecting himself. If someone is listening to you talk with his chin supported by his hand, it means he's bored and literally holding up his head to help himself pay attention. If someone lifts his chin at you, it means he feels superior, or he seriously questions what you just said. If he strokes the chin with light movements, he's probably concentrating hard on what you're saying. However, if he holds the chin, or rubs it forcefully, then he doesn't believe or agree with what you've said.

Several head positions are mentioned by Mr. Walters. These include the one where someone tilts their head as he's listening to you speak. This seems to be a signal that the person is interested in what you're saying and is listening intently. The person may also place a hand on one side of the face while doing this. But there's a big difference when he props up his head with the hand alongside the cheek or under the chin. In this case, he doesn't like or agree with what you're saying, or he's bored and may well be having thoughts of his own and not listening to what you're saying at all. And if the head is thrust forward, says Dr. Glass, that's definitely an aggressive posture. The man may even be hostile toward you.

Another head position is one that parents sometimes use when a teen returns home late. Let's say that Dad is standing in the foyer with his hands on his hips, head tilted downward, and with his chin drawn inward. I'll bet he might even exhibit a tight mouth or a slight scowl. This position shows that he's not willing to consider or accept what you're telling him as an excuse.

➤ **Other gestures of note.**

Rocking back and forth, says Dr. Glass, is a signal that a person is anxious or uncomfortable and is trying to soothe himself. A person who spreads out and takes up a lot of room is someone who feels confident and strong. He will extend his legs in front of him, and he may lean back in his chair with his fingers laced behind his head. A person who is insecure will often pull his legs back toward himself, sometimes tucking them under a chair or entwining them around each other or around a chair leg. And he'll cross his arms in a self-hugging type way.

If a person acts restless and moves a good deal, it indicates he may be nervous and doesn't want to be there. Hand wringing and finger drumming and foot tapping might signal that a person is uneasy and apprehensive. And take a look at his eyes, because it might be that the man is irritated, and you'll probably see some confirmation in the hard look he's shooting your way.

➢ **Nodding.**

If people nod their head slightly while you're talking to them, it can mean they agree with what you're saying. But if they do so vigorously and often, it may suggest that they're insecure and fear rejection. They're trying to get you to like them, making you think they agree with whatever you say.

➢ **Other signals to watch for.**

Dr. Glass says that a bowed head definitely shows a person is unsure of himself, and he's possibly depressed, as well. Such a person is probably not a happy camper, and he's likely affected by low self-esteem. I've interviewed people who exhibited this body language. They're hard to deal with because they don't say much, and it's difficult to read their signals because they don't exhibit much emotion. They're like shells of people who can't be reached. They seem rather like remnants of that long ago attack of the Pod People.

Hartley mentions two types of personalities to watch for when you're considering confronting someone to ascertain the truth of a certain situation. He terms the first type of person a "judger." By this he means someone who is neat, orderly, and organized. This type doesn't like clutter, and he has the preconception that there is a right way to do things in life. He plans his activities (and those of others he controls) using calendars, notes, lists, goals, and deadlines. And he doesn't much care for someone who doesn't share the same values.

The other type is a "perceiver." They tend to have piles of papers and materials all over their office. They don't get concerned with deadlines. They often put off making decisions until the last possible moment. They are apt to rethink the decisions they've already made. If they make a list of things to do, they'll probably misplace it. And whereas the "judgers" plan all their activities in advance, including vacation trips, the "perceivers" will wait until the last minute to decide what to do for the weekend. They are not bothered by clutter and messiness.

It could help you in questioning one or the other of these types of persons by knowing what they value concerning order and organization and deadlines. Life styles of people are important and meaningful to them. Some people want to sit on the porch and visit about the weather and how the crops are doing before you can get around to asking for whatever information you may need. Some are busy, driven, and impatient. They want you to get down to business. Give them the "bottom line" of what you're interested in. Of course, if you want to throw them off guard, you'll do just the opposite of what makes them comfortable and operating "in the groove."

Dr. Dimitrius mentions that you can discern people's attitudes and methods of approaching life from clues you pick up in their workspace or home. Such situations as a home where the grass is eight inches high, the house in poor repair, and the inside is cluttered and dirty suggest a different type of personality and set of values from those of a person with a manicured lawn, a fresh coat of paint, and clean floors and furnishings within tidy rooms. She also suggests that if a person's home and office send different signals, she gives more credence to the message sent by the home. In my work, I've been in many houses and apartments that suggest the people living there are slovenly, disorganized, and apparently uncaring about cleanliness and orderliness. I expected such people to have little or no regard for authority and the law, and that usually turned out to be the case.

Walters states that various meanings can be attached to the behavior of a person touching parts of the face and head with her hand. He says that when a person's hands are moving around her mouth, nose, eyes, or ears while she's speaking, the gestures act as a kind of concealment. They're collectively known as "negation behaviors." That is, they cancel the meaning of what is being said, and thus, they're associated with deception. The most telling and consistently used movements are the touching of the mouth or the nose.

With regard to the mouth, during many interviews of suspected felons, I've noticed that the mouth or the area around it is like a magnet to a person's hand when they're feeling stressed by having to answer difficult questions. Covering the mouth with the hand almost always indicates that a falsehood is about to emanate from that tricky orifice. I've seen this one a lot, especially with nervous criminals. They will also often touch their nose or their cheek. Watch out for a finger placed beside or below the mouth, or any part of the hand partially blocking it, sometimes even when they're actually speaking, because you're about to get punked.

> **Watch for these signals.**

We've mentioned that when a liar touches his mouth, or covers it with a finger, part of his hand, or his fist, this is the monkey's equivalent of the "speak no evil" gesture. The person is afraid that he'll say the wrong thing, or he's already lied to you and he's trying to cover up his misstep. And if he's also exhibiting a number of nervous swallows, you'll have yet another indication that his pants are about to burst into flames. Along the same lines, Walters notes that putting objects into the mouth serve as the same denial signal. People will chew on their fingernails, pens, toothpicks, gum, or pipe stems. They may also nibble their lip as a means of controlling their speech.

Chewing on an object means fear or denial.

Being under stress, says Navarro, will cause a person to have a dry mouth, and the person may lick his lips to keep them wet and pliant. Sometimes people will rub their tongues back and forth across their lips to calm themselves. They'll likely display other signs of being under stress, such as nibbling on their lip or an object. These signs of insecurity may also indicate that the person is being dishonest with you.

Dr. Glass mentions that anytime a person touches the face frequently during a discussion, he may not be telling the truth. He feels uncomfortable with his deception, and the moving of the hand to the mouth, nose, or eyes right after telling a lie is a way of placing an obstruction between him and you. In a sense, it's a blockade that he can hide behind in case of retaliation against him for his lack of candor. And when a person rubs his eyes, Dr. Glass says it indicates that he's signaling for you to stop what you're doing. He wants you to quit questioning him, and he wants to escape the uncomfortable situation he's in.

Navarro adds that we should watch for situations in which someone is talking with us and trying to explain away some crime he's suspected of doing, and his response is made with passive statements that are not bolstered by strong physical gestures. This is because someone who is lying tends to lack confidence in what he's saying. So, his nonverbal signals tend to be weak and unconvincing.

 ➢ **Other physiological changes.**

Lying also causes the blood pressure to increase, and this is one of the bodily changes that is monitored by a mechanical lie detector. The nose also receives more blood, and it expands. It's not enough to be seen by the naked eye, but this "Pinocchio effect" is quite amusing, and it probably also contributes to the liar wanting to touch or brush or rub his nose after telling a fib. His nose may be itching from the extra blood. A man who tells a lie will also have a resultant swelling in other nether regions. This may or may not be detectable, depending on his natural endowment and the situational ability for you to be able to observe such a function.

Hadley mentions that stress will cause some people to blush. But prior to the blushing becoming obvious in the person's facial complexion, usually in the cheeks, it will first go to his ears. I've had this happen to me when I was embarrassed or thought I was about to be embarrassed by some situation. My ears will turn bright red and will burn as if I'd been in the sun for hours. It's a very uncomfortable feeling.

When someone hears another person saying something that makes him uneasy, says Dr. Lieberman, the person listening will move his head away from the speaker. This may be a quick jerk of the head, or a slow turning. It's an unconscious way to get away from the person and his message. On the other hand, a slight tilt of the head indicates the person is interested in what's being said.

A shoulder shrug may mean a person is emphasizing that they don't know the answer to a question. But Dr. Glass suggests that if a person gives a shoulder shrug very quickly, it could mean they're actually denying what they're telling you. In other words, they're trying to appear calm, but they're nervous because they've just told you a lie, and the quick shoulder shrug is a "tell" signaling that they're being deceptive. Also, Navarro says that a partial shoulder shrug (with only one shoulder lifted) is indicative that the person doesn't know the answer to your question or that he's not committing strongly to his answer (perhaps because he's just lied to you). Also, when a person's shoulders rise so far that his neck vanishes (what Navarro calls the "turtle effect"), the resulting pose is a strong indicator that the person displaying the posture is insecure and/or dejected.

> **Touch me not.**

Dr. Lieberman makes the point that if a person never touches you during a conversation, it might be an indication that he's lying. Lieberman says that when a person lies to you, he will avoid this level of intimacy. Of course, many times when you're talking with someone, you may not be in a position for them to touch you, such as if you're sitting across a desk from each other. Or there may be a certain formality between the people that would obviate such a gesture. And if a law enforcement officer is talking to a suspect about a crime, such touching would not be expected in the normal course of the interview.

> **Stress.**

Other such motions of withdrawal that signal discomfort with what the speaker's saying include actually moving farther away from the speaker and also turning sideways to him. Gestures that include fiddling with one's hands, clothing, or other parts of the body can indicate that a person is nervous about talking with you. Ever run across someone who's a habitual pen clicker or who jingles the change in his pocket or plays with his keys? Those people are really feeling some stress and need an outlet through movement.

A person who is not coming clean with you will be less expressive with his hands, says Dr. Glass. Such a person will often clench his hands into fists or keep them folded in his lap or even stick them into his pockets. The tighter the clasping of the hands, the more nervous and stressed the person is. And remember, a supinated hand, where you can see the palm, is a gesture indicating honesty. A pronated hand, with the palm down or pointed away from you, will signal deception.

> **The legs and feet speak volumes.**

Walters comments that the legs often show when a person is under stress. You'll need to assess whether his leg fidgeting is just from general discomfort, or whether it's caused by stress from the questions you're asking. Such movements include crossing or uncrossing the legs, crossing the legs in the other direction, pumping them up and down like pistons, wiggling them back and forth, or turning them away from the questioner and toward an exit (which signifies they want to leave). Also, jiggling the foot of the leg that's crossed on top of the other one is a sign of nervousness and sometimes irritation.

Dr. Glass also mentions the foot jiggling, and she says the feet are the most honest parts of the body. She states that when a person's feet are planted on the ground, it indicates truthfulness. However, if he has a foot resting on the heel, or on the outer edge of the foot, it means that the person may well not be telling the truth. I've noticed this posture many times when talking with someone I suspected of criminal activity. He'll usually slump in his chair, with one foot stuck forward and the other one pulled back, with the forward foot turned to the outward edge or resting on the heel.

Many times, an interviewee will jiggle a foot nervously while she talks. Dr. Glass mentions that the foot tap and jiggle are ways of saying, "I want to get out of here." A person who slaps her thighs in a rhythmic manner is also signaling she wants to leave. Navarro adds that when a seated interviewee begins kicking the upper foot of her crossed legs at a certain point in an interview, she's probably become uncomfortable about what you're asking her. On the other hand (or foot), when a person continuously kicks or jiggles her foot during an interrogation, then suddenly stops, Navarro says this "foot freeze" is indicative the person is feeling threatened by your question. Also, if an interviewee suddenly withdraws her feet beneath the chair, she's been made uneasy by what you just asked her.

Not interested in answering questions.

Locking one foot around the other ankle, says Dr. Glass, signals that a person is withholding either her true emotions or some information that you're seeking. I've found that people who do this will also often cross their arms. And they're usually very closed-mouthed individuals.

Of course, a person may simply do these things because she's normally not that self-confident or she's just plain nervous about talking with you. I had to be aware of that when I spoke to people, because many individuals are intimidated by talking with an FBI agent. This could be because they've done something illegal that they're worried might be detected, or else they're just thrown off stride about how to interact with an agent, as they've never done so before. Many people told me that I was the first FBI agent they'd ever had contact with.

➢ **Watch the body.**

A person's torso, claims Navarro, will adjust itself to perceived danger. If you're asking questions that make an interviewee uncomfortable, he'll probably move away from you, turn his torso away from you, and possibly blade his body to you. If he's in a position where he can't lean away from you, he will use something to create a barrier between himself and you. He may cross his arms over his chest, place objects on the desk between you and him, or deliberately fiddle with items within his reach, such as soft drink cans, or pens, or paper weights. When people move closer to you or lean toward you, they probably like what you're saying or appreciate your looks. If they imitate your posture, which is called mirroring or isopraxism, this shows they agree with you and want to get along with you.

However, if someone exhibits a splaying out posture, with the legs and arms spread out in an exaggerated fashion, they're showing you and your position of authority an attitude of disrespect. This is a powerful nonverbal signal. It can often be seen with criminals in jail interviews and with teenagers in any sit-down discussion with their parents.

➤ **Take note of disposition.**

A person may be naturally shy or self conscious or even have a social avoidance disorder that makes him uncomfortable even making small talk. But if he's not nervous when you are chatting with him about unimportant topics, then he begins to exhibit signs of self-awareness and discomfort when you switch to the questions you want answered truthfully, then this could well be a strong signal that he's lying to you or considering giving you some non-truths and some partial truths.

Another signal that a person may be shy or withdrawn is when she tucks her feet underneath her chair. Sometimes, she'll cross her feet at the ankles and then pull them beneath the chair. Walters says this may indicate the person feels a little inferior. As I mentioned before, I think it's also a sign that she's protecting herself by drawing in physically as a defense mechanism. This is often accompanied by the person crossing her arms across the chest. It's the old Missouri "show me" gesture, or even worse, it may indicate that you'll never convince her or sway her to your way of thinking. Co-operation from a person using these bodily signals will not be easy to attain.

People will transmit signs of anger with their body language, says Walters. And the anger they're showing may have occurred because they're feeling hostile toward you for questioning them, or that they're feeling trapped by a situation in which they may be found out for their bad behavior. Such signals include thrusting out the chin and/or tilting up the head. This is a common signal of defiance and challenge. Navarro adds that people who are angry with another person and are about to start a fight with them will often puff out their chest at that person, somewhat like a gorilla trying to intimidate a rival or a foe. A heaving of the chest or panting will signal extra oxygen intake which is also a built-in response to a potential battle.

And I've sometimes witnessed a person who is growing more agitated begin to clench his jaw muscles until they actually ripple. Another sign of anger, says Walters, is when a person has his eyelids partially closed, as though he's squinting. The eyebrows will lower into a "V" shape, as well. Crossing the arms high on the chest and clenching the fists are other signals of being upset. Drumming the fingers or a pen on a tabletop will signal irritation and potential aggression.

When a person scratches behind her ear, says Dr. Glass, it sometimes means she doubts what you've said, or at the least she thinks she's misunderstood or is confused by your comments. If she tugs at an ear while talking to you, unless she's Carole Burnette, she's trying to delay the conversation. She wants to think about something she's previously seen or heard before she responds. And if she rubs an ear between the thumb and forefinger while you're speaking, it means she's not really interested in what you're saying, or else she just flat doesn't believe it.

> **The hands and arms as indicators.**

Dr. Lieberman notes that the hands and arms are often good signals of deception. A person who is not revealing something to you, or is outright lying, will tend to move his hands and fingers less often than a more forthcoming person. He may make fists of his hands or stick them into his pockets. He might keep them in his lap or stiffly at his side. And I've noticed that some-times when people don't want to answer your questions, they'll become obsessed with something that's sitting on the table or attached to their person and will toy with it during the conversation.

Arms crossed across the body and legs crossed at the ankles both indicate that the person is either not interested in what you're saying or that he's not receptive to discussing the subject, possibly because he'll have to lie to you about it. Dr. Lieberman says that the person is probably "keeping something in." Also, if the person's arm movements seem stiff and robotic, this indicates that the person is likely being evasive. If he uncrosses his arms and leans forward, he's either ready to be more co-operative, or he's about to terminate the conversation. You'll soon find out which.

When a person sits with his arms held behind his head, fingers interlaced, and often leaning back in his chair, this also signals that he's a person of authority in the situation at hand. Navarro calls this a "hooding effect," as it resembles the look of a cobra that has expanded its hood to threaten others. This posture, along with spreading the arms when talking with someone else, whether standing or sitting, shows the person feels in charge of the situation and he can claim as much territory around him as he wishes.

A person who stiffens his legs out in front of him while stretching his upper body back and away from you is not interested in whatever you're discussing and wants to move on. I've found myself doing this during countless boring business meetings. And Walters mentions that sometimes a person will lean noticeably to one side, often toward an exit. We know that means he wants to make a break for it. If he sits straight upright, with rigid posture, it suggests that he's trying to control himself physically and emotionally. The reason may well be that he's not being open with you or candid in his responses to your questions.

Arms akimbo, notes Navarro, is a way of showing a person

is claiming his territory. It projects authority in the situation at hand. It may be simply saying, "I'm in charge here," or it may be confrontational in that it signals the person he's addressing that he's about to be called on the carpet to answer for some transgression.

Another posture to watch for is when a person leans in toward you. Walters warns that this may not be because he finds you fascinating. It may well be an attempt to control the conversation. Be aware of whether his speech patterns are aggressive and whether the person seems to want to dominate the discussion and you.

Sometimes if a person, particularly a child, exhibits little movement of his arms, a phenomenon Navarro calls "arm freeze," he says that this may be a protective device. The child may have been abused at home, and he's learned not to attract attention by being too noticeable. Adults will sometimes use this posture if they're trying to avoid attention. Or they'll grasp their fingers behind their back as a way of telling those around them to stay away and leave them alone.

Aldert Vrij says the causes for a person to manifest the above mannerisms would include fear of being found out and being punished for his actions, emotional feelings of guilt, and excitability (possibly indicating a "duping delight") that are being felt by the deceiver. He notes that when a liar becomes anxious that he might be caught by a questioner, he will try even harder to make an honest impression. So watch for the extra strain in the person who's trying to impress you with his earnestness and rectitude.

Other items to be aware of, adds Navarro, include the phenomenon that people have a definite space requirement for their person (called proxemics), and that if you invade that space, they'll become uncomfortable, uneasy, and even angry. Their hearts will beat faster, pulses race, and they may get red in the face and neck regions. He suggests not invading someone's personal space when you're interviewing them for information. The resultant discomfort caused by such an infringement could

Mark Bouton

cost you the ability to make the interviewee calm, relaxed, and possibly more talkative and co-operative. Also, take note of whether the spread out person suddenly withdraws into a smaller space when questioned about something that distresses him.

Vrij comments that a person trying to deceive you might show behavior that seems rigid, rehearsed, and without spontaneity. He says a person feeling fear will automatically raise his eyebrows, and that they'll pull together, as well. The man or woman's voice pitch will rise, although only slightly, and it may be hard to detect such a slight difference. I *have* noticed this circumstance before, though. And the person will usually begin clearing his throat at about the same time. Vrij comments that a fearful individual may exhibit raised upper eyelids and tensed lower eyelids.

Trembling or shaky hands, says Navarro, can be caused by excitement, uncertainty, fear, or stress. If a person is a chronic alcoholic, his trembling may be part of the baseline of his normal behavior. However, if the interviewee seems relatively calm and in control, then he begins trembling when a new question is asked him, this may be something to take note of. When someone is stressed, neurotransmitters and hormones can surge through his body, causing severe trembling of the hands and fingers.

If a person is listening to you speak, states Dr. Lieberman, and she touches her face or throat, it indicates she doesn't want to be participating in the discussion. Navarro adds to be aware when someone purses her lips while you're talking, as this usually means she doesn't agree with what you're saying, or she's thinking of another idea she may perceive is better. And if she grips her ear, she's doubtful about the truth or validity of what you're saying.

When people steeple their fingers (touch them together in a way that it seems they've constructed a pointed top much like a slanted roof of a house), the result is a display of great confidence. People who use such a display will feel more authoritative and self-assured than those who don't. They also appear to be more truthful to others who are watching them, although there is not a correlation. Both honest people and stone cold liars can use the steepling position. Truthful folks don't have a patent on it.

Navarro also points out that people who display their thumbs, as when putting their hand into a side coat pocket with the thumb outside, are sending a signal of high confidence. In contrast, anyone who sticks his thumb into a pants pocket with the rest of the hand left outside sends a message that they're of low status and have little self-confidence. Also, if a person displays his thumbs in a raised position, such as when he grasps the lapels of his coat (as we see lawyers do in older movies), this is another positive display.

Another set of signals can be sent by the hands. When people wring their hands or interlace their fingers, especially after a particular question is asked, this is usually interpreted as a stress reaction or possibly a display of low self-confidence. A stroking of the palm with the fingers of the other hand, as well as touching of the neck by an interviewee while he's talking are both indicative of self-soothing mannerisms intended to lessen the stress the person is feeling at the moment. He may also stroke his arm with his other hand as a way to ease his nervousness. And the stress he experiences may be caused because he feels that he has to lie.

> **Posture and positioning make statements.**

Walters relates that if a person sits or stands with his shoulders squared to yours, then he's ready to talk with you "on the level." If he turns his shoulders away from you, he's not mentally or emotionally involved in the conversation. And if he rotates his shoulders while he's talking, it could mean he's not telling the truth at that particular moment. A slight and quickly executed shoulder shrug, or a shrug with only one shoulder also both indicate that the speaker doesn't really believe what he's been saying to you. It's a way of negating what he's just told you.

> ➢ **Smiles can show wiles.**

Also, be alert when someone smiles at you. If the smile seems "painted on," with the person's face looking stiff and unnatural, the person is more than likely giving you a false smile. Dr. Lieberman characterizes it as a "lips only" smile. If you spot such a smile, you might want to pay careful attention to the words that come next from that man or woman. Allan and Barbara Pease note that smiles are controlled by the zygomatic major muscles, which tug up the corners of one's lips. These muscles can be controlled willfully, and a phony smile can easily be produced.

Watch politicians, talk show hosts, and salesmen for displays of these artificial smiles. A phony smile will only involve the lower part of the face, and the mouth often appears asymmetrical, with usually the left side of the mouth rising higher when a person is trying to slip one past you. The eyes will remain relaxed and unaffected.

Such reactions as fake smiles are important to notice. The best and most reliable gestures in terms of detecting truth or attempted deception are those that a person makes automatically. This is because he can't consciously control those gestures, so they are good indicators of how a person is reacting to a question or interaction.

When a smile is real and heartfelt, another set of facial muscles, the *orbicularis oculi*, are involved in making it. These muscles can't be voluntarily controlled by a person. They are activated when an individual projects a true smile, and the muscles pull the eyes back. They also affect the upper face, making crinkle lines alongside the eyes and bunching the skin beneath them. Hopefully, your sweetie will usually greet you with one of these warm and welcoming expressions, and not the artificial and sterile WalMart™ greeter's grin.

A true smile.

The Pease's further note that when people are telling the truth, they will increase their smiling frequency. This is an effort by an honest person to convince the listener he's being genuine and truthful. So, watch for the opposite behavior. Paul Ekman states that when people lie, they smile less than usual. This especially applies to men.

Of course, in this instance, you'll need to be familiar with the person's normal smiling behavior. I've seen a few criminals as dour and deadpan as the guy in the movie *Fargo* who, after a petty falling-out, stuffed his partner into a wood chipper. Not your hail-fellow-well-met type. Other individuals, regardless of their jobs or activities, are as sweet as Labrador puppies or as mean as Mamba snakes.

And you've probably noticed and had a negative reaction when someone seemed to smile too quickly and hold it for too long a time. This can give the impression that the person is wearing a mask. Indeed, it's likely a mask of deception.

➤ **Check out the threads.**

The clothing that a person wears also sends some signals. Recalling the neatness of the Shah of Iran, I was interested to read that Dr. Glass feels that people who dress immaculately in a sharp, buttoned-down manner may be very disciplined and organized people. Or they may be inflexible types with rigid behavior and overly-controlled emotions. She mentions that they may be the ones who press their blue jeans and iron their underwear. I don't know about his underwear, but I knew an FBI agent who always had a sharp crease in his jeans. I'm lucky if mine are clean and not too wrinkled.

I usually interviewed suspects who would never make it into the pages of *GQ*. Dr. Glass says that slovenly people usually suffer from poor self-esteem. I presume that the guys I'm thinking of would be classified as slovenly. Soiled and wrinkled clothing, unkempt greasy or dirty hair, gritty fingernails, and a general lack of style, proper deportment, and fashion sense would characterize most of these people. Dr. Glass thinks that they may be depressed or not care what other people think about them and their appearance.

I believe she's right about that. Many of the people that I interviewed were living in a manner that was way outside the norm, and they probably didn't know, and certainly didn't care, what people's reactions to them were. Use and abuse of drugs and alcohol, poor sleep patterns, lousy diets, and lack of good physical and dental hygiene certainly added to these people's woes. And a lack of respect for the law and for honesty and decency seemed to be a side effect of such a lifestyle.

Another aspect of dress to watch for, according to Dr. Glass, is when a person dresses inappropriately for the occasion. She says this shows he's a rebel who has a need to be noticed. I wonder what her thoughts are on the tattoos and piercings so prevalent today. Display of such accouterments used to be a way of being a nonconformist. Now, it's close to being the norm, especially among younger folks. But I still think it indicates a desire to be rebellious.

Dr. Dimitrius mentions that a person's clothing reflects not only his personal taste, but also his economic status. He may be showing that he's rebellious, cool, wealthy, a blue collar worker, or just a casual person by the way he chooses to dress, especially in social situations that usually call for a certain type of outfit and decorum. Dr. Glass thinks that improper attire is a sign of hostility and a wish to control situations. She says such people are insecure and want to bully others.

A person's vehicle, says Dr. Dimitrius, will also show volumes about him. His car will reflect both his values and his wherewithal. Nowadays, much can be surmised about someone depending on whether he's driving a Hummer, a Volkswagen, or a hydrogen hybrid. Also, the cleanliness of the vehicle, inside and out, will show much about the person.

I found in my job that often a person's history and lifestyle choices were reflected in the tattoos he chose to display. And it was almost always a way of life that was outside the normal pattern of behavior in a civilized and law-abiding society. Skulls, daggers, and Nazi swastikas are the choice of a certain type of person. Whereas, the butterflies, angels, or hearts, which are chosen by others, definitely send their own messages.

Dr. Dimitrius observes that often much can be determined about a person's attitudes and values from the type of friends or associates he hangs out with. Especially if he belongs to certain groups or mingles mainly with certain types of people, much can be inferred about his beliefs. There are different strokes for members of a motorcycle gang or Skinheads from people who belong to reading clubs, quilting circles, or yoga and meditation classes.

Also, be observant of how someone treats others, says Dr. Dimitrius. You'll see his true character displayed in his actions, not in what he tells you. To know with whom you're dealing, it's a good idea to watch a person when he's not aware he's being seen. His attitude and methods of interacting with other people will show a great deal about what kind of person he is on the inside.

> **Phony emotions transmit signals.**

Dr. Lieberman refers to an "emotion commotion." This is when someone makes a response to a stimulus that's not spontaneous, and therefore it's not real. There will be a delay between the stimulus and the reaction. The duration of the response will be longer, and the expression will fade abruptly. When someone fakes emotions, observers will usually notice the effort. Lieberman mentions the phony facial expression that shows surprise as being a particularly noticeable one. It's a look that we see often on daytime soap operas. And the actors who do the expression often exaggerate it to the point that they resemble Charlie Chaplin in his silent films.

And then there are the wigs and overdone hairdos. Dr. Glass suggests that people who do comb-overs or wear toupees are insecure and not open with others. She didn't mention hair plugs or other hair restoration methods. But her feelings are that such people tend to hide things. I've interviewed men with hair loss situations before, but I never considered that they had more to hide than their balding pates, and that they were less honest than their hirsute counterparts. Besides, I've noticed that my hair is thinning a bit, and I don't want to cast stones in case I should eventually join the hair-challenged corps.

➤ **Other grooming oddities.**

Dr. Glass mentions that people with nails so long as to be impractical are likely saying, "Notice me!" I read this not long after seeing a woman on television who claims to have the record for the longest existing fingernails. They were about two feet long, curved, and made her hands practically unusable. She had to hold her hands out in front of her as she walked, drawing stares from passersby. Dr. Glass also says that people with nails bitten to the quick may be nervous and anxious people.

She also thinks that folks who are too meticulously groomed, with perfect hair and clothing, may be overly rigid and inflexible. I've noticed that this type of man and woman also tends to go heavy on the cologne and perfume. And they're often the type to belittle others. Reapplying makeup too often is a signal, says Dr. Glass, that a woman is overly self-conscious and probably insecure. None of these situations overtly signals deceptive practices, but I think it's wise to make an assessment of the type of person you're dealing with in seeking true and accurate information.

➤ **Behavioral patterns.**

According to Walters, we all use consistent behavior when

it comes to telling lies. We'll give out pretty much the same signals each time we are brandishing falsehoods. Also be aware that even though a person is exhibiting a signal that in most people would mean they were being dishonest, it may be a form of movement or posture that the person has adopted in his ordinary repertoire of actions. So, when he performs the action, it doesn't necessarily mean he's being untruthful. That's why it's good to watch for several bodily indicators of lying, as well as paying attention to verbal hints that all is not kosher in the state of Denmark. And, as a reminder, we're usually detecting lying by noting stress reactions and signals, but not all symptoms of stress are caused by a person telling lies.

"Illustrators" are hand and body movements that complement a verbal statement. Walters compares them to movements a street mime might make. I think of them as some gesture that an actor would use to amplify or clarify his speech. Dr. Ford says that illustrators are movements that are linked with speech, and that people use them to add to, emphasize, or make clearer what they're trying to say. With people that use their hands when they talk, especially if they do it frequently and constantly, it might suggest that they're lying if they suddenly stop or even decrease using the movements. This happens because they're more intent on monitoring the words they're saying when they lie, instead of allowing their gestures to normally accentuate their speech flow.

Dr. Ford states that "emblems" are facial expressions, or types of posture, or body language that have a particular meaning within cultural groups where they're used. Actions such as lifting an eyebrow (Remember The Rock?), shrugging one's shoulders, or head nodding or shaking have certain understood meanings in the American culture. (In some cultures, the head nod means the person is not in agreement.) Dr. Ford suggests that when an emblem (which is an automatic movement) seems to contradict what a person is saying, then it could well be a signal that he's lying.

"Adapters" are movement or the lack of movement, and

they act as stress relievers. Grooming behaviors, such as brushing back one's hair, adjusting one's tie, or smoothing one's clothing are indicators of adapters. We all use such movements when we're anxious about meeting someone new, about to do public speaking, or going on a job interview.

Walters suggests watching for changes in the pattern of the usage of emblems, adapters, and illustrators by an interviewee. He feels that increased movement in these types of signals would indicate a rise in the stress and anxiety level felt by the interviewee. The higher the level of stress, the more movements you'll see. And he discusses the "dismissal gesture," describing it as a sweeping gesture of the arm and hand away from the body that shows the person giving it doesn't want to talk about or deal with the situation at hand.

❖ **A riddle within an enigma.**

I worked a case in Kansas in which money was determined to be missing from a teller's cash box that had been padlocked inside her locker and closed inside the locked bank vault overnight. Talk about your sealed room mystery. However, when I interviewed the teller whose money was missing, let's call her Mary, a young woman who was roundly suspected by the bank management to be a thief, I tended to believe her near-tears protestations that she didn't take the money and had no idea how it disappeared. And it made sense to me that from her sound work record at the bank, her seemingly sound monetary situation, and her apparent personal stability, that she wouldn't be the type to take money which she would obviously be suspected of stealing.

Of course, that made solving the case a bit more difficult. I started by learning the bank's routine about how employees got access to the vault. Naturally, there were many employees who walked in and out of there during the day. But before I went about interviewing all of those folks, I knew I had to determine how someone could get into the teller's locker that was sealed with a combination padlock. And there were no signs that the locker had been forced open, nor was it the loose kind that you sometimes find in health clubs.

After reviewing the routines of the employees, I found there were three other tellers who also put away their cash boxes into their own lockers at about the same time that Mary stowed her cash. Two of the tellers were young women, and the third was a young man I'll call Charles. The women seemed as shocked as Mary was when I asked them about how the money could go missing. But Charles was very calm, collected, and confident. Not that there's anything wrong with that, but he also gave me a phony smile and was rather glib in his answers. I quickly got the impression that he was playing a game—that he fancied himself as a bystander who was watching a puzzling scenario that was confounding everyone, but to which he alone knew the answer.

I don't usually base the way I work on hunches, but I definitely kept Charles in mind when I worked to unravel the mystery posed by this situation. For instance, the locker that Charles used was only a couple of ones away from Mary's. The other teller's lockers were more removed in distance. Still, there was that padlock.

I questioned Mary again about her routine in placing the money into the locker. Did she ever put her cash box down anywhere in the process? Did she ever put the money into the locker and then pause to do anything else before she closed the padlock? She assured me that there would be no opportunity for anyone to snatch the money out of the closed cash box before she secured it into the locker. And the vault was locked down soon after the money was placed inside.

So I asked her to physically go through the motions for me. She did, and it seemed that she followed the processes she'd described. She was adamant that her previous evening's routine had been no different than usual. I asked if she recalled anyone else being inside the vault at the same time she was. She thought she remembered that Charles came in when she was leaving the vault, but she wasn't sure because they'd done the routine so many times that she wasn't paying that much attention.

Telling her thanks for her help, I let her return to work. I stood alone in the bank vault and stared at the lock. I thought about the process the tellers went through. I mused about all the various key locks and combination locks and vaults we had in our own FBI office space. And I reached up, grabbed the padlock, and gave it a good yank. It came open. Aha!

It turned out that the lock in question, although when shut appeared to be securely locked, would not actually engage until the tumblers were rotated after closing it. So, I asked the other tellers to show me their usual routine. All of them twirled the combination padlock's dial after they'd closed the lock. I asked Charles why he did that. He smiled (you know the kind) and said that it was to complete the locking process. I interviewed him twice more before the smug young man admitted that he'd opened Mary's lock and grabbed the missing money from her cash box.

Even though body signals can't always be said to be proof positive that a person is trying to deceive you, they can sometimes lead you to take a closer look at what a person is doing or telling you. And they can make you even more vigilant in watching for other signals when dealing with the person. While I was interviewing Charles again, though he was smart and wily and calm, he put his finger beside his mouth a couple of times when answering questions, which is a strong indication of lying. Also, he turned his legs away from me during the second interview.

When the interviewee turns his legs and body away from the interviewer, it signals that he is uncomfortable and that he wants the present situation to end. If his feet are pointed toward the door, that's a strong indication that he wants to get the heck out of Dodge (or whatever town he happens to be in). So the phony smile, smug attitude, finger beside the mouth, and the turned away legs all pointed me toward Charles as a strong suspect in the crime.

> **Woe is me.**

One other useful signal to be aware of is the head drop. This is when someone you're questioning visibly lowers their chin to their chest, usually with their eyes downcast. Often they'll sigh audibly when they do this. These are signs that the person is about to confess that he did the actions that you're trying to find out about. Walters does caution that a similar motion is used by people who are experiencing depression. But the person's comments will signal you about their depression, as he'll mention such things as how bad things have gotten, or how blue he's been feeling, or how nothing seems to be going right for him. Of course, he may be depressed because he's done something wrong, and now it seems that you are about to prove that he's done it, and he'll have to face the unpleasant consequences.

➤ **Stress and signs of deception.**

According to Walters, all signals of deception are caused by stress. However, just because someone is stressed doesn't necessarily mean they're lying. Some behavioral symptoms we've touched upon that probably do indicate deception are profuse sweating, wringing of the hands, and biting one's lip.

Psychologist Aldert Vrij says in his book that other signs that someone is being deceptive would include when they blush or go pale, and/or have sweaty or cold hands. I've seen all of these during my interviews of criminal suspects. Of course, some people may be introverts or socially anxious, and they could exhibit blushing or sweaty hands just from nervousness. Navarro concurs that having sweaty hands does not necessarily mean that a person is lying to you. However, if it occurs in conjunction with another signal or two, it can be considered as a confirming sign that the individual is being deceitful.

In fact, Vrij states that expressive, extroverted people are usually more comfortable conversing with others, and they're more often believed by listeners than are introverts. This is ironic, because introverts tend to lie less and to commit fewer crimes than their more outgoing peers. But because of his outward friendliness and confidence, we seem to trust the social person more implicitly. (Once again, beware of the hearty smile and firm handshake of the salesman who doesn't know you from Adam's canary, but he's interested in you as a potential means of meeting his monthly sales quota.)

Often when a person considers the consequences of being caught in a lie, which could be severe, his nervousness causes him to feel generally fidgety, his cheek and neck tingly, and his mouth dry. But if he tries to consciously suppress his normal and natural reactions to these feelings, he'll come across as acting in an unnatural or wooden manner, and this should be noticed by the questioner.

Vrij comments on the importance of motivation in the way a person might act under questioning. For instance, if a person is a suspect in a murder case, he would be highly motivated (and probably highly emotional) during the interview, inasmuch as he wouldn't want to be thought of as a liar (or found out as a liar and a killer).

Also, he will make a strong effort to be seen as truthful. In such a case, Vrij states that the liar will likely suffer from what he calls a "motivational impairment effect." This will cause the person to exhibit rigid behavior and to seem as though his performance is rehearsed (which it likely is). After all, no guilty person is going to go into a critical police interview without a well-thought-out story to tell.

Vrij also makes what I consider a valid point by citing experiments that he was involved in with Winkel and Koppelaar in 1991. These experiments were a study of possible "cross-cultural non-verbal communication errors" that could be made during cross-cultural interviews. The studies asked both white and black volunteers to use assigned white or black gaze behavior, self-manipulations (such as scratching one's arm), speech disturbances, and hand and finger movements. The outcome of the interviews was that regardless of whether the interviewee was white or black, the white police interviewers determined that a higher percentage of the people who used the "typical" black patterns of behavior were thought to be lying during the interview. That is, 72 percent of the people using black non-

verbal responses were thought to be "suspicious" in their answers, irrespective of their actual race. Only 41 percent of those
using typical white behavioral responses (no matter what race)
were considered "suspicious."

➤ **Movement.**

Vrij mentions in his book that many people who are lying
show a decrease in movements in their legs, hands, and fingers.
He comments that many law enforcement personnel think that
the opposite behavior is a sign of lying. They watch for a suspect to be jittery in his behavior. But Vrij contends that liars
will be thinking harder to tell their story so that it will seem believable, and they will, therefore, show fewer movements.

I think from my experience that they will also, especially if
they're experienced criminals, attempt to act relaxed and honest
during the interview. Another arm signal to watch for is what
Walters calls "cocooning," in which the person appears to be
hugging himself, wrapping his arms and hands around his body.
This indicates that the person is experiencing emotional pain
and that he's withdrawing from the conversation. I've noted
several suspects performing this particular movement during jail
interviews.

Variations from the usual way that people look or act when
they're talking could be indicative of deceptive behavior. The
better you know a person's normal reactions and expressions
and mode of talking, the better chance you have of noting when
these things change. Once you're alerted to the possibility that
the person has altered his usual ways of acting, then you can
pay attention to what he may be trying to put over on you.

➤ **Truth in microexpressions.**

You should always be alert to watch for microexpressions
that show what the person is truly feeling. Dr. Lieberman refers
to these as "initial reaction expressions," and he notes that they
reflect the person's true feelings. He also gives the cogent suggestion that even if you can't read what the expression was relating, the fact that the expression changes quickly from the initial one to another one could be a clue that the person is now

trying to mask the way he really feels.

You might have noticed these expressions when you run into someone and they flash a look of "Oh, no. Not now." Maybe they're in a hurry to get somewhere and don't have time to talk to you. Or perhaps they'll show a look of "Oh, damn, here he comes" when they know you're probably going to chastise them about a mistake they made at work. In regard to the question of whether a person is lying or not, these expressions will usually be one of shock or dismay when the interviewee realizes that you know more about the situation than he gave you credit for.

Another type of expression denotes anger. While we usually recognize this particular look, it could be given as a microexpression that only lasts a split second before the person who shows it is able to control it. And sometimes you've just made the person upset by asking indelicate questions. But anger is a response that is not unlikely from a person who's been asked something that makes him feel vulnerable to being caught and punished for doing something.

Another item to watch for, notes Dr. Lieberman, is whether the expressions a person makes are consistent with what he's saying, and whether the timing of the expression and the verbal statements seems natural. For instance, if someone says they're angry with you, but they don't show an angry expression until after they make the statement, it's likely faked. If a person nods when he is saying something, it's probably true. But if he doesn't nod until after he's finished making his statement, then he's consciously trying to look honest.

Tension causes people to show a number of expressions, and Navarro lists some of these as squinting, compression of the lips (to where they seem to disappear), nostril flaring, quivering of the mouth and lips, and tightening of the muscles along the jaw line. Tension also produces stiffness of the neck and a lack of movement in the body. As tension is produced by the stress of lying, these can all act as possible indications that a person is not being forthcoming.

Paul Ekman, a psychologist who specializes in studying how to detect body language and facial expressions related to lying, has found that anger causes a person to lower the eyebrows. I'd suggest that there will probably be a look of menace in the person's eyes, as well. Also, anger will create a narrowing of the lips. This will create a hard look, I assure you. So, you should be able to discern whether the person is angry with you or is under stress from trying to answer your questions. Decide whether he looks more like a panther or a trapped rabbit. That should give you your answer.

Vrij comments that these microexpressions must be watched for intently during an interview. They won't always occur, and when they do, they may happen in 1/25th of a second. Thus, if you blink at the same time (which usually takes about a tenth of a second), you will miss the expression altogether.

Supposedly, an observer trained in how to read microexpressions can detect with accuracy up to 80 percent of persons who are lying. And when Ekman, O'Sullivan, Friesen and Scherer conducted a study in 1991, they found that if observers also watch for other clues to deceptive behavior, in addition to being aware of any microexpressions displayed, the success rate in identifying both truthful and deceptive behavior was 86 percent. This might be a reason for having another investigator watching the interview. The interviewer is often not positioned where he or she can observe all of the bodily movements of the person being interviewed. There may be a table between them, and also the interviewer may miss some signals when he jots down a record of the interview.

The other investigator can even observe the interview through a one-way mirror. Through this method, he can take notes or record what the interviewee says. He might catch a microexpression that the interviewer misses. He will be able to see expressions and other body language the interviewee uses while the interviewer is distracted by writing down notes. And he'll be much better positioned to watch all the body language signals that the interviewee is sending out through movements of his trunk and extremities. He'll likely be better able to observe when a comment that the interviewee makes is incongruent with his bodily actions. Also, he'll be in a position to offer another opinion as to whether the man acted guilty of the crime in question.

I didn't notice O.J. Simpson making many body movements during his trial. He seemed almost in a state of stupefaction during most of the trial. But he was quite animated and demonstrative when trying on the glove found at the murder scene and the one found at his residence (which matched). And why did they have him wear that pair of underlying gloves? Anyway, he pulled and tugged and strained visibly, and quite helplessly, as we could all see, eventually shrugging and giving a pitiable expression indicating that he just couldn't get the gloves on, no matter how doggedly he might try.

And did you catch the expression on his face when he heard the verdict of "not guilty" of the stabbing murders of his wife, Nicole Brown Simpson, and her friend, Ronald Goldman? I got the feeling that it was more than an expression of relief or justification. I've seen people be judged not guilty, and they usually inhale in relief and smile. They don't wince and look as if they're about to cry as O.J. did. To me, it looked like an expression of "Oh, my God, I can't believe it; I got off."

➤ **What about the <u>polygraph</u> and other machines?**

Concerning possible bodily responses that occur when someone lies, Aldert Vrij comments that when a person experiences a fear of getting caught when he's being questioned, or he has guilty feelings when lying about what he did or didn't do, or even when he gets excited during his periods of lying to someone, small physiological reactions occur in his body. These include an increased heart rate, higher blood pressure, and additional palmar sweating. The modern polygraph machine (or lie detector) will measure a person's pulse rate, blood pressure, respiration rate, and skin conductivity (sweaty palms).

The examiner will <u>measure</u> the tested individual's responses when asked control questions, then compare the results to differences in the physical changes that the person exhibits when he's being questioned about the crime or another matter. Studies by psychologists have reported that examiners are accurate in their assessments of truthfulness about 80 percent of the time. They will find false indications of lying more often than they err in concluding someone is telling the truth.

Of course, the examiner's training, experience, and individual skills in interviewing and operating the machine will affect the outcomes. And there have been indications that pathological liars, who feel little remorse or anxious reaction when they lie, are more apt to "beat" the polygraph than folks who react more normally. Also, certain ways of causing false readings have been put forward that seem to work, such as tightening the anus, or pushing a toe against a tack in one's shoe, biting the tongue, or other similar methods of causing oneself pain and thus stress at the times that one wishes to combat or confuse the readings the examiner receives.

Just as a side note, there was a particular defense attorney in Kansas who always used to comment, when mention was made of the use of the polygraph machine, that he'd once had a client who claimed he was Jesus Christ, and the man had been given and passed the polygraph as to that unlikely scenario. Also, just as when we attempt to assess a person's truthfulness by the way he reacts to a question, the telltale signs he may give only indicate anxiety or anger or fear. We often associate these reactions with lying, but they can occur independently.

There's no specific physiological reaction that occurs in the body that will specifically show a lie has been told. Everything must be read in relation to the way the person usually speaks and acts, as well as in relation to the particular situation in which the person is being questioned. I've interviewed men who were very nervous and anxious, but they were later determined to have no guilty knowledge of the crime in question, and they didn't participate in it.

However, if a person you've interviewed or questioned has

displayed several signals that are associated with stress and nervousness, and there are logical reasons to think he was involved in the wrongful act in question, then you can be reasonably certain that you should continue to suspect him. You can question him further or check other pertinent facts about the wrongdoing with respect to whether he could have been involved. You won't drop him as a good possible person to have carried out the illegal or immoral act.

The polygraph machine, which I've asked examiners to use on several occasions in cases I was working, is a simple-looking affair, packed in a case the size of an ordinary briefcase. It has dials with knobs, a roll of paper, ink vials, and styluses that move back and forth to record the various readings. The machine makes heavy black marks on the scrolling paper when questions are asked of the subject. A blood pressure cuff, an elastic band that encircles the chest, and fingertip clamps of the type you'll see in a hospital will all be placed on the subject of the test in order to obtain the readings that need to be recorded.

There are two different types of polygraph examinations usually given. The first is called the Control Question Test, and it's the one used by the FBI examiners. In this type of exam, the subject is given three types of questions. Neutral questions are ones which are of no relevance to the crime or other matter being investigated and which should not cause any emotional response in the interviewee. This type of question might be something like: "Is your name Sally?" (A truthful answer in this hypothesis is yes, and it should cause Sally no consternation.) Another such question could be, "Are we currently in Chicago?" Again, if they are, the interviewee can answer "yes" with no concern and no physical reaction.

Then the polygrapher will ask a control question. This should be a question that in a general way has to do with the crime (such as asking about having ever stolen anything when the crime in question is the theft of a rare and highly valuable diamond pendant). The object of asking these questions is to elicit a guilty response by the interviewee and to (hopefully) note some guilty physiological response from him or her.

The question might be in the vein of: "During your school years, did you ever take anything from another student without his or her knowledge?" (The examiner will have previously embedded in the interviewee's mind that he is seeking any indications that the person may be the type of individual to have done the crime in question.) Thus, if the interviewee lies and says "No," he should react to the question. And he will have shown an arousal, which the examiner can use as a baseline to determine when the person is lying. (Incidentally, I don't know whether I'd mess up the baseline questioning in an instance such as this. Just because I personally don't believe in stealing other people's property, I can't recall any instance when I ever took anything from anyone. This is considered a rarity.)

Then when a relevant question is asked concerning the crime in question, the polygraph examiner will have a basis for detecting whether the person is telling the truth or lying in response to that question. The question would then be along the nature of, "Did you steal the diamond pendant that belonged to Jennifer?" The person's reaction to this question should be indicative of whether he or she is lying or telling the truth.

Another method of questioning used with the polygraph machine is called the Guilty Knowledge Test. In this format, the examiner will attempt to detect lying or truthfulness about whether the person knows anything about how a crime was committed and who was involved in it. So, a question might be, "Do you know who took the diamond pendant?" The idea is that a person with guilty knowledge about a crime should react physiologically when asked or shown something associated with the crime that only the perpetrator or someone who knows about the details of the crime should be aware of.

For instance, if an examiner were asking O.J. Simpson a question in this format, he might say something like, "The killer lost something at the scene of the crime. Did he lose this?" Then he would, in order, show him a handkerchief, a T-shirt, a pencil, a face mask, and a black glove. If O.J. had done it, he would show a definite reaction to the black glove and no reaction to the other items displayed. Or if the knife had been found at the scene, they might show O.J. a series of knives, including the actual knife used in the killings.

As you might imagine, there should be no interruptions of the test. No noise or other distractions should be allowed in the vicinity of where the examination is being conducted. The test should be done in a simple room with only the examiner and the person being questioned present in the room at any time during the test.

Aldert Vrij noted that the results from studies of the effectiveness of the tests showed substantial differences between the two types. In the Control Question Test, it was determined that the machine and examiner do a good job of detecting guilty persons. The detection rate was 73 percent for them. The rate for detecting innocent people was lower at 66 percent. However, 9 percent were incorrectly classified as innocent, and 13 percent were falsely determined to be guilty. There were some inconclusive tests that were not entered into the results.

In the Guilty Knowledge Test, there was a good deal of accuracy in detecting when people were innocent of the deed in question. The detection rate was 96 percent. So, only 4 percent of innocent people were falsely found to be guilty of lying. It should be noted that in this type of test, there is no inconclusive reading for the results. The detection rate for guilty suspects was 82 percent, however, this meant that there was a false positive rate of 18 percent, wherein the test detected innocent people as being guilty.

> **The super lie detector?**

Mention is made in an article called *Duped*, written by Margaret Talbot in the July 2, 2007, issue of *The New Yorker* magazine about a new method of detecting lying. It's called fMRI (functional magnetic resonance imaging), and it is a form of MRI scanning of the brain. The premise behind the procedure is that when the brain uses oxygen to perform certain tasks, there will be a necessary rise in the level of blood in the area of the brain that controls those tasks.

This will be visible through use of the machine because oxygenated blood has magnetic properties that make it readable by the machine. Thus, a scan will produce images of glowing parts of the brain. And since the brain supposedly must work harder in order to fabricate lies than to initiate true statements, those areas of the brain will require more oxygenated blood, and they'll show up more brightly on the scan results.

Joel Huizenga has started a company in San Diego, California, that's based on this technology. He calls it No Lie MRI. Although the fMRI has been used primarily to detect neurological disorders, Huizenga wants to use it to provide a foolproof method of detecting lies for clients with presumably large bank accounts (each machine costs three million dollars).

Huizenga got the idea when he saw an article in *Time* magazine about Daniel Langleben, a psychiatrist and neuroscientist at the University of Pennsylvania, who had performed an experiment with the fMRI concerning deceptive behavior. When people were inside the MRI machine, he would ask them to make statements, some of which were true and some of which were lies. Langleben noted that when the subjects told lies, three areas of the cerebral cortex of the brain would show extra activity. To Huizenga, this meant he should leap into action.

He had enlisted about a dozen clients at the time of Talbot's article, at a clip of ten thousand dollars per test. Companies and the U.S. government are supposedly interested in the idea. In fact, Huizenga has hired a former FBI agent (not me) to liaison with government agencies. So, the future of lie detection may or may not be greatly affected by this technology. Obviously, the people who are reading this book to learn about how they can detect lies will probably not place a call to California for a ten thousand dollar appointment. (That's presuming that they can get the object of their distrust to agree to lie down motionless in the machine in the first place.)

> **The future of lie detection?**

Some influential people seem convinced of the validity and effectiveness of the fMRI method. Ms. Talbot mentioned an article in *Wired* magazine called "Don't Even Think About Lying." The writer of the article was effusive about the future of the fMRI, stating that it would alter many entities, including the judicial system and the security business. However, it seems that there are some problems with the procedure. Technicians have reported that the machines are very touchy (grumpy, perhaps), and that some days they don't perform well. Also, just as in any MRI, if the person being tested is too fidgety, the results won't be accurately recorded.

When Langleben conducted a test with volunteers attempting to lie about playing cards they'd seen, the results were that the fMRI procedure was able to tell the truthful subjects from the ones who lied in 77 percent of the tests. And, remember, the accuracy rate of the polygraph examination has been around 80 percent. It seems that more refinement of the fMRI procedure could well be in order.

Nancy Kanwisher, a cognitive scientist at M.I.T., has been critical of the potential use of the fMRI procedure in detecting falsehoods. She points out that when the brain is required to do any task that is somewhat complex, such as making up a believable lie, many parts of the brain light up, not just three particular ones. And Elizabeth Phelps, a cognitive neuroscientist at N.Y.U., makes the argument, which I consider to be valid, that perhaps someone who is a pathological liar or a sociopath who doesn't react strongly when he tells a lie, will not show the same cognitive results during the test as a normal, socialized individual.

> **Another technological possibility?**

As I was describing this book briefly to my optometrist, Dr. Verne Claussen, of St. Mary's, Kansas, he held up a twelve-inch-long, black, cylindrical object about an inch in diameter, and said, "Did you know that a long time ago they used this retinoscope in a lie detecting test?" I said that I didn't, and he told me that he believed the test was done at Ohio State University in Columbus, Ohio, sometime in the nineteen-fifties. The idea was that when someone was asked a question to which he gave a truthful response, there would be no change in the focus of his eye. However, it had been observed that when a person lied, a change of focus of their ocular lens could be seen through the retinoscope.

According to his memory, Dr. Claussen said that the retinoscope was tested against the polygraph machine of the day, and that it performed just as well as that machine. My research did find a mention of a Dr. W.D. Bates of New York who had mentioned the lie-detecting properties of the retinoscope when interviewed for a book in 1971. Otherwise, I could not find that this method of lie-detecting had been explored. Perhaps it will be in the future.

➤ **More technology in catching lies.**

Another method for detecting lies was explored by Aiden Gregg, a British psychologist, which he calls a timed antagonistic response alethiometer test (Tara). In his testing, subjects were asked to answer questions using a computer keyboard. Gregg found that when the interviewees lied in response to a question, they were slower in beginning to type their answers than when they told the truth. The quantifiable results were that the people tested began their answers in 1.2 seconds when they were giving truthful responses, and in 1.8 seconds when they were responding with falsities.

This seems consistent with other results of tests to discern liars, in that people who lie verbally are often hesitant in their responses, and they speak more slowly than those who tell the truth. They also have more pauses during their comments. And they may stammer and/or use a greater number of "uhs" or "ers" in their remarks.

➤ **The ultimate in lie detecting.**

In fact, I recently saw a former means of supposedly scientific truth-detection on the TV sitcom *Scrubs*. In this episode, Heather Graham was playing a doctor who had befriended Elliot, a regular female doctor on the show. Elliot was imagining

Heather in a Wonder Woman costume, and in that getup, Heather proceeded to use her golden "lasso of truth" on another person on the show. Of course, the guy immediately spilled his guts. Perhaps the circular design of the MRI machine was a subconscious effort to replicate the round loop of the lasso. Let's hope it proves as effective.

➤ **Other possibilities.**

An article dated April 15, 2008, on the msnbc Health & Fitness website, written by Rob Shmerling, Harvard Health Publications, was titled "The Lie of Lie Detectors." This article spoke about two recent studies showing new ways of detecting when someone was lying. The first method used a brain scan. It showed that when volunteers lied, the anterior cingulated gyrus became activated as shown by an increase in blood flow to that part of the brain.

The other study used a method called "thermography," in which a high-resolution thermal imaging camera was used and showed that when people lied, there was an increased blood flow in the area around the eyes and other parts of the face, which produced a rise in heat in those areas. When people in the test told the truth, they didn't have the increased level of heat in those areas. And the technology used to measure the results was much simpler and easier to operate than a standard lie detector machine.

Thus Shmerling indicated that these two methods might become more important in determining lying than the standard lie detector machine. This is because the current lie detector doesn't directly measure when someone lies, but rather shows the amount of stress produced in normal, healthy persons when they lie. Today's machines measure an increase in respiration, galvanic skin responses, blood pressure, and heart rate. And it's been shown that these reactions can be manipulated by someone knowing how to do it, with a resultant false outcome.

So, I think the best course at this time is for you to learn and remember the various "tells" that people show when they're lying. The machines—polygraph or fMRI—will likely not be available to us for use. And it seems that we can probably achieve about the same results from a knowledgeable approach to detecting deception with our own mental powers.

8

How Lying Affects Daily Life

> ## ➢ Deception in our world.

Dr. Lieberman states the premise succinctly: "But we live in a world of deception. And whether you want to play or not, you're in the game." And as you've undoubtedly surmised by now, that's the current state of the matter in America and probably throughout the world. So, in order to play the game the best we can, I believe we should learn all we can about how to detect deception.

If you ever question what difference it really makes, consider the study results released in January, 2008, by the Center for Public Integrity and the Fund for Independence for Journalism, which are both nonprofit journalism organizations, about the false statements made by top Bush administration officials which led the U.S. into war with Iraq in March, 2003. The study noted 935 false statements made in the two years preceding the start of the war. The campaign to shape U.S. opinion about the potential attack included many claims that Iraq had weapons of mass destruction or was trying to make or obtain them, and that they had strong ties with al-Qaeda.

The study said flatly that these assertions were made by the usual suspects—Bush, Powell, Rice, Rumsfeld, Wolfowitz, and White House press secretaries Fleischer and McClellan—and they were plainly false. Therein lies the lesson. If <u>lying can start</u>

a violent war that threatens to destabilize Mideastern countries and set them at odds with the Western World, causing death and destruction for years on end, then you must admit it's a powerful force of evil.

On a more mundane level, an online article by Hara Estrof Marano for *MSN Health & Fitness*, on November 7, 2007, related that, "Lying is one of the great facts of social life." She mentions that most people fib once or twice a day. Relationships involving adolescents and their parents are riddled with lies. College students practice important deceptions with their mothers in every other telephone conversation.

Dating couples tend to deceive each other both about past relationships (number and intensity), and about current attractions or indiscretions which they'd rather keep secret. Married couples lie to one another less regularly, but the lies tend to be of more importance. Considering the crucial nature of their bond, the damage that can be done to the relationship makes the deception more critical.

Lying certainly affects all of us in our romantic relationships. I'll use the most familiar pattern of a man and a woman in a relationship as the most usual example of a social interaction. Several studies indicated that men and women are affected differently both when they lie and when they're lied to. In the studies, women asserted that they felt quite guilty and uneasy when they lied. Men were apt to be less concerned about the matter. When asked about serious lies they'd told and been told, the women described themselves as having been more affected emotionally by these lies than the men did. They tended to think more often about the fact they'd been lied to, and they were more resentful about the fact than men. Also, women more often felt that the lie seriously affected their relationship with the liar than the men seemed to feel.

At any rate, deception in one form or another is used regularly in the interactions between men and women. Dr. Ford notes that women often dress in a sexy mode to attract men, even though they may not be that interested in sexual activity.

And they will flatter the ego of their male partner in order to further the relationship.

In an article in *Redbook* magazine, 1993, Pamela Redmond Satran puts forward the idea that most deceptions used during interactions between the sexes are white lies that are meant to help preserve the relationship. Both men and women will use these types of deceits. Sometimes it relates to things they've done in the past (both sexes, but especially women tend to reduce the number of sexual partners they've had in the telling), and sometimes it speaks to things they've done during the relationship that they'd rather their partner didn't find out about.

Of course, it's well-documented that many men, in order to enter into sexual contact with a woman, will profess intimate feelings that they may not have, or claim unfelt love for their present partner, or even offer the possibility of marriage. The downside of all this play-acting is that when deception is detected in the dynamics of a love relationship, the outcome is usually negative for both parties and damaging to the stability of the bond between the partners. Such deceptions will sometimes even end the relationship.

Dr. Joyce Brothers, a well-known psychologist, related in an article in the June, 1996, edition of the *Reader's Digest* entitled "7 Lies That Men Tell Women," that men often lie because of their egos, and their deceptions usually relate to trying to conceal some damaging or embarrassing information, or to inflate their image. The first lie Dr. Brothers notes is: "Me? I graduated at the top of my class." This is an obvious attempt to impress a woman the man is interested in. But it will, of course, be found out if the relationship lasts very long.

Another prevarication is, "Of course I like your friends." I'd suggest that this might also be used regarding her mother. The man is trying to make his latest lady friend like him. George Strait sings about this in a country song named, "You Know Me Better Than That," about how he's told his new girlfriend that he loves the opera and her cat, but . . . .

Two other exaggerations are: "That dress isn't too tight. It looks great!" and "Honey, you're the best (sexually)." Of course, he's just trying to make her feel good. But say, for instance, the dress really is too tight and her girlfriend tells her so, or she splits it when sitting down. Then the relationship is damaged because the woman realizes he was lying all along.

Another sample of the seven lies includes, "No, I can't call you. I don't even know where I'll be." This may be true, or it may be a cover-up for a drinking bout with his friends, or a way to hide an affair. He's either avoiding his significant other or hiding something he doesn't want her to know. I'd suggest that most women won't fall for that one, especially in this age of the ubiquitous cell phone. The old "I couldn't find a pay phone" bit just won't wash anymore. I suppose the new take on that one is, "My cell phone lost its charge."

Dr. Brothers furnished another common lie: "They're downsizing at work. But don't worry, they won't get me." In this deception, he's both protecting his partner from pain and uncertainty and massaging his own ego. He's trying to convince both his partner and himself that he's too important and useful to be let go. This one could potentially be catastrophic if he does succumb to the riff in workers. And with the way jobs are being slashed in the present economy, this has become a major and critical lie.

"Sure, I'll mow the lawn—as soon as this crick in my back goes away." Dr. Brothers says that in using this type of lie, the man is trying to avoid a woman's ire. He often feels that his mate is nagging him or giving him a big hassle about doing some work or going somewhere, and he's trying to avoid the task and not be thought badly of. He might even be able to assuage the woman and also earn her pity. I'm sure this one is used universally and often. And to my mind, it somewhat smacks of the old excuse, "Not tonight, honey, I have a terrible headache." Different strokes for different sexes, I suppose.

Just as an informal experiment to see how prevalent lying is in our society, I checked the movies available on television for one evening's fare. I didn't even write all of them down, because almost every one included some thematic element concerning lying. But here are some of the ones I saw:

Brokeback Mountain, with Heath Ledger, 2005, is a movie where two cowboys have a secret romance, even though one is married. I saw that one, and there was a lot of deception, avoidance, and lying going on there. The cowboys were lying to their boss, to the one man's wife, and to the rest of society in general. But it was all in the name of love, I suppose. And we'll do a lot of things for that, won't we?

Rosanna Arquette starred in a 1998 movie called *Crimes of Passion: I Know What You Did.* In that one a female defense attorney kills a rapist, then she must keep the evil deed secret from her detective boyfriend. Of course, most of us have secrets to hide, but hopefully, they don't approach the level of having committed a murder or other heinous crime. Still, the premise makes for good drama.

Another feature available on the evening's fare just happened to be one that is almost a classic for our study of lying. In *A Few Good Men,* 1992, starring Tom Cruise, Jack Nicholson, and Demi Moore, Navy lawyers defend Marines for a murder committed at Gitmo (Guantanamo Naval Base). And if you've ever seen that one, you'll likely not forget the scene in which the character played by Tom Cruise (a Navy defense attorney) tells the character played by Jack Nicholson (a tough Marine officer) that he wants to know the truth about what happened the day in question. Jack Nicholson gives Cruise a look that would mow down a hayfield and says, "The *truth?* You couldn't *handle* the truth."

Nick Nolte stars in a 2006 movie named *Off the Black,* in which a dying umpire asks a young ballplayer to pose as his son at the umps upcoming high-school reunion. I haven't seen that one, but I would imagine it follows the pattern seen in many sitcoms where the characters try to pull off some ruse and the whole thing embarrassingly unravels. Still, there's usually a lesson learned that goes deeper than that of not trying to deceive people. The participants often learn something about themselves that they didn't fully realize before.

In the 2005 movie *Into the Blue,* with Paul Walker, Jessica Alba, and Scott Caan, four divers cross paths with drug smugglers. In that one, everyone's lying about how they haven't found a sunken treasure. And with the drug dealer's lost load improbably ending up in the same locale as the sunken treasure, everyone lies about not having seen that and not being able to bring it up, as well.

Tom Hanks gives us the leading performance in *The Da Vinci Code,* a 2006 thriller based on Dan Brown's runaway bestselling novel. In this story, dark secrets from the past of the Catholic church are about to be exposed if Hanks doesn't get killed first. Of course, in real life, there was much controversy over what was true and what was false in this fictional tale, showing that we do sometimes get passionate over the veracity of certain ideas.

The title gives it away in the 1991 movie starring Goldie Hawn and John Heard named *Deceived.* I don't recall having seen this one, but from the description, there seem to be layers of deception going on. An art expert suspects her husband of forgery, and then she suspects him of not even being her husband. And we thought we had troubles.

I happened to have recently watched the 2006 movie starring Nicolas Cage, Ellen Burstyn, and Kate Beahan, called *The Wicker Man.* It's described as being one in which a lawman finds sinister forces at work as he searches for a missing child. I won't spoil the plot, but there is a huge secret being kept from the detective as those he investigates conspire to fool him.

Non-disclosure is a big part of many of these movies. And when the non-disclosure leads to not revealing the whole truth about a matter, to the point where someone doesn't understand the concept of the matter involved, then it's deceptive. When the audience knows or suspects that there's a big secret being kept, they'll wait through a lot of scenes to find out what it is. After all, most people want some mystery in their lives. And they want to see if they're clever enough to guess or figure out what the answer is. Hopefully, the techniques you'll learn in this book will help you be more effective at doing so.

Julia Roberts is caught in a terrible situation in the 1991 film *Sleeping With the Enemy.* As the battered wife of a yuppie neat-freak, she realizes the only way to get out of her abusive relationship is to concoct a lie. She fakes her death at sea, and then she flees from Cape Code to Iowa. No, not heaven—Iowa. I suppose that's about as far as she can get from water activities, so she feels safe. However, we all realize that her ruse must be found out, or there's no plot.

In the 2005 movie *Walk the Line* with Joaquin Phoenix and Reese Witherspoon, the description tells us that it's the story of music legends Johnny and June Carter Cash. I thought it was a powerful movie with terrific portrayals by the stars. However, it did reveal that Johnny had some problems that he tried to keep hidden. He was shown as being a drug user, and he didn't walk the loyalty line too steadfastly before marrying June.

Blind Trust, a 2007 film starring Jessica Capshaw, Chad Willet, and Art Hindle, shows an innocent woman who learns sinister secrets about her lawyer after he defends her for murder. I'm not familiar with this one, but it seems there are deceptions abounding. And, once again, there are those deep dark lies which we love to learn about.

Another big secret is kept by Ben Stiller in the 2007 version of *The Heartbreak Kid.* Michelle Monaghan appears in this romantic comedy in which Stiller, while on the honeymoon with his new bride, falls in love with another woman. Didn't something like this happen to Jerry Seinfeld? I'll bet it's tough to tell your new partner while on your honeymoon that you're trading him or her in for a new model. Ah, well. It seems the rich and famous play by different rules.

More ordinary folks are afflicted by deception, too. For instance, in the 1999 film version of the comedy, *The Out-of-Towners,* starring Steve Martin and Goldie Hawn, the Ohioans, after suffering many adversities in the hostile environs of New York, find themselves also being victims of each others' deceptions. Martin hasn't told Hawn that he lost his job. She has withheld information about their daughter which has hurt them in their metropolitan adventure.

When Hawn confronts Martin about his lie, he retaliates with a comment about her evasiveness. She says she didn't really lie about the matter. Martin asks what she did, then. And Hawn provides a response that's very telling in our passive acceptance of lying in America. She tells him, with a bit of irony, "They weren't lies, they were an incremental accumulation of half-truths."

In the 2008 movie, *Transsiberian,* Ben Kingsley plays a police inspector assigned to a Russian narcotics squad. He tracks a couple who transport large amounts of drugs and money. He questions a woman he thinks knows where the man who last had the knapsack full of drugs is located, During the interview, he says, "In my country we have a saying: 'With lies you can go forward in life, but you can never go back.'" I guess lies do leave a noticeable trail in their wake.

The last example I'll mention is the 2006 movie, *Basic Instinct 2,* with Sharon Stone, David Morrissey, and Charlotte Rampling. In this story, the character Catherine Trammel finds herself on the wrong side of the law in London. It sounds to me as if she's been lying again. Come to think of it, I may tune in to see if she's up to any of her other old tricks.

Yep, just a glance at one night's offerings on the boob tube shows us there's a whole lot of lying going on. Fiction does imitate reality, even though it often exaggerates it. And I'm convinced that the powers that be in Hollywood fully appreciate that lying and cheating and deceiving are ubiquitous in our society. Besides, those darker elements of the human condition do make for good drama, comedy, and romance stories.

❖ **Lie detection solves a major case.**

In a strange way, I'm convinced that the prevalence of lying in our society helped the FBI identify Tim McVeigh and Terry Nichols as being the Oklahoma City bombers. Having worked on that case, I was in a position to learn just how that dynamic unfolded. The bombing of the Alfred P. Murrah Federal Building in Oklahoma City took place on April 19, 1995, at 9:02 a.m. The powerful bomb hidden in a Ryder truck demolished the entire north face of the nine-story building, killing 168 people and wounding and maiming over 800 others. Nineteen children, most of them playing in a day care facility on the second floor of the building, were among the casualties.

A man parked his small red sports car about a block from the Murrah Building that morning. He had just stepped out of the vehicle when the blast went off. He stood there in shock, looking toward the scene of the explosion. Suddenly, a large piece of metal, the axle-housing of the Ryder truck that contained the bomb, came whirling in his direction like a giant boomerang and smashed into the windshield of his car, stopping just short of striking his ten-year-old son who was sitting in the back seat.

Law officers cleaned a layer of grime off the truck part in order to find the vehicle identification number stamped thereon. With the number located, a telephone call ascertained that the Ryder truck was a rental. FBI agents then conferred with the Ryder Truck Corporation at their headquarters in Florida to determine that the truck in question had been rented in Junction City, Kansas.

The Ryder Truck had been rented at a business located in the territory in which my Topeka Resident Agency investigated crimes. Two of our agents drove to the rental business and obtained a copy of the rental contract, as well as getting a sketch drawn of the renter from descriptions of those who had seen him. The man used the name Robert D. Kling when he signed the contract.

The agents also obtained a physical description of the man, as well as various pieces of information that indicated he'd been in the Junction City area for several days prior to the bombing. The location seemed inconvenient—a five-hour-drive from the target. The natural assumption, what with the knowledge of bomb-making required, was that the man may have had some connection with nearby Ft. Riley, an Army base.

I realized we'd have to canvass the area in Junction City and possibly at Ft. Riley to see if we could find some connection between the renter's description, sketch, and the name used on the truck rental contract, in order to fully identify the suspect. I drove to a location on Ft. Riley that we were using as a Command Center, where Army Office of Special Investigations agents, FBI agents, Bureau of Alcohol, Tobacco, and Firearms agents (experts in analyzing bomb blasts), Geary Co. Sheriff's Office members, and detectives from the Riley Co. Police Department were gathering.

I spoke with the agents who had questioned the man who rented the truck to the suspect. They had a copy of the rental contract, a description of the renter, and a sketch. The sketch looked like that of a young man who, from his short haircut, could likely be in the military.

We decided to go out in teams of two in order to canvass the town to see if anyone could identify the renter of the Ryder truck. Investigation would include contacting people at hotels, motels, gas stations, liquor stores, cafes, fast food places, and anywhere else it would be logical that a person coming to town for a few days might visit.

Garry Berges of the Geary County Sheriff's Office was my partner in the search. Soon, we went out to cover leads, trying to identify the renter of the truck. First, we tried half a dozen places in the area that were associated with the name Kling, in order to determine whether people there knew anyone named Robert D. Kling. With that accomplished with negative results, we turned to trying motels.

As I turned off the highway, I spotted two motels within a hundred yards of each other. I drove into the parking lot of the Dreamland Motel, a one-story place with about forty rooms. In the office, I talked with the manager of the motel, one Lea McGown. I said that we were investigating the Oklahoma City bombing, and I discussed how horrible it had been, with children and other people being killed. She agreed and seemed co-operative.

I told her the man had probably been in Junction City for three or four days prior to the bombing, and that he might have been driving a Ryder Truck. She said that one man who stayed there had driven a truck, and she thought he'd acted suspiciously with it. I asked her what he'd done.

She told me he had wanted to park the truck behind the motel, but she insisted that he park it in front. He parked on the asphalt, then got out and made sure the back end of the truck was locked. But as he knew Ms. McGown and her son were watching at the time, instead of raising the door and slamming it down, he leveraged the door down with his forearm to close it, and then he locked it. I knew this was strange behavior, and I could only conclude that he didn't want anyone seeing what was in the box of the truck.

I asked her, "Do you remember the man's name and what room he stayed in?" She looked out the glass window behind her and said, "He stayed in room 25, right there." It was thirty feet away. She'd seen him several times over the days he was there.

I asked to see the registration receipt, and she placed it on the counter. My partner and I studied the card as it lay there. The man had registered in the name Tim McVeigh. He had stayed there for four days prior to the bombing, checking out the day before the explosion. He had listed an address in Michigan and an Arizona license plate for a car he was driving when he arrived.

Another important factor was that the man had written the information on the receipt in a backward slanting handwriting, just like the name Robert D. Kling was written on the rental contract for the Ryder truck. Only four percent of people write with a backward slant. I was getting a good feeling in my gut.

I scooted the registration receipt into a paper bag, telling Ms. McGown that we needed to keep it as evidence. "Can you describe the man to me," I asked. She provided a description that matched the man who rented the Ryder truck. Then I showed her the sketch.

"That's him," she said. We'd go on to find three other people in the motel who had seen McVeigh and said he looked like
the man in the sketch. They'd also seen the Ryder truck and
could provide details about the man's comings and goings from
the motel.

Ms. McGown provided records of telephone calls made
from room 25. McVeigh had made four calls, two calls to a
Terry Nichols in Herrington, Kansas, and two to a local Chinese
restaurant. At the restaurant my partner and I learned they'd
been phoned by a man giving his name as Kling. They delivered
an order of food to him at Room 25 at the Dreamland Motel.

We sent the information by teletype to FBI Headquarters
and to our offices in Michigan, Arizona, and Oklahoma City.
The license tag listed on the registration card was invalid. Subsequent investigation by the FBI office in Michigan showed that
the address McVeigh furnished was good, and that McVeigh
and Terry Nichols had lived there for a year with James Nichols, Terry's brother. James stated that Tim McVeigh was an actual person, and that he believed that was his true name. The
Michigan office of the FBI found a valid Michigan driver's license registration for McVeigh. They obtained his height,
weight, and birth date from the driver's license bureau records.

Then a check of the FBI's National Crime Information
Center (NCIC) computer revealed that McVeigh had been arrested for speeding by an Oklahoma Trooper about sixty miles
north of Oklahoma City about 90 minutes after the bombing. A
search of the car had turned up a pistol, so McVeigh was being
held in custody for a hearing. The FBI then got an arrest warrant
served on him before he got out of jail. And we had a material
witness warrant issued for Terry Nichols.

A long interview was conducted with Terry Nichols. Afterwards, a search of his house and garage turned up a great deal
of incriminating evidence, including blue plastic fifty-five-
gallon barrels of the same type used to construct the ammonium
nitrate bomb, a receipt for the purchase of twenty-three gallons

of diesel fuel, a diesel fuel pump, and a receipt for the purchase of 1100 pounds of ammonium nitrate with McVeigh's finger-prints on it. (All these items included components of the type of bomb used in Oklahoma City.) Nichols was also arrested for the bombing and for having obtained materials for the bomb through theft and deception.

Subsequent investigation would show that the two of them conspired to build the bomb. They stole detonation fuses and used an alias to buy ammonium nitrate, and they constructed the bomb at a small lake outside Junction City. McVeigh drove the truck to Oklahoma City, parked it in front of the federal build-ing, and hustled away as the fuses to the explosives burned down.

A question that lingered in my mind was that we knew that McVeigh used the alias Kling to rent the Ryder truck and also to order the Chinese food, so why would he write his true name on the registration receipt when he checked into the motel? I asked Lea McGown if she had any idea why he might have done that. She had a theory which I found plausible.

"I thought he was a little suspicious. I've gotten some bad checks here," she said, "and sometimes damage to the rooms. So I talk to people when they're filling out the registration card to make it harder for them to think of some phony name to write down. If there's trouble, the police can find them easier with their real names and addresses."

So, once again, lying rears its ugly head. If people hadn't ripped off the manager of the Dreamland Motel, the FBI might not have gotten McVeigh's real name, at least, not before he was released on the speeding and gun charge. And if he'd been set free on bond, who knows where he might be today?

➤ **You mean we deceive *ourselves*?**

Another interesting facet of deception in daily life is the self-deception that we sometimes develop in order to help us face life and its disappointments. Ernst Kris, a psychoanalyst, wrote a paper in a 1956 issue of the *Journal of the American Psychoanalytic Association* called: "The personal myth: a problem in psychoanalytic technique." In this paper he explores self-deception and its ramifications, terming the result the "personal myth." He suggests that often people will develop this myth as a "story to live by." This is a person's own view of his idealized self in his relation to the world.

The personal myth is often used to deal with the low or questioned self esteem that people feel in dealing with the harsh realities of life. It helps protect them from psychic trauma. It is a delusion that a person uses to help him operate in the cruel and unforgiving world he faces. E.P. Lester mentioned in the Psychoanalytic Quarterly in 1986 in an article entitled "Narcissism and the personal myth," that such tendencies and actions are closely related to if not identical to a narcissistic personality.

I know that working as an FBI agent requires one to play many roles in dealing with people. Sometimes we have to be tough and aggressive. Sometimes we must be merciful and forgiving. Often we must commiserate with people about the afflictions they've received at the hands of members of the criminal element.

We learn to talk with people from all walks of life. Not just to make small talk, but to be able to communicate with them and earn their respect and co-operation and help in our efforts to solve crimes. It's not a form of self-deception or an outright deception of the other person, but it's a way to interact in the most advantageous way that will allow us to perform our job effectively.

Of course, everyone plays a role, or more accurately, various roles during their ordinary day. We may be loving and considerate parents, hard-nosed and blunt executives, brave firefighters, beneficent patrons of the arts, helpers in soup kitchens, ardent lovers, true and faithful friends, social cut-ups, patronizing supervisors, or reverent parishioners. Various circumstances call for different responses and even for different personas to handle them.

> **Sing those lyin' blues.**

Another influential part of our society is the song industry.

As anyone who has ever listened to country or pop or blues music well knows, there are many titles and voluminous song lyrics about cheating and lying. Much of it refers to relationships between men and women. But then, don't most of our social interactions have to do with that, too?

Toni Braxton sings a song entitled "Lies, Lies, Lies," in which she catches her man coming in late with the scent of cheap perfume about him and a guilty look on his face. That's all the evidence she needs that he's been cheating on her, and she sings that everything he says is just lies, lies, lies. At this point, she's had enough, so she packs up and says, bye-bye.

One of the early great country songs was written and sung by the all-time superstar of country music, Hank Williams. In "Your Cheating Heart," he admonishes his significant other that she'll cry and pine and toss and turn and walk the floor because her heart will punish her for the way she's treated him. It's a great salve to the feelings of the person who's been cheated on. And what could be better than a good country song to express your pain?

In "Little Lies," the lyrics of the song by Fleetwood Mac deal with the social white lies we've mentioned before. The song says that even though the couple can't make it together, and they're better off apart, that the singer would settle for a day to believe in her lover. The chorus is bittersweet, saying that the partner really can't disguise the way he feels. Still, she'd like for him to tell her some sweet little lies. And we know those would include professions of love and faithfulness.

Check out Pauline Hoegberg and "Feelgood Lies," talking about a plethora of white lies that run rampant through our relationships. She's mad at her boy friend, who thinks he's irresistible, saying that he's predictable and a faker with an alibi. She challenges him to look her in the eye and tell her those real good, feel good lies. But she doesn't want to play, and she's going to run away.

Dave Frishberg and S. (Josh) Frishberg wrote a song, recorded by the Short Sisters on *"The Short Sisters Short Tape,"* that epitomizes the message of this book, so I'll definitely have to include it here. It's called *"Blizzard of Lies,"* and it describes many of the lies with which we're bombarded regularly in our daily lives. You may have heard some of these phrases: He's in a meeting; you've won a prize; let's have lunch sometime; I'll get right back to you; I won't say a word; this is a great deal; the check's in the mail; it's fresh today; and this won't hurt a bit. Yep, as the song so rightly puts it, we're marooned in a blizzard of lies.

As the former U.S. President Harry "Give 'em hell" Truman was quoted as saying in *Look* magazine, April 3, 1956, "I never give them hell. I just tell the truth, and they think it is hell."

In the movie, *Swimming with Sharks,* 1994, Kevin Spacey utters the line, "Life is not like the movies. Everyone lies, and love does not conquer all." This is a sad realization, but probably true. Still, I believe we can learn to deal with life's untruthful situations more effectively.

On a more positive note (if perhaps sarcastic in tone), Clare Booth Luce comments that: "Lying increases the creative faculties, expands the ego, and lessens the frictions of social contacts." And as I study the content a bit more, I must admit she banged home a lot of nails with those hammering comments.

In the movie *Galaxy Quest,* Enrico Colantoni, plays the part of Malthesar, the leader of the Thermians, an alien race who has modeled its society on an American sci-fi adventure show they've seen from the television signals beamed into space. The Thermians believe the shows to be "historical documents" of true events. Four representatives of the Thermians travel to earth to try to convince Captain Taggart, played by Tim Allen, to help them fight against an evil General Sarris, who is intent on destroying their race.

Captain Taggart tries to explain that the show is just actors "pretending" to be space heroes. Malthesar reflects that their culture has only recently become aware of the concept of lying. He notes that General Sarris had lied by saying he would do one thing, and then doing the opposite. Sarris had promised them a peaceful treaty arrangement, and then he attacked them.

Still, Malthesar and the rest of the Thermians maintain their naïve faith in Captain Taggart and the rest of the crew, who seem somewhat able to play their parts in the real-life spaceship the Thermians have constructed based on the model from the TV show.

But when push comes to shove, Tim Allen is no match for the fierce General Sarris in the flesh. Sarris forces Allen to tell Malthesar the truth about who he is.

Jason Nesmith: "Malthesar, there's no such person as Captain Taggart. My name is Jason Nesmith, I'm an actor. We're all actors."

Sarris: "He doesn't understand. Explain as you would a child."

Nesmith: "We, uh, pretended."

(Malthesar gives a blank look.)

Nesmith: "We lied."

The show is based on the concept that the actors who play space adventurers in the *Galaxy Quest* television show must live up to their parts and carry out heroic acts in actual situations of life and death. They're forced to face many deadly foes and dangerous situations. And they find out whether or not they have the "real stuff" as brave wanderers in space. They must somehow be true to Captain Taggart's tag line, "Never give up. Never surrender."

And once again, to put the usage of deceptive words in historical perspective, we can go back to 496 BC, when Sophocles wrote in *Creusa*: "Truly, to tell lies is not honorable; but when the truth entails tremendous ruin, to speak dishonorably is pardonable."

Allow me to use one more comment by Mark Twain, who so often knew just how to phrase something so that humor would blunt the sharpness of the dagger thrusts of his words. He told us that, "A lie can travel halfway around the world while the truth is putting on its shoes." Well put, Samuel Clemens.

My purpose in this chapter was to show a bit of how our lives are saturated with various kinds of lies, deceptions, pretenses, falsities, and confabulations. I'm hopeful that by now you're convinced that what I've said is true, and that you must be more aware of deceptiveness around you, learn to spot it, and know how to deal with the person using it on you. In a way, we all have to look out for ourselves and our friends and loved ones.

Perhaps the methods you've learned in this book will help you do that. In the last chapter, I'll summarize the ideas we've mentioned in the earlier chapters. I hope that this will jog your memory and keep the basic principles of lie detecting uppermost in your mind.

9

Summary: Ten Secrets to Spotting Lies

> **O**kay, so people lie. What should you do about it?

You're now aware of how often people lie and that you
need to remain alert for signals of deception. In this chapter, I'll
recap the main points we've covered in the earlier parts of the
book. At the end, I'll provide a page that will encapsulate the
gestures and movements and postures that people often make
when they're trying to deceive. Also, I'll include the speech patterns, voice inflections, and syntax to be wary of when watching
for signs of lying. And though there are a great many mannerisms and actions to watch for, with concentration and practice, I
believe you'll soon find yourself being effective and confident
in spotting most of the lies that are sent your way.

Once again, I think it's best not to flaunt your new skills or
even to mention that you possess them. Your new abilities are a
good secret for you to keep close to the vest, like a great poker
hand. It lets you make your bets from a position of strength and
confidence. And I'll wager that you'll come out ahead more often in life now that you've acquired the knowledge set forth in
this book. It's akin to having a pair of aces in the hole. Don't
give away your advantage or reveal your special knowledge until all bets are down. If you never explain your secret, you'll
keep playing great hands for the rest of your life.

If you like, the summary page at the end of the chapter can
be removed or photocopied to give you a quick reminder of the

basic principles involved in detecting lies. This page will be set up under the first letter headings that spell out "To Spot a Lie." It's hoped that this shorthand manner of setting forth some of the highlights of our ways to detect deception will help you better recall the mannerisms to watch for. And if you don't recall some of the specifics involved in the summary, you can always go back and review the particulars of the various items of which you should be aware.

The Ten Secrets

1. Touching (mouth, nose, neck or throat, eyes, ears, objects)

Remember to watch for people who touch or partially cover their mouth when they're responding to something you've asked them. It's the old "say no evil" principle, where the person is basically trying to mask what he's said, or he's trying to prevent himself from saying it. At any rate, this particular mannerism is a strong one for indicating that the person is probably tossing some bull in your direction. Don't forget to dodge, partner.

The same principle applies when a person touches his neck or throat, or scratches his neck or cheek, or rubs the back of his neck. He's uneasy with the question you've asked or the situation you've said you want to discuss with him. He doesn't want to go there. These mannerisms are ones that indicate nervousness and/or anxiety. And there's a good likelihood that those feelings are produced because the person is uneasy thinking that you know or suspect something he doesn't want you to know. He's now trying to think of a way to lie his way out of the tight situation in which he finds himself.

Remember that chemicals called catecholamines will be dispersed in the prevaricator's system, causing his nose to swell slightly, which is uncomfortable. Also, his blood pressure will rise, accentuating the effect. He'll likely touch, or scratch, or vigorously rub a finger beneath his bothersome appendage to soothe the distressing feeling. Called the "Pinnochio effect," this is a reliable indicator that the person is telling a falsehood or is contemplating doing so.

The fibber may also rub his eye vigorously, which is a signal that he wants you to quit asking him questions and go away. It's a "see no evil" signal. He also may rub or tug at his ear, the "hear no evil" sign, reflecting his unease. Sometimes the liar's ears and cheeks and the back of his neck will get warm and red and even sweaty. Such blushing will often indicate that the person is either embarrassed or ill-at-ease because you've caught him in a lie, or you've put him into a situation where he feels he must tell a falsehood in order to avoid being found out about something he's done. He could even get that reaction from thinking that he must come clean and face the possible unwanted consequences of his prior actions.

Sometimes people being questioned become nervous and fidgety, and they'll use objects as a protective barrier between themselves and you. They may place a cup of coffee or a cold drink on their desktop between the two of you. They could start toying with a pen or paperclip or some other object on their desk or nearby table. This indicates tension and insecurity on their part. The object acts as a psychological shield for them against your intrusive questions and comments.

2. Omission (words, ideas, answers, clarifying statements)

Acts of omission are often difficult to detect. Someone may give you an answer to your question that seems to make sense and to be innocuous in content. Then, upon some reflection and study, you'll realize that what he said was incomplete. He hasn't addressed the core idea of what you asked him. He's been guilty of using nonspecific words or phrases, or he may have verbally danced around the subject. In this way, he's avoided answering the question you asked. He's probably leaving out telling details, thus making the answer seem frothy and without real meat to it.

Evasiveness by a person in answering your queries is a

strong sign that he is hiding the truth as to what he's done, said, or thought about something that affects you. You need to be aware of this failure to directly and specifically give a full and true answer to the gist of the question you've asked. It will take some more fishing, and exploring, and digging for the truth on your part in order to get the complete and authentic answers to your questions.

Also, you'll need to piece together various comments he's made to see whether they hang together as substantial answers to your inquiries. Don't get upset or rattled. Time is on your side if you stay calm and collected and just reason out what it is that he's not saying in response to the queries. If you question him evenly and incisively, he'll either have to answer more completely, or he'll have to more or less admit that he doesn't want to answer your questions. And that will tell you something about what's going on with him, won't it?

A good signal that someone is omitting something in the answer to your question is that he will use no clarifying details in his response. Most people will want to make sure that you understand their answer to a question. And while almost no one is as articulate or eloquent as to compose sentences that completely and thoroughly answer questions, we tend to fill in whatever blanks or uncertainties or possible ambiguities there are in our original comments by making additional statements that explain or refine or add texture to those previous remarks. If someone fails to add these clarifying details, he's likely to be hoping that you'll take his answer at face value and move on to some other subject. He doesn't want to dwell on the subject that you've brought up, as there's information there that he would rather you not know.

3. Speech (stuttering, mumbling, pausing, scrambling phrases, slurring, bad syntax, high voice pitch)

I think most of us tend to notice, at least subconsciously, when someone answers us and is afflicted by such verbal maladies as those mentioned above. We probably tend to think about the responses as being the result of the person being nervous about something, or perhaps having had too much to drink. Those may both be contributing factors, of course, but there are psychological factors at work in this situation, as well.

The person may be uncomfortable in answering your question because, once again, there is information associated with a full disclosure answer that he simply doesn't want you to know. The pauses in his normal speech pattern may indicate that he's taking longer to construct an answer that he feels will sound plausible to you but won't give away certain facts he wishes to keep hidden. And the longer such a conversation goes on, the more there is for the fibber to recall that he said earlier that he must make sure jibes with his present story.

The tension will mount for this person to the point where he may begin to stutter or slur his words and phrases. Now it should become clear to you that the person is overly nervous about the conversation. And if you don't already know the reason that particular line of questioning may be making the person uneasy, you should begin to ask yourself why that's the case.

Another signal of possible prevarication on the horizon is when a person who is normally well-spoken begins using bad syntax in his speech pattern. In this case, his desire to present an answer that makes sense but doesn't give away certain information probably overpowers his current capacity to smoothly and articulately phrase such comments.

Unusual speech errors are a strong signal that someone is lying. Most psychologists will mention that a person may have a higher-pitched voice when he's nervous about lying to you. I've noticed this phenomenon before in subjects I've interviewed. Some psychologists insist that the pitch won't rise enough to be discernible to human hearing. But I do think if you pay attention to the person as he speaks, you'll definitely notice a certain strain in his speaking voice which should indicate to you that nerves are influencing him as he attempts to answer your queries. If there's no special reason you know for this occurrence, you should review the question and answer in your mind to search for details that are omitted or portions of the answer that are glazed over without particular comment. The Devil may well be hidden in those unspoken or poorly articulated details.

4. Posture (stiff, leaning away, stonewalling, leaning sideways, shoulder roll, head jerks or shifts, blading the body)

Both the conscious and subconscious parts of your mind will note when another person exhibits body language that doesn't seem relaxed and normal. This is helpful, because often a person will give himself away as being uneasy or nervous in answering questions by his posture or body movements. If a person stiffens when you broach a certain line of questioning, you can be sure that he or she is not comfortable talking about the subject at hand. Of course, it won't always be because he's going to try to deceive you concerning certain aspects of the matter—he might just be uncomfortable talking about the subject—but you should consider that he's fibbing as a definite possibility.

Particularly if a person suddenly leans away from you, or he becomes rigid in his body language and tends to stonewall you in his response to your question, you should immediately become suspicious about his reaction. He may very well be trying to hide some piece of information or his feelings about a certain subject from you. It's possible that he's just trying to protect you from certain knowledge that he knows could possibly hurt your feelings.

Or it may be that he's trying to cover up for or disguise some action he took that he knows you won't condone. I would suggest that hesitation on his part might signal the first reaction about protecting your feelings. However, the other more abrupt and stronger signs such as his jerking his head away from you or doing a sudden shoulder roll might indicate that he's affected by a need to protect himself from getting in trouble with you.

5. Obfuscation (fake smile, ill-timed gestures, words unlike emotions, no use of contractions)

This type of behavior is simply an extension of the nervousness that the person trying to answer your query is feeling. It goes along with the stiffness in posture and the head jerks or other evasive body language she's using. It's a manifestation of her unease in trying to answer your questions in a reasonable-sounding way that won't give clues that she's lying or leaving out some important information. She's attempting to use what she considers to be normal gestures in presenting her answers to your questions. But because she's thinking so hard about how to phrase and articulate her answers, the additional attempts to present gestures that seem natural will often be ill-timed, awkward, and phony in appearance.

As we recall, a real smile cannot be faked. A phony smile only involves the lower part of the face, without engaging the muscles of the face that will cause a person's eyes to crinkle. It looks painted on and has no real liveliness to it. Be sure to assess why the person would be giving you a fake smile while making a statement or answering a question.

Also, we usually use contractions in our everyday speech patterns, and when a person suddenly begins speaking without them, her remarks will sound stilted and unnatural. Be aware that this is another signal she's feeling nervous and uncertain. Analyze not only her unusual physical appearance and stilted way of speaking, but be sure to scrutinize the content of what she's telling you for any omissions, weaknesses, holes, evasions, and illogical thinking.

Also, if the person is saying something that should evoke a corresponding emotion, but the emotional display doesn't seem to be there, she may be faking the statements. If you pay attention, you can usually spot when someone doesn't seem to be feeling and expressing the emotions you'd expect in connection with the content of what she's saying. If she's congratulating you on some accomplishment, but you sense her smile is lacking and her heart doesn't seem to be in what she's telling you, then she may actually be jealous of you or she doesn't really feel you deserve your award. And if she's responding to a question, you are right to be suspicious of her answer.

6. Tells (mimicking, denial, bridging, modifying, blocking, displacing, stalling, inclusion)

One indication that someone may be telling you a falsehood is when he repeats or mimics part of the question you just asked. This may be because he's been caught off guard by your query, and he realizes he's hesitated a bit too long in giving an answer. So, in order to get started on his response, he'll begin by repeating part of what you just said. His response may be something like, "No, I wasn't flirting with Linda. She just brought up something I found interesting, and we were having a discussion about it." You may draw your own conclusions about that answer.

When you're dealing with denial, the person is basically rejecting the reality of what happened and trying to suck you into buying his version of how the facts of the matter should be interpreted to give a more favorable impression of how he acted in the situation. He's actually trying to convince both you and himself, and possibly a jury, of his innocence. The best way to approach dismantling the façade he's trying to construct is to keep coming back to the actual facts that refute his reconstruction of the events. Keep returning to reality and the basics of what happened that make his argument fallacious and ridiculous. Don't buy into his pipe dream. Stay cool and collected and on track with your message, letting him know that you'll only see the facts in a reasonable and sensible way.

The use of bridging is a means of evasion. That is, the person will tell his story up to a certain point, and then he'll fast forward to another part of the story, as if the part that was "bridged" was not important. In actuality, it was probably the most crucial component as to his involvement in whatever activity you're asking about. Be sure to pay close attention to gaps in a story. They may not be oversights or ways of speeding up the story. They may actually "be" the story as far as you're concerned. When the details are determined about what was left out of the original telling, the story will likely take on a whole new dimension.

A person may use modifiers to make his statements sound as if they are valid and make sense. But in effect, he's allowing the person an escape hatch, a loophole, a way out of the tight situation he's in. Such phrases as "I almost never go there" might qualify. Or he might hit you with, "That's not something I would ordinarily do." The key to watch for is that the person is not totally denying that he did something, he's qualifying or modifying his possible participation in a way that seems to be indicating he did nothing wrong.

7. Attitude (creased forehead, grimaces, clenched fists, arms crossed, hands stuffed into pockets)

It always pays to take note of a person's general attitude when you're conversing with him. This makes it easier to assess whether his body language is commensurate with his verbal comments. It also may show whether he's inclined toward being deceptive. If someone is accused of performing an ugly act, and he doesn't exhibit some indignation or arousal, then something is definitely askew with his attitude. Most folks would not merely accept such awful accusations without some anger and resistance.

A person is certainly projecting a negative attitude when he grimaces and has a creased forehead. Whether he's just being defensive, or whether he's upset because you've caught him doing something wrong, you'd best analyze carefully what he's saying. If the man is fiddling with his clothes, hands, or other parts of his body, he's nervous about talking with you, and this could most probably be because he's being deceptive.

When a person has his arms crossed, it usually means that he's not being receptive to what you're saying, or that he's guarding himself against your questions. He's being reserved in his attitude and will likely not be very forthcoming in whatever comments he makes. His answers to your questions will probably be incomplete or indefinite or inconclusive. You'll have to work hard to get an open response, much less an honest one from him.

The body language of a person having his hands stuffed

into his pockets is also a reserved attitude. It may mean that he is just shy in his manner in dealing with others. Or, it may be that he's not going to be truthful in his answers to your questions. When a person is not expressive with his hands, he's not being expressive with his responses. It's almost the opposite of a person who has his hands out, showing the palms, which is considered a sign of openness and honesty. The analogy may be that if you can't read the hands, you can't read the person's mind, either. It may pay to spend some time trying to get the person to relax and open up before asking him any of the critical questions you're trying to get answered.

8. Legs (bouncing, swinging, crossing, pointing, tucking)

Some psychologists and other observers of body language feel that the legs and feet are the most expressive parts of the body when it comes to signaling deception or uneasiness. You can feel the tension when you discuss a matter with a person who bounces her legs or jiggles or swings her feet when listening or talking. She is definitely apprehensive about the conversation. She'd rather not be there discussing that particular matter with you.

When someone crosses her legs, it may signal a closing in of her attitude. She's not as open and straightforward as she seemed before she crossed her legs. Of course, a lot of women do this habitually, so that might not be indicative of deception with them. But watch to see if the woman also nervously jiggles her foot or dangles a shoe. If so, there's some uneasiness there that you should be aware of.

When someone tucks her leg beneath her as she's sitting, this often indicates a personal withdrawal and a defensiveness of posture. She's not being totally open with you. She's protecting herself physically, psychologically, and emotionally.

Also, you will recall that when a person turns her legs away from you, or points her feet away from you, especially when her feet point toward a door or other escape route, you can be certain that she is not comfortable in the situation. She literally wants to get out of that space. It might be because she doesn't

252

enjoy being with you, but if you know that's not the case, then she's probably uncomfortable with the situation and with the conversation. She doesn't want to be answering your questions. She wants to escape and be free of the hounding she feels you're giving her.

9. Incongruity (gives partial shrug, smiles when saying something serious, exaggerates actions)

When a person says something, then at the end of his sentence gives a quick or partial shrug, you can be sure that he's telling at least a partial falsehood. The shrug unconsciously relates that the person feels uncertain about his comment, especially about whether you will accept it at face value, or whether you will question him further. We almost innately pick up this signal as meaning something is not simple and straightforward about the presentation.

The out-of-place smile is easy for us to spot and to analyze. Something is not right. We sense the incongruity and the falsity of the gesture in connection with the verbal comment. The person is trying to win us over or to make us overlook or accept something he's said at face value.

The same feeling comes over us when we observe a person making an exaggerated action or signal. We know it's not right. We've seen gestures all our lives, and we notice when they're overemphasized, ill-timed, or not in keeping with what's being said. You should make it a habit to question in your mind whether the person is trying to deceive you through making false statements or by trying to gloss over a particular subject.

10. Eyes (acute lack of contact, blinking, darting, closing, glancing away, shifting, aversion, "mercy stare"

The eyes are very expressive, and we need to watch them closely. But also remember to pay attention to the other areas of the body and the ways they pose or move. Sometimes a person who is nervous about talking with you (for whatever the reason) will have a decided lack of eye contact with you. However, the amount of eye contact will vary among cultural and racial groups. So, you need to be aware of what the norm is for eye contact in a general conversation. Also, blinking too rapidly, eyes darting toward different objects in the area, and constant glancing away from you during a conversation are signs of nervousness, and they may well signal deceptiveness if the person is being questioned about criminal or other bad behavior.

Often when a person is lying, she will close her eyes longer than normal. She will shift her focus more often than normal. And if you've caught her in a position where she feels compelled to confess some activity, she may give a protracted "mercy stare," where she's looking into the distance or upward, as though seeking some divine guidance or intervention. This usually indicates she's about to come clean with you and reveal all.

➢ **And now you know.**

Those are the principal indicators you should watch for. I'll set it out below in a shorthand version that should help jog your memory if you consider it from time-to-time. In the meantime, you should be learning and remembering the signals as you practice them. And soon, they will become second nature to you. You'll be confident and accomplished in spotting lies and in knowing how to deal with whoever is trying to put one over on you. Here's wishing you the best of luck in using your new knowledge and ability. And may you have a long and happy life, protected from the evils of deception.

–30–

Mark Bouton

TEN SECRETS FOR SPOTTING LIES
*Watch for clusters or groups of behaviors.

Touching – mouth, nose, neck or throat, eyes, ears, objects

Omission – words, ideas, answers, clarifying statements

Speech – stuttering, mumbling, pausing, scrambling phrases, slurring words, bad syntax, higher-pitched voice

Posture – stiff, leaning away, stonewalling, turning sideways, shoulder roll, head jerks or shifts

Obfuscation – fake smile, ill-timed gestures, words unlike emotions, no use of contractions

Tells – mimicking, bridging, modifying, displacing, stalling, denial, inclusion

Attitude – creased forehead, grimaces, clenched fists, arms crossed, hands stuffed into pockets

Legs – bouncing, swinging, crossing, pointing, tucking

Incongruity – gives quick or partial shrug, smiles when saying something serious, exaggerates reactions

Eyes – no contact, blinking, darting, glancing away, closing, shifting, aversion, "mercy stare"

*Remember to value and honor your close personal connections and family ties. Use the above techniques to inform yourself and to protect your health, money, and above all, your important relationships.

Bibliography

Dimitrius, Ph.D. Jo-Ellan and Mazzarella, Mark. *Reading People*. New York: Ballantine Books, 1999.

Ekman, Paul. *Emotions Revealed*. New York: H. Holt, 2003.

Ford, Charles V. *Lies, Lies, Lies*. Washington, D.C.: American Psychiatric Press, Inc., 1996.

Glass, Ph.D. Lillian. *I Know What You're Thinking*. Hoboken, NJ: John Wiley & Sons, Inc., 2002.

Hartley, Gregory and Karinch, Maryann. *How to Spot a Liar*. Franklin Lakes, NJ: Career Press, 2005.

Lieberman, Dr. David J. *Never Be Lied to Again*. New York: St. Martin's Griffin, 1998.

Nance, CFE Jef. *Conquering Deception*. Kansas City, MO: Irvin-Benham, LLC, 2004.

Navarro, Joe. *What Every Body is Saying*. New York, Harper Collins, 2008.

Nierenberg, Gerald I. and Calero, Henry H. *How to Read a Person Like a Book*. New York: MetroBooks, 2001.

Pease, Allan and Pease, Barbara. *The Definitive Book of Body Language*. New York: Bantam, 2006.

Smith, Dr. David L. *Why We Lie*. NY: St. Martin's, 2004.

Walters, Stan B. *The Truth about Lying*. Naperville, IL: Sourcebooks, Inc., 2000.